THE GRAND TRADITION
British Art from Amherst College

THE GRAND TRADITION
British Art from Amherst College

Frank Anderson Trapp

THE AMERICAN FEDERATION OF ARTS

This catalogue has been published in conjunction with *The Grand Tradition: British Art from Amherst College*, an exhibition organized by the American Federation of Arts.

The exhibition and publication have been made possible through the generous support of the National Patrons of the American Federation of Arts. Additional support for the publication has been received from the J. M. Kaplan Fund and the DeWitt Wallace Fund through the AFA's Revolving Fund for Publications.

EXHIBITION TOUR

Bass Museum of Art
Miami Beach, Florida
May 7–July 2, 1988

Brevard Art Center
Melbourne, Florida
October 8–December 11, 1988

Palmer Museum of Art
The Pennsylvania State University
University Park, Pennsylvania
January 7–March 4, 1989

The Fine Arts Center at Cheekwood
Nashville, Tennessee
April 15–June 11, 1989

Paine Art Center
Oshkosh, Wisconsin
July 2–August 27, 1989

Montgomery Museum of Fine Arts
Montgomery, Alabama
September 23–November 18, 1989

The American Federation of Arts represents a merging of the nation's two oldest and largest non-profit educational organizations serving the visual arts community: the Art Museum Association of America and the American Federation of Arts. One of its primary activities is the organization of exhibitions and film programs that travel throughout the United States and abroad. Other services to museums include a fine arts insurance program, technology services, design awards to the field, workshops and institutes for museum professionals, and discount services.

Published by The American Federation of Arts
41 East 65 Street, New York, New York 10021
Printed in Japan
AFA Exhibition #134

Library of Congress Cataloging-in-Publication Data

Trapp, Frank.
  The grand tradition

  Catalog of an exhibition of art works selected from the Mead Art Museum. The exhibition will be held in the Bass Museum of Art, Miami Beach, Fla. and 5 other cities from May 1988 to Nov. 1989.
  Bibliography: p.
  Includes index.
  1. Art, British—Exhibitions. 2. Art, Modern—17th–18th centuries—Great Britain—Exhibitions. 3. Art, Modern—19th century—Great Britain—Exhibitions. 4. Mead Art Museum (Amherst College)—Exhibitions. I. American Federation of Arts. II. Mead Art Museum (Amherst College) III. Bass Museum of Art. IV. Title.

N6766.T7 1988 709'.41'074013 87-33458
ISBN 0-917418-86-7

Designer: Michael Shroyer
Editor: Martina D'Alton
Photographer: David Stansbury
Composition: U.S. Lithograph, typographers
Printing: Dai Nippon Printing Co., Ltd.

Front cover: *Portrait of Sir Jeffery Amherst*,
  Sir Joshua Reynolds (No. 6)
Back cover: *Pentedatilo*, Edward Lear (No. 35)

Contents

FOREWORD

In 1985 the AFA collaborated very successfully with the Mead Art Museum, Amherst College, to organize a traveling exhibition drawn from their esteemed collection of American art. It gives us great pleasure to follow up that rewarding experience with *The Grand Tradition: British Art from Amherst College*, an exhibition that illustrates the range of British art of the eighteenth and nineteenth centuries.

Since 1940, when the Mead Art Museum received the pivotal gift of Gainsborough's portrait of Lord Amherst, the Museum's collection of British art has grown steadily. Today it includes outstanding examples of history, portrait, landscape, still life, and genre painting in oil and watercolor, as well as prints, furniture, and other decorative arts. We are delighted to be making such an outstanding collection accessible to a wider public.

We are deeply indebted to Frank Anderson Trapp, director of the Mead Art Museum and curator of *The Grand Tradition*. His intelligence and enthusiasm have made the exhibition and this handsome publication possible. We are also grateful to Dr. Trapp's staff for their able assistance.

At the American Federation of Arts, I want to acknowledge the important contributions of Harold B. Nelson, chief administrator for exhibitions; Michaelyn Mitchell, publications coordinator; Victoria Hertz, registrar; and Sandra Gilbert, public information and promotion director.

We also wish to thank our museum partners who will be presenting the exhibition in their galleries: the Bass Museum of Art, Miami Beach; the Brevard Art Center, Melbourne, Florida; Palmer Museum of Art, The Pennsylvania State University, University Park; the Fine Arts Center at Cheekwood, Nashville, Tennessee; Paine Art Center, Oshkosh; and the Montgomery Museum of Fine Arts, Alabama.

Finally, we would like to thank the National Patrons of the AFA, who, under the direction of Margot Linton and Nani Warren, have designated the project as the National Patron exhibition of 1988.

Myrna Smoot
Director
The American Federation of Arts

Introduction

Visitors to the exhibition and readers of this catalogue will doubtless ask just how so fine and varied an array of British art came to exist at a small, liberal arts college in rural Massachusetts. As with virtually all collections of art, the Amherst collection was assembled by a happy combination of chance and design. For years, the college's holdings in British art were quite miscellaneous and sparse, consisting mainly of household furniture and other works of decorative art bequeathed from the estates of alumni or other friends of the college. Thanks to what my predecessor, Charles H. Morgan, aptly characterized as "a series of unrelated accidents," further works were in time accumulated.

Eventually, the process was given a focus. In 1940 Mrs. George D. Pratt gave Gainsborough's portrait of Lord Jeffery Amherst to the college, an altogether appropriate addition to the collection. Lord Amherst was Britain's commander-in-chief during the French and Indian Wars in the mid-eighteenth century. Under his command, the British enjoyed their first decisive victory. To celebrate this feat, several New England towns were named in Amherst's honor, including the town that surrounds the college also bearing his name.

Soon after this nucleus gift was made, the portraits of Lord Amherst's parents and, somewhat later, those of his grandparents came on the market. They were purchased by the college out of an admixture of "piety and sentiment." In 1959, the Amherst family's porcelain dessert service was procured by a group of generous alumni at the college, with the participation of the current Lord Amherst himself. The single most auspicious acquisition, however, was made almost a decade later, in 1967, when Reynolds'great portrait of Sir Jeffery entered the collection. Thanks to the generosity of Mrs. Richard K. Webel, a third portrait of Jeffery Amherst, painted by Joseph Blackburn, was later acquired by the Museum. This group of Amherst family portraits is an unusual, probably unique, historical document, the most significant of its kind outside Great Britain.

This whole process of gradual accumulation was ably orchestrated by Professor Morgan, the founder of the art gallery at Amherst College. He shared in the prevailing sentiment toward the project and guided and animated the enterprise as a whole. In addition to the Amherst family depictions, related treasures came as gifts from friends and alumni of the college. These include a number of portraits and decorative objects from the estates of Herbert L. Pratt (class of 1895) and of Miss Isabel Turner. The children of another alumnus, Dwight Morrow (class of 1895) and his wife Elizabeth, were also beneficent. Mrs. Winifred L. Arms deserves special mention for her many fine gifts of decorative objects.

In 1951, the collection was further augmented by the handsome donation of a collection of fine prints given by Edward C. Crossett (class of 1905). Included amongst the rich and varied contents of the Crossett Collection was a small treasure trove of British prints, many of which are included here. Given that working nucleus, purchases have been made over the years to fill out the print collection selectively. Further museum purchases have also been made in the fields of oil painting and watercolor. The process of judicious enlargement and enhancement of the Mead Art Museum collection continues as means and market opportunities permit.

The evolution of a collection rich in British examples is especially opportune at Amherst College for reasons other than a British namesake. The representation of American art at the Museum is well known for its size and excellence, and a strong tradition of American studies has long been maintained at the college. It is difficult to consider the early days of American art without reference to transatlantic ties, particularly those with Great Britain. Indeed, certain

major figures such as Benjamin West or John Singleton Copley remained lifelong British subjects and
concluded most of their professional careers in England. Despite birth in the American colonies and
their close identification with the emergence of an
artistic heritage unique to our own shores, they were
at the same time products of British culture.

To some extent, such ambivalence of allegiance
would recur from time to time. Philadelphia-reared
Charles Robert Leslie, for example, found himself
more at home in England than in America, as did the
more famous later expatriate James A. McNeil Whistler. From that point of view, even the career of John
Singer Sargent was closely tied to his British experiences—as were those of earlier artists Gilbert Stuart,
Washington Allston, and Thomas Sully.

In organizing this exhibition, an arbitrary decision was made to consider West, Whistler, and Leslie
as British subjects (having been naturalized in Britain, so to speak), while Allston, Copley, and Sully
remain American. In the case of Copley, the Museum's strong portraits date from his colonial period
and are generally regarded as "typically" American,
so they do not appear.

Like the collection of American art at Amherst
College, the reserves of art from Britain are richest in
eighteenth- and nineteenth-century examples. Accordingly, the selection of works in the present exhibition
centers on that historical span.

Paintings in oil by British artists are first to
attract our attention, and works in this medium are
the focus of Part 1 of this catalogue. Among them,
the portraits at the Mead Museum recall the eminence
attained by advocates of that branch of representation
during the eighteenth century. The commercial importance attached to portraiture in earlier historical
periods is implicit in the number of portrait commissions awarded to the painters of Britain during the
eighteenth and nineteenth centuries. Almost every
artist of good reputation was employed as a portraitist
at one time or another.

Curiously, portraiture was long considered as
but an auxiliary branch of art by academic theorists of
those times. The intellectual worth of the object at
hand was judged according to a hieracrchy of comparative values attached to the subject matter. History
painting was of transcendent importance, with portrait, landscape, still life, and genre painting rele-
gated to positions of lesser prestige. History painting
was construed at the time to include subjects drawn
from classical or religious lore or from the recorded
course of the human past. Such categories are not
always rigidly observable in the present context, however. Genre painting—depictions of scenes of everyday life—for example, may border on allegory on one
hand, portraiture on the other. The arrangement here
reflects that duality, and some genre subjects will be
found among the history paintings, even though purists
of a former age would probably have been offended by
such blurring of topical boundaries. Landscapes round
out the group of oil paintings in Part 1.

Watercolor painting, in which many British artists came to specialize and excel, comprises Part 2 of
the catalogue. In Part 3, the record of British accomplishment in the print medium will be substantiated
with fine examples from the collection. While the
practical limitations of selecting for a traveling exhibition have restricted the choice of works of decorative
art, a sampling of British attainments in those allied
arts adds further dimension to this display of the
material culture of Great Britain.

The complexities of selection and arrangement
notwithstanding, it is hoped that the ensemble of
works brought together in this exhibition and catalogue will afford visitors and readers alike an attractive and instructive picture of British art in the grand
tradition.

Every exhibition is the product of the efforts of

many persons. *The Grand Tradition: British Art from Amherst College* would not have been possible without the talents and devotions of the staff of the Mead Art Museum. Irene Farrick has coordinated the effort throughout, not only in the phases of catalogue preparation, but in organizing the practical details of shipping, insurance, and other necessary procedures. In this she was ably assisted by Lois Mono. Our technician, Alfred Szarkowski, has tended to the essential preparatory tasks. David Stansbury took new photographs of all the objects for inclusion in the present publication. The initial notion for the exhibition was suggested by Judith A. Barter, Curator of the Collection, and Harold B. Nelson of the American Federation of Arts. The encouragement of both has been much appreciated. The support of this enterprise by Peter R. Pouncey, President of Amherst College, was of course an essential condition to its realization and is warmly acknowledged. Ultimately, sincere appreciation is to be expressed to the many generous donors, both living and dead, who have contributed over the years to the artistic substance of the exhibition which you are hereby invited to enjoy.

Frank Anderson Trapp
Director
Mead Art Museum

1. OIL PAINTING

For historical reasons that have yet to be adequately explained, Britain was curiously lacking in a native tradition of painting for many years after its emergence as an important, modern nation of the sixteenth and seventeenth centuries. This lapse is the more curious in view of the singular artistic contribution in Britain during Medieval times and the continued enthusiasm of the English as collectors.

For the most part the needs of royal and aristocratic patrons for works of art were long served by foreign craftsmen, most of them imported from The Netherlands and Germany or, occasionally, Italy. The most conspicuous of these visitors was Peter Paul Rubens (1577–1640), whose services both as painter and diplomat while in England were rewarded with a knighthood bestowed by Charles I. Some of the other artists are also well known for their contributions to the culture of their adopted land. The succession of great portraitists who were naturalized in England included Hans Holbein the Younger (1497/8–1543), Sir Anthony van Dyck (1599–1641), Sir Peter Lely (1618–1680), and Sir Godfrey Kneller (1648–1723). Characteristic pictures by both Lely and Kneller are included in the present exhibition, examples of the protracted Baroque traditions of portraiture introduced into England by Rubens and van Dyck and his followers.

It was not until William Hogarth (1699–1764), however, that a significant school of native-born British painters began to form. To be sure, occasional predecessors had emerged, some of them with a modicum of lasting reputation. Sir James Thornhill (1675–1735), for example, may have been distinguished as a painter in the late Baroque tradition of history painting, but it was Thornhill's son-in-law Hogarth who brought Britain into the international mainstream of post-Renaissance developments in painting.

Hogarth's contributions were multiple, for he was active as a teacher and printmaker as well as a painter. His originality is especially to be appreciated in the moralistic genre subjects for which he gained wide reputation. His portraits and "conversation pieces"—group portraits given a domestic or landscape locale—also assumed a pronounced personal, and by extension "English," character. Although Hogarth's painting is not represented in the Amherst College Collection, a portrait by his contemporary, George Beare (active 1741–1749; No. 9) is very close in quality and kind to Hogarth's own performance. Beare too portrays the middle-class clients whose rising status and expectations had begun to exert a distinctive influence on the tastes of the time. The unknown lady who was Beare's plain, but appealing subject is strikingly similar to her counterparts being painted in New England by John Singleton Copley (1737–1815) just a decade later. The relationships between these subjects is tantalizing to contemplate.

With the foundation of the Royal Academy in London in 1768, the emergent British School was afforded a new intellectual focus. The academy served artists' longstanding need for opportunities to exhibit their work as well as for an educational structure suitable for inculcating professional standards among aspirant artists. The practice of portrait painting was especially well served by that new institution, many of whose members revived the traditions of aristocratic portraiture in the Grand Manner which had fallen rather fallow since the heyday of the Baroque. As the first president of the Royal Academy, Sir Joshua Reynolds (1723–1792) played a primary role, not only as a distinguished painter, but as an intellectual luminary. His annual *Discourses*, delivered before the members of the academy and their students, stand as great accomplishments in their own right.

Portrait works by Reynolds and his colleagues at the academy constitute the most important single aspect of the collection at Amherst College. A mere listing of the artists makes this clear. They include not only Thomas Gainsborough (1727–1788), Reynolds' greatest rival both then and now, but also Reynolds' two successors as president—Benjamin West (1738–1820) and Sir Thomas Lawrence (1769–1830). Among other representatives of this golden age of portraiture are Allan Ramsay (1713–1784), Richard Wilson (1714–1782), Francis Cotes (1729–1770), and Sir Henry Raeburn (1756–1823). Interestingly, many of the sitters of these distinguished masters were members of the Amherst family.

West is represented by his *Portrait of Dr. Enoch Edwards* (No. 8). This portrait of a middle-class sitter continues in the mold of informal portraiture that was maintained somewhat apart from the mainstream of fashionable representations even by such masters of the formal portrait genre as Reynolds and Gainsborough. Similar qualities of directness are to be appreciated in two studies by Lawrence, one of them addressing the sober countenance of West himself.

The difficulties of respecting strict boundaries of classification by subject matter are exemplified by two further works, both of which are portraits, yet verge on being genre depictions. The charming little interior setting in *The Dutchess of Bedford* by Sir Edwin Landseer (1802–1873; No. 16) flows so naturally onto the stretch of land Her Grace is surveying that we could almost regard the work as a landscape. In *Light Thrown on a Dark Passage*, James Sant (1820–1916; No. 17) quietly invites us to share in the thoughts of a charming subject he (and we) have just chanced upon in a private moment. Again, our literary expectations are alerted.

There was also a British fascination for history painting, an area well represented in the Amherst College Collection. Works of the kind constituted a mainstay of the production of Benjamin West, as may be seen in his interpretation of a biblical theme, *David Prostrate, Whilst the Destroying Angel Sheathes the Sword*

(No. 18). In this case, the highly adaptable West harks back to much the same sources of inspiration in Italian late Baroque that had served Thornhill before him.

Another of the founding members of the Royal Academy, the Swiss-born Angelica Kauffmann (1741–1807) also gained favor with her efforts as a painter of history, as may be seen in her Homeric scene, *The Return of Telemachus* (No. 19). Sharing in the Neoclassical predispositions of her era, Kauffmann was quite understandably favored as a decorator by such leading British advocates of that international fashion in architecture and decoration as the brothers Adam.

A darker, less reassuring side of the classical coin also surfaced in the art of British interpreters of the classic past, however. In the brooding scene painted by Thomas Barker of Bath (1769–1847; No. 20), Marius (or some other heroic personage of those honored circumstances) ponders the vulnerability of mortal fulfillment amidst the ruins of a metropolis resembling Rome strangely ruined before its time. Romantic adumbrations in the art of Britain are apparent here in remarkably vigorous terms. Once again, transatlantic connections are made; there is similar imagery in the work of Washington Allston (1779–1843) or, later, the English-born Thomas Cole (1801–1848), whose *Daniel Boone in His Cabin on the Great Osage Lake* (ca. 1825/26) directly recalls the thematic heritage Barker has here called upon.

Given the strongly literary bent of English culture it is hardly surprising that many artists were attracted to narrative subjects derived from the theater. Two of many interpretations of the kind are included in the present exhibition. One of them, painted by Charles Robert Leslie (1794–1859; No. 22), shows a scene from Shakespeare's *Henry VIII*, in which Queen Catherine of Aragon receives the king's ambassador. Leslie's sense of theatrical aptness distinguishes this and other reenactments by his hand. He is allied with

a good number of his colleagues who specialized in
this form of history painting. An *Ophelia* by Thomas
Francis Dicksee (1818–1895; No. 23) at a later phase
of the development of British painting exudes Pre-
Raphaelite overtones in the overtly sentimental nature
of its characterization of Shakespeare's pathetic heroine.
Expressive and technical characteristics linked with
mid-Victorian tastes are also recognizable in the
charming *Family Portrait with Two Children* by Sir
George Hayter (1792–1871; No. 21) and *The Stone
Mason* by John Ritchie (active 1858–1865; No. 24).

Also deeply implanted in the British sensibilities
was a love of the natural scene which saw the rise of a
thriving school of landscape painting during the late
eighteenth and early nineteenth centuries. An early
example of that turn of emphasis is the landscape by
George Morland (1763–1804), in which the British
affection for the rural scene is convincingly expressed.
To some extent, the predisposition for landscape was
also capably served by British watercolorists whose
contributions are discussed in Part 2. By all standards,
however, the leading lights were Joseph Mallord
William Turner (1775–1851) and John Constable
(1776–1837). Unfortunately, their work in oil is yet
to be represented in the Amherst College Collection,
although their mastery of printmaking mediums is
shown and discussed below in Part 3. To a limited
extent, Constable's approach to rustic landscape is
suggested in a small, but appealing painting, *Landscape
with Cattle*, convincingly attributed to Frederick
William Watts (1800–1862; No. 32), Constable's
successful imitator.

There is no counterpart in the form of a surrogate
Turner or Bonington amongst the Amherst College
pictures, but by compensation of sorts, there is a
lively little topographical study of a piazza in Bologna,
probably painted by Thomas Shotter Boys (1803–1874;
No. 34). It comes acceptably close to the remarkably
seductive skills of Richard Parkes Bonington
(1801-1828), whose meteoric talents briefly closed the

arc of British landscape depiction that ranged from
Constable's veristic "rustic" modes to Turner's poised
position between the scenographic traditions of Italy
and the classical magic of the "divine" Claude Lorraine.
Also representing the topographical traditions is a
precisely rendered evocation of William Beckford's
Fonthill Abbey, painted by the little-known, but gifted
Scottish artist, Robert Gibb the Elder (1801–1837;
No. 33).

Throughout British landscape painting of this
remarkably productive age, certain other interpretive
partis-pris came to pertain. They had to do with the
concepts—or perhaps, more properly, the poetic
conceits—of sublimity and the picturesque. Those
notions, which are discussed more fully in individual
catalogue entries, are admirably represented in
Landscape with Carriage in a Storm by Philippe Jacques
de Loutherbourg (1740–1812; No. 25). Altogether, it
constitutes a veritable essay in the vision of Nature
possessed of the power to strike terror into the hearts
of a humanity helpless in its grip. Similarly, *Pentedatilo*
by Edward Lear (1812–1868; No. 35) embodies the
spell of Nature's innate majesty and forbidding
strangeness of proportion and shape. The lurking power
of those configurations is converted into no less solemn,
but somehow less threatening, mysteries in *Salamacis
and Hermaphroditis* by John Martin (1789–1854; No.
29).

The wonders of Nature are regarded more calmly
but with equally Romantic ardor in landscapes by
David Cox (1783–1859; No. 28) and John Linnell
(1792–1882; No. 30). They, too, bear witness to the
remarkable evolution of British accomplishment during
the early maturity of that flourishing school.

The paintings in Part 1 are divided into the
three groupings just discussed: portraiture, history
painting, and landscape. Within each group, the
entries are arranged chronologically according to the
year of the artist's birth.

PORTRAITURE

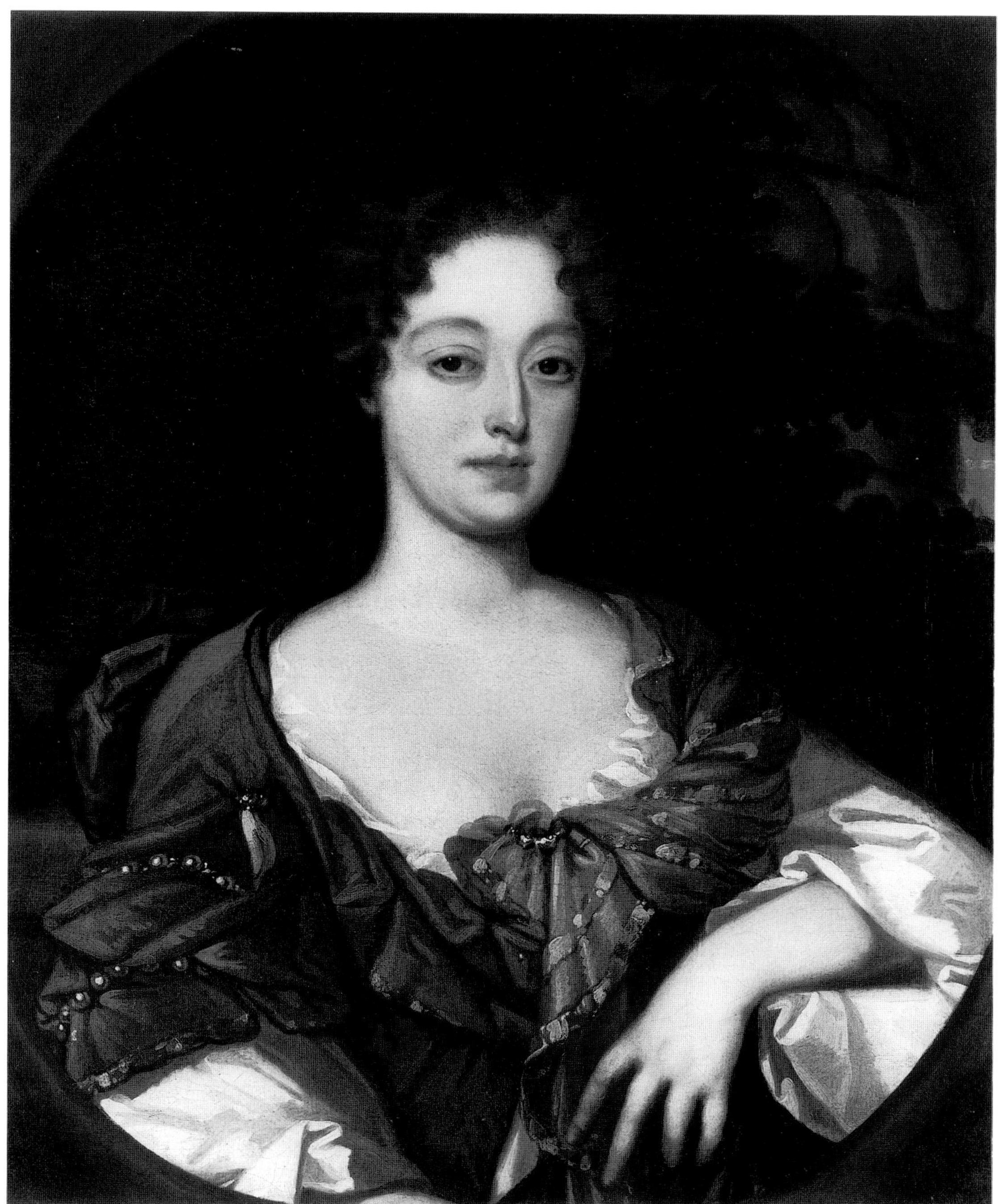

SIR PETER LELY (1618–1680)

1. *Portrait of Anne, First Wife of Sir Francis Warre*
    Oil on canvas, 30 x 25 in. (76.2 x 63.5 cm)
    Bequest of Mrs. Ives Washburn
    1964.82

It has always seemed odd that England of the Renaissance and Baroque periods produced no prodigy in the visual arts equal to those in literature. Although a scattering of works of quality recall the activity of a few native artists such as the miniaturist Nicholas Hilliard (ca. 1547–1619) or Hogarth's most distinguished predecessor, William Dobson (1610/11–1646), the wants of British patrons were mostly satisfied by artists from abroad. The presence of Hans Holbein the Younger (1497/8–1543) at the Tudor court or the sojourn of Sir Anthony van Dyck (1599–1641) were memorable examples of the success sometimes enjoyed by imported talent.

Sir Peter Lely assumed a comparable role during the years after the Restoration of the Stuarts and, if anything, left an even more pronounced mark upon the future practice of portrait painting. Born in Germany of Dutch parents, Lely was trained in Haarlem and had been accepted into the Guild of that artistic center before his arrival in London in the 1440s. Trained to undertake the full range of subjects that might be demanded of a painter by continental patrons, Lely attempted to employ those skills in decorative projects he proposed to Parliament at the time of the Common-wealth, and he did in fact paint some mythological themes during his earlier years in England. For the most part, however, portraiture was the commodity in demand. It was in his capacity to satisfy those interests handsomely that he won later and lasting acclaim as the leading artist of the court of James II. As a technician, Lely at his best rivals van Dyck, whose works he clearly studied. While he can hardly be accounted an artist of so high a rank, he did popularize a mode of placing his portrait subjects in a garden setting. This arrangement occurs once in van Dyck's

oeuvre but would survive for well over a century after Lely's time as a tradition in fashionable British portraiture.

Lely's portrait of Lady Anne is exemplary of the qualities that mark his portraits of Restoration beauties, with their sensuous features and practiced elegance. Quite naturally, his skill at putting a flattering gloss upon actuality won the artist a flood of commissions. He achieved wealth and fame, and a knighthood was bestowed upon him late in life. A series of portraits of the fairest maids of honor at the Royal Court—his famous "Windsor Beauties"—commissioned in the 1660s by the Duchess of York, epitomizes the flattering voluptuousness of his feminine sub-jects. More in tune with subsequent taste perhaps, are his "Flagmen," now at Greenwich. His powers of characteriza-tion are exhibited in this series of strong portraits of admi-rals, painted in 1666/7, at the peak of his powers. To satisfy the demands for his services to a fashionable clien-tele he employed a number of studio assistants, but to his credit, the standards of quality in his shop were carefully monitored, as even his lesser products testify.

SIR GODFREY KNELLER (1646/9–1723)

2. *Portrait of James Radcliffe, Earl of Derwentwater*
   Oil on canvas, 30 x 25 in. (76.2 x 63.5 cm)
   Anonymous Gift
   1979.8

Born in Lubeck and trained in Amsterdam in the studio of Rembrandt's pupil, Ferdinand Bol (1616–1680), Sir God-frey Kneller eventually succeeded to the preeminence Lely had enjoyed among high-born patrons of his adopted land. While Kneller based his approach to portraiture largely on the formulas Lely had employed, it is generally agreed that he exhibited more perspicacity in his interpretations of individual character. Qualities of the kind are most notice-able in the series of forty-two portraits he painted of mem-

bers of the Kit Cat Club, formed by socially prominent Whigs. The format of those rather small, bust-length portraits, normally showing one hand, was widely adopted thereafter.

Respectful of the value of the professional traditions that had served him so well, Kneller was appointed gover-nor of London's first Academy of Art (founded in 1711), a forerunner of the Royal Academy that was established much later in the century. By precept as well as example, he thus prepared the way for the eventual emergence of a prosper-ous school of native-born artists. These later artists would profit from the professional foundations laid by Lely, Kneller, and their lesser colleagues from abroad. In that sense, William Hogarth was his chief—though indirect—successor.

Kneller's *Portrait of James Radcliffe, Earl of Derwent-*

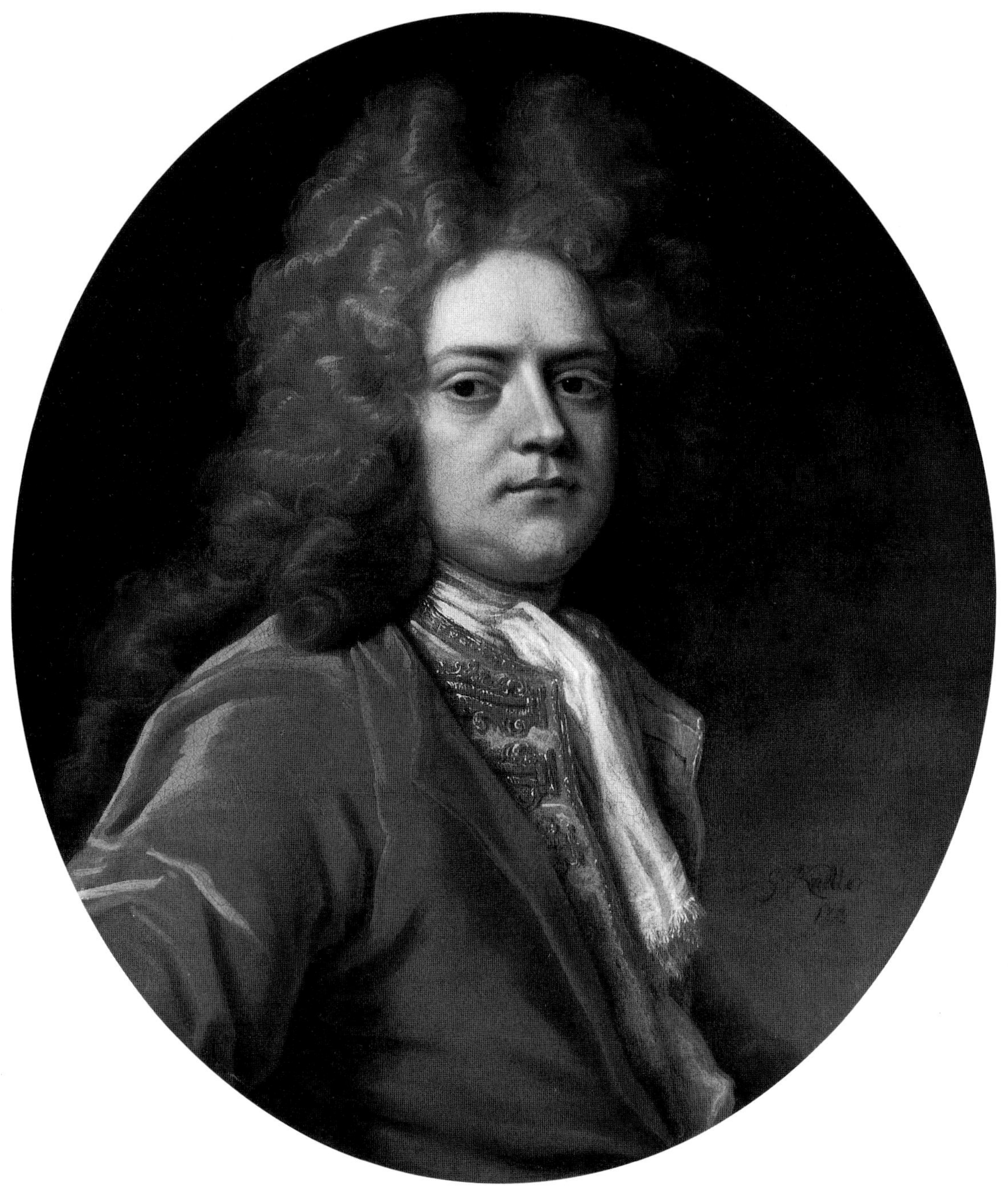

water, is an attractive example of his painterly skills and ability to capture an engaging sense of individual likeness. His aristocratic sitter was a person of uncommon biographical interest. Known as "Handsome Derwentwater," James Radcliffe was born in London but raised at the Stuart court in France. Since his mother had been Lady Mary Tudor, natural daughter of Charles II, the young nobleman was deemed a suitable companion to Prince James Edward, the "Old Pretender" to the English throne.

Loyal to those blood ties and to the Roman Catholic faith, Radcliffe had returned to England in 1710 and was party to the unsuccessful Jacobite uprising in 1715. Brought to trial after his surrender at Preston, where the rebels suffered defeat, Radcliffe stubbornly held to his allegiances and was accordingly beheaded on Tower Hill, 24 February, 1716. Kneller's skills as a draftsman, so ably demonstrated in this oil portrait are confirmed in a fine drawing, *A Head of a Man*, purchased for the collection some years ago.

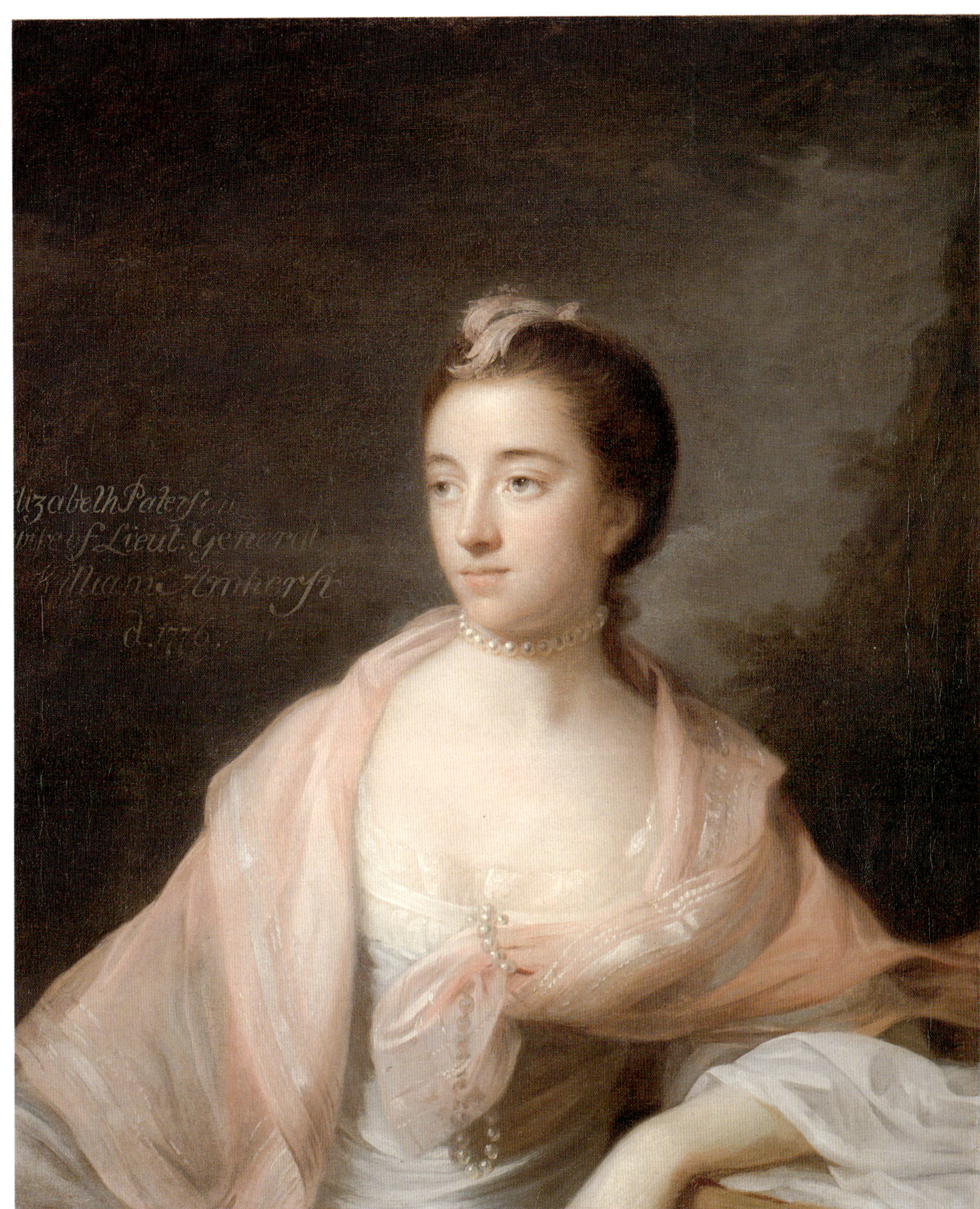

3

ALLAN RAMSAY (1713–1784)

3. *Portrait of Elizabeth Patterson Amherst*
    Oil on canvas, 29 x 24 in. (73.7 x 61 cm)
    Museum Purchase
    1967.84

A prominent figure among those who served the livening demand for portraitists in the 1740s was Thomas Hudson (1701–1779), a painter distinguished more perhaps by industry than talent. One of the many assistants trained by Hudson to help turn out his wares was a young Scotsman of far greater gifts and ultimate contribution, Alan Ramsay. Son of a well-known poet and himself a person of breeding and experience abroad, Ramsay was well prepared to rise above the pedestrian levels avidly maintained by Hudson. Ramsay was favored by experience in Rome (1736–38) where he associated with the leading masters of the day. There he acquired of a feeling for introducing an easy cosmopolitan grace into his portraits, making him a more worthy rival to Hudson, once he settled in London around 1739. In addition, while in Rome he gained a deep understanding of Classical archeology—one that was deepened by further visits to Rome later in his life. In fact, his learned views on Classical topics earned him the abiding respect of personalities eminent in matters of the sort, such as Giovanni Battista Piranesi (1720–1778) and the noted architect Robert Adam (1728–1792). Imbued with the intellectual spirit of the Enlightenment, he was equally at home in philosophical discussion with David Hume or Adam Smith, whom he also counted as close friends. More than any other artist of the time, he matched the gifts of mind of a Reynolds.

Historically, Ramsay thus linked the plainspoken openness and curiosity of a Hogarth with the Grand Manner formulated by Reynolds. Indeed, even earlier than Reynolds, Ramsay daringly paraphrased a classical model (the Apollo Belevedere) in the portrait of a tartan-clad *Norman, 22nd Chief of Macleod* (1748). One of Ramsay's fortes, however, was his ability to endow his female subjects with an appealing gracefulness of facial feature, pose, and dress—tendencies of his art that were apparently refreshed by return visits to Italy.

Ramsay's *Portrait of Elizabeth Patterson Amherst* bears witness to an appealing style. Particularly in the pale,

delicate restraint of the artist's palette, there is a foil to the discreet reserve of the sitter. Here, Ramsay's admiration for certain of his French contemporaries is to be recalled. A second visit to the Continent in the 1750s brought him into fresh touch with the portraits of Jean-Marie Nattier (1655–1703) and Maurice Quentin de la Tour (1704–1788). Like Gainsborough, he responded to the special niceties of the French mode. Lady Elizabeth was the wife of Jeffery Amherst's younger brother William, who was to become a lieutenant general in the course of his successful military career. William and Elizabeth's son William Pitt Amherst was the first of the line to be named an Earl.

Despite the success of his mature years, in which he emerged as a major figure in the development of fashionable British portraiture, Ramsay turned down a knighthood and declined involvement in the newly founded Royal Academy, while still remaining on friendly terms with Reynolds. Having indulged for a time in strictly commercial, shop production of commissions from George III, he turned his own hand, but rarely (though successfully), to work for friends. Perhaps because of the effects of an apparent stroke that affected his right arm, Ramsay seems to have given up painting altogether around 1769. His many remaining years were devoted to literary and archeological pursuits and the company of his friends.

RICHARD WILSON (1714–1782)

4. *Portrait of Vice-Admiral John Amherst,* 1749
    Oil on canvas, 29½ x 24 in. (74.9 x 61 cm)
    Museum Purchase
    1967.86

Remembered primarily as a landscape painter, Richard Wilson here shows his gifts for portraiture. The son of a Welsh clergyman, Wilson served an apprenticeship in London in the shop of a lackluster portraitist, Thomas Wright. By the 1740s Wilson had achieved some reputation in that branch of his chosen profession, as may be seen in his likeness of Vice-Admiral John Amherst (1718–1778). Perhaps less forcefully realized than Hogarth's portrayals and more reticent in statement of character, Wilson's portrait

nevertheless shares many qualities with those of the somewhat older master. Most of all, Wilson cultivated a rather comparable briskness of surface handling that relates both artists to the Rococo tastes dominating developments of their time on the Continent.

Unlike the xenophobic Hogarth, Wilson chose to interrupt a well-established career to make a prolonged visit to Italy (1750–58). There he was attracted most of all to the Roman Campagna that has enchanted so many other pilgrims to Italy before and since. His subsequent role as the virtual founder of a native British landscape school took shape in Italy. He had previously depicted an occasional landscape, and as a mature artist he evolved a distinctively personal approach to landscape. Despite persistent reservations about the importance of that branch of representation, Wilson enjoyed a sufficiently flourishing

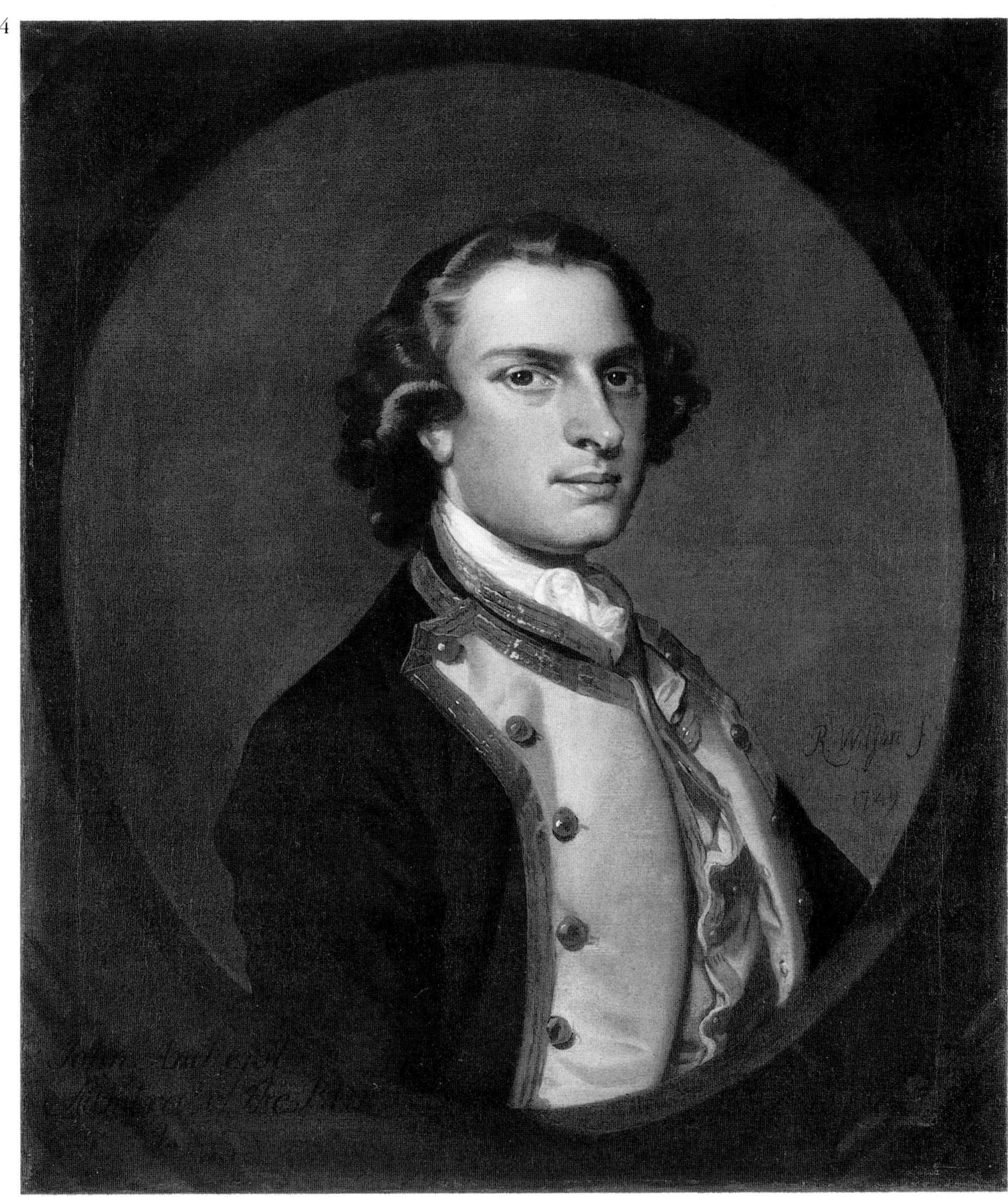

reputation to be numbered among the artists who joined Joshua Reynolds, Benjamin West, and others in founding the Royal Academy of Arts in 1768.

Wilson's portrait shows John Amherst as a young officer, long before he had attained his eventual, high rank in the admiralty. Some years later, in 1758, he was one of three members of the family to serve in the British campaigns against the French for dominion over the North American territories. Captain William Amherst was aide-de-camp to General Jeffery Amherst during the siege of Louisburg (1758), and Naval Captain John Amherst commanded the ship aboard which his brother Jeffery made his way to Boston following that victory. It was during that period when General Amherst was quartered in Boston that a notable portrait of him was painted by the Anglo-American painter, Joseph Blackburn (1700?–1763). (That earliest of the three portraits of Jeffery Amherst now owned by Amherst College is considered too fragile to be subjected to extensive travel, hence it has been excluded from the present selection of works.)

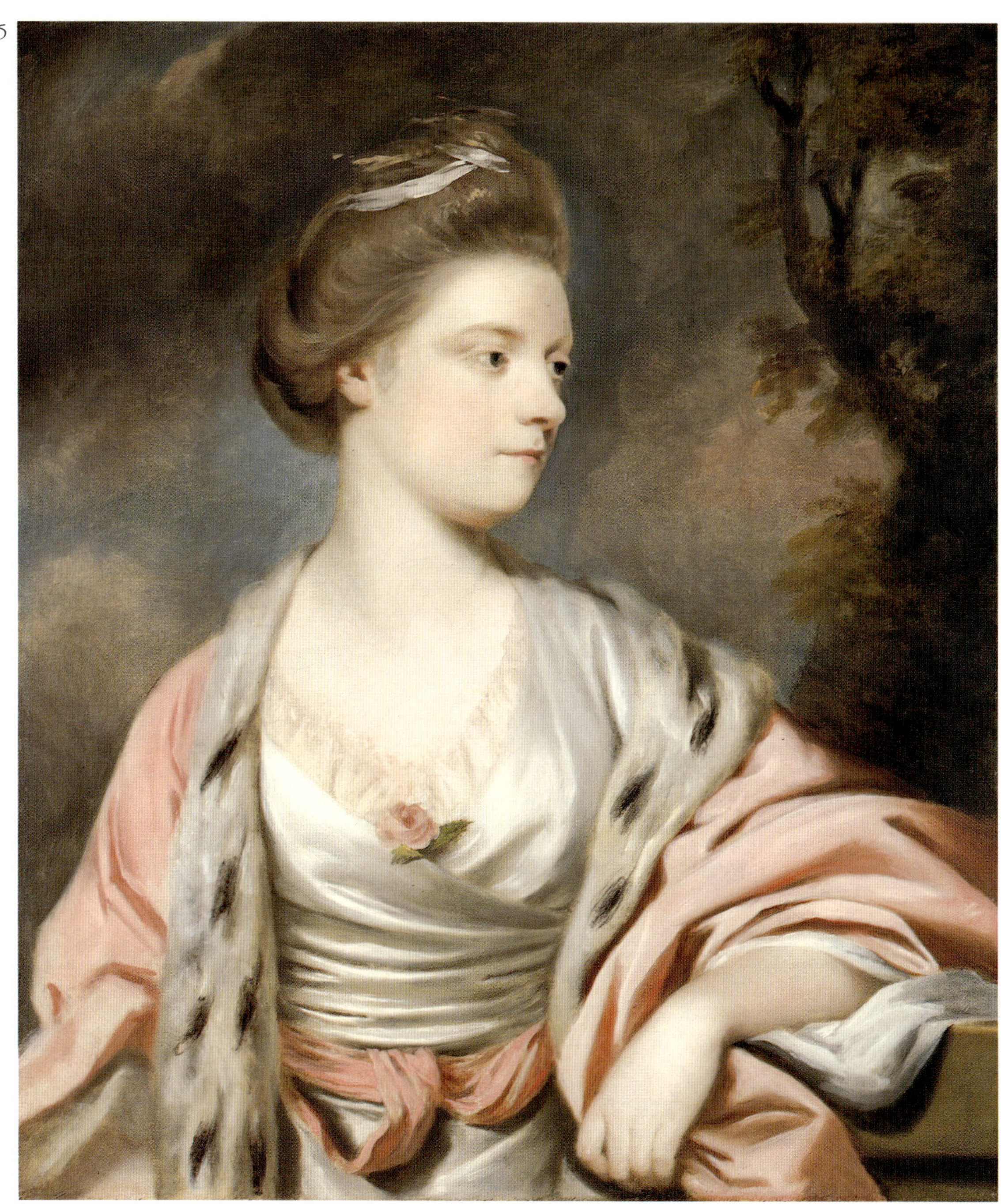

FRANCIS COTES (1726–1770)

5. *Portrait of Elizabeth Carey Amherst, Second Wife of Jeffery, Lord Amherst*
   Oil on canvas, 30 x 25 in. (76.2 x 63.5 cm)
   Museum Purchase
   1967.80

Jeffery Amherst's first wife and second cousin, Jane Dalison, is not represented in the collection, but her successor, Elizabeth Carey Amherst, is handsomely recalled in a portrait by Francis Cotes. At the peak of his reputation as a

painter of fashion, Cotes vied with Reynolds and Gainsborough for the patronage of the prosperous and high-born persons of his era. Only posthumously was his enormous reputation shaded both by his early death and by the advent of a brilliant younger portrait artist, George Romney (1734–1802). In the absence of a work by Romney in the Amherst College Collection, we benefit the more in having a fine example by his successsful predecessor who did so much to set the tone of expectations that both he and Romney profitably satisfied.

Cotes' *Portrait of Elizabeth Carey Amherst* is typical of

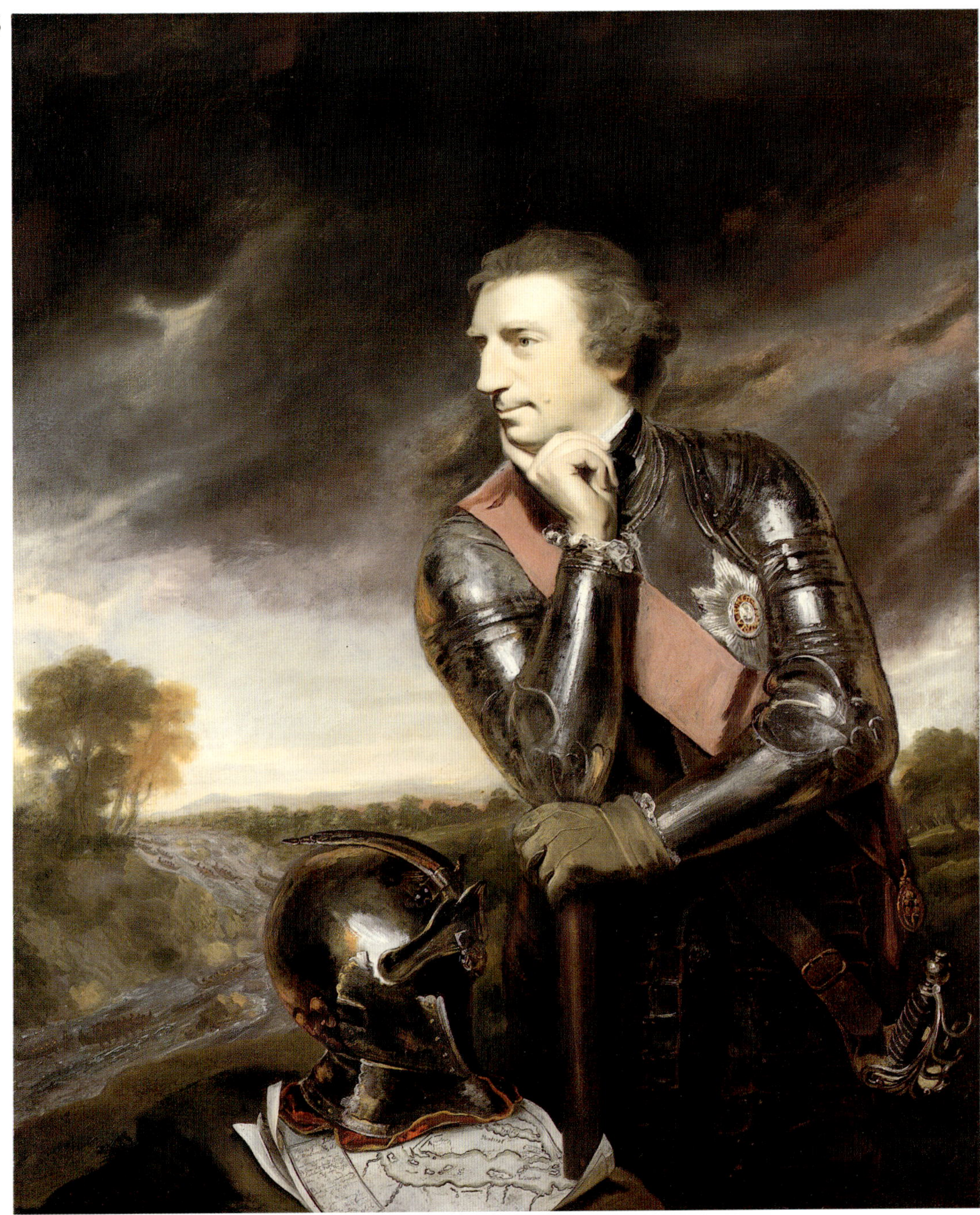

its maker's production. With her look of sudden diversion from the viewer's attention, she is shown against a dark fragment of landscape that sets off the pale tones of her tastefully arranged dress. (Cotes' assistant Peter Toms often provided the costume accessories.) The relative pallor of the tonalities of the figure may well reflect Cotes' early involvement in pastel painting, a medium that had then become popular, especially on the Continent. Whatever the case, Lady Amherst's genteel presence is evoked, not without fragrance of effect, in Cotes' sympathetic portrait of her.

Sir Joshua Reynolds (1723–1792)

6. *Portrait of Sir Jeffery Amherst*, 1765
   Oil on canvas, 50 x 40 in. (127 x 101.6 cm)
   Museum Purchase
   1967.85

The keystone of the Museum's collection of British art in the Grand Tradition is its great portrait of Sir Jeffery Amherst by the dean of English painters, Sir Joshua Reynolds. If Hogarth may be regarded as the founder of an independent school of painting in England, it was Reynolds who enlarged upon that initiative, bringing British standards in the arts in line with those that had so long pertained in Europe.

One aspect of that process was the establishment of the Royal Academy of Art in 1768. As first president of the academy, Reynolds was an eloquent spokesman for the noble lineage of the artistic past and its meaning for both present and future. He shared Hogarth's belief in teaching and public service, but he translated those intellectual goals into academic terms in the root sense of the word. The key to artistic success, by those precepts, could be codified and transmitted to future generations with regard to the proper understanding of the accomplishments of the great masters of the Renaissance and Baroque traditions.

In the Grand Manner that was realized in the High Renaissance, Reynolds saw the touchstone of artistic fulfillment in his own day. He had become fully aware of those sources of inspiration in an extended stay in Italy (1749–53) which served to inform the rudimentary experience of apprenticeship to Thomas Hudson, followed by a term of work on his own. With his talents galvanized by the direct experience of the Italian legacy, he was greeted by immediate success upon his return from there to London.

Reynolds' gift for reconciling those attributes of grandiosity, deduced with such rare intelligence from his study of the old masters, with his innate shrewdness of pragmatic observation is well demonstrated in his portrait of the future Lord Amherst. The military hero is here shown in ceremonial finery, proudly displaying his well-earned decorations as a Knight of the Order of the Bath. He appears dramatically posed, as though studying the unfolding campaign against the French, with his helmet resting on a map of the territory under dispute. The landscape stretching dramatically beyond the general reflects the actual terrain that had to be traversed, as Amherst's forces were transported down the rapids of the St. Lawrence toward Montreal. That successful maneuver had been illustrated in a drawing made by one of Amherst's officers, Thomas Davies, in 1760, now preserved in the Public Archives of Canada, Ottawa. Reynolds is known to have employed visual documentation of the kind in preparing his composition. A masterpiece of portraiture in the heroic Baroque tradition, the Amherst icon ranks high in the gallery of its artist's many glorifications of the notable personalities of his era.

THOMAS GAINSBOROUGH (1727–1788)

7. *Portrait of Lord Jeffery Amherst*, ca. 1785
    Oil on canvas, 30 x 25 in. (76.2 x 63.5 cm)
    Gift of Mrs. George D. Pratt
    P1940.5

For the benefit of posterity Jeffery Amherst also turned to Reynolds' greatest competitor, Thomas Gainsborough, for a likeness painted during later life. We thus have the opportunity of observing the same subject treated by the two dominant personalities in English painting of their generation. Gainsborough's career evolved very differently from that of his learned colleague. Although he had come to London for his preliminary studies, he spent his early professional years outside the capital, first at Ipswich, then at Bath. He had for a time devoted his attention mainly to landscape and never abandoned those interests, even though portraiture came to be his mainstay.

From early on, he was more responsive to the Netherlandish traditions and the French Rococo than to the Grand Manner which held Reynolds in its spell. Gainsborough was, in fact, the English artist who most successfully translated the elegant lyricism of the French advocates of the Rococo into an unmistakably personal yet also English idiom. He was experienced in that idiom from having assisted the Parisian engraver, Hubert François Gravelot (1699–1773), who had for twenty years maintained his illustrator's shop in London. At the same time, Gainsborough transformed his admiration of van Dyck and the realistic persuasions of the seventeenth-century Dutch landscapists such as Ruisdael into thoroughly original terms. From that curious and complex amalgam he arrived at a style that stands out indelibly at whatever stage of its evolution one may encounter it.

While still resident in the fashionable resort city of Bath, Gainsborough had been sought as a founding member of the Royal Academy. But subsequent disagreements with the hanging committee led to his eventual withdrawal from participation in academy exhibitions. Gainsborough had moved to London in 1774. He enjoyed an outstanding success with a fashionable clientele, not least of whom were members of the royal family, who found his style more to their liking than that of Reynolds. Showing his works only at his home, and not in public, Gainsborough more and more indulged in a sketchy, generalized manner. It is that phase of his later performance that is to

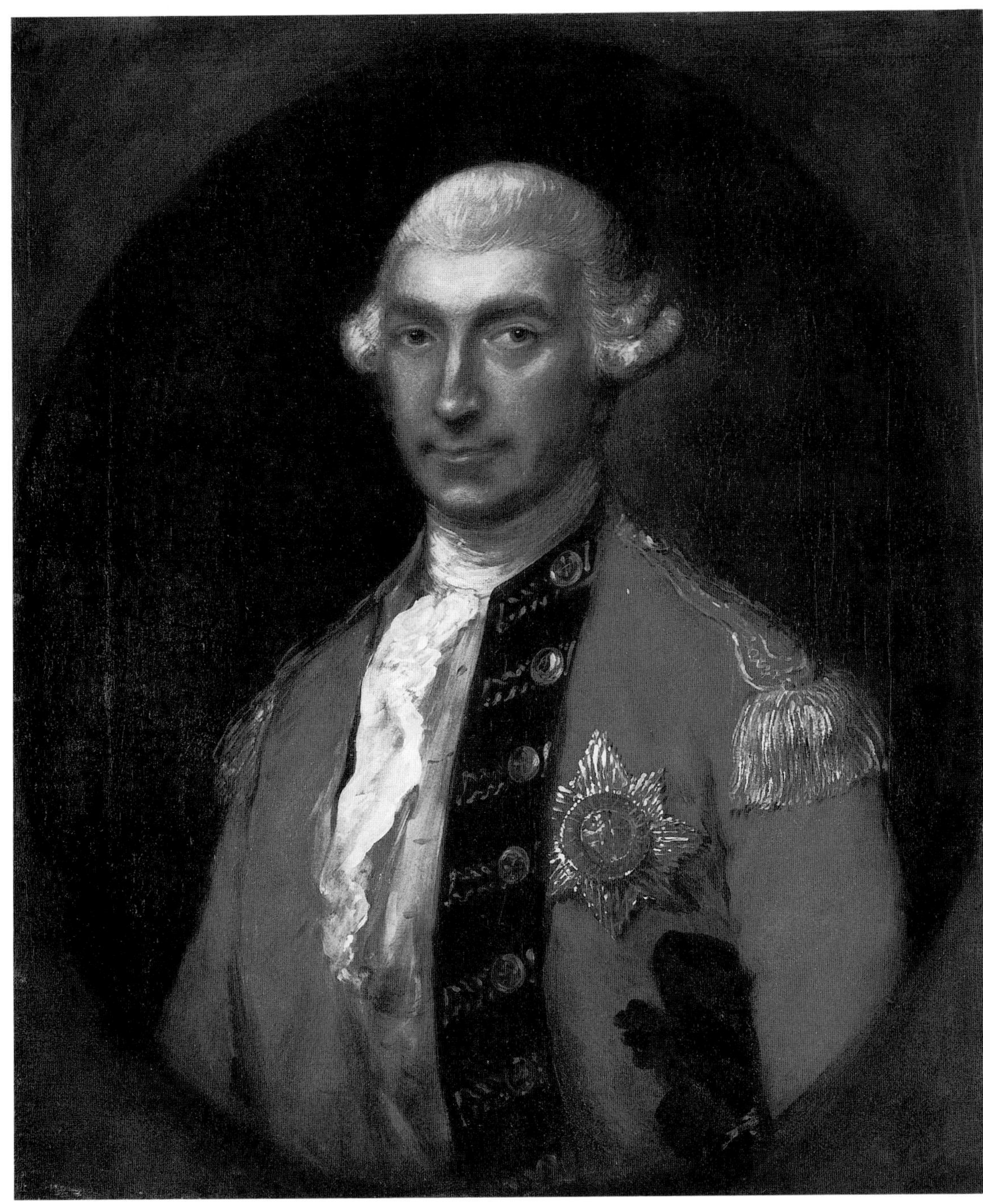

be recognized in the Amherst portrait. If not an outstanding Gainsborough product of those years—when he was more apt to evoke feminine presence than male—it is at least an amiable reminder of his outstanding contribution to the history of British portraiture in what is now regarded as its "Classic Age."

Generalized and "impressionistic" though it may be, Gainsborough's portrait of Jeffery Amherst says something about the subject himself. Here shown as Baron of Holmesdale, later to become Baron of Montreal, Amherst was for most of those later years entrusted with charge of the British armies as commander-in-chief. Shortly before his death he was made marshal. He was thus in a position to enjoy the fruits of demanding years of military service across the Atlantic. Still portrayed as an army general, but relieved of the air of the hard-bitten officer portrayed by Blackburn or of a leader pondering the outcome of his decisions, as Reynolds conceived him, he now appears —still remarkably youthful in feature—as the fashionable image of successful service to the Crown.

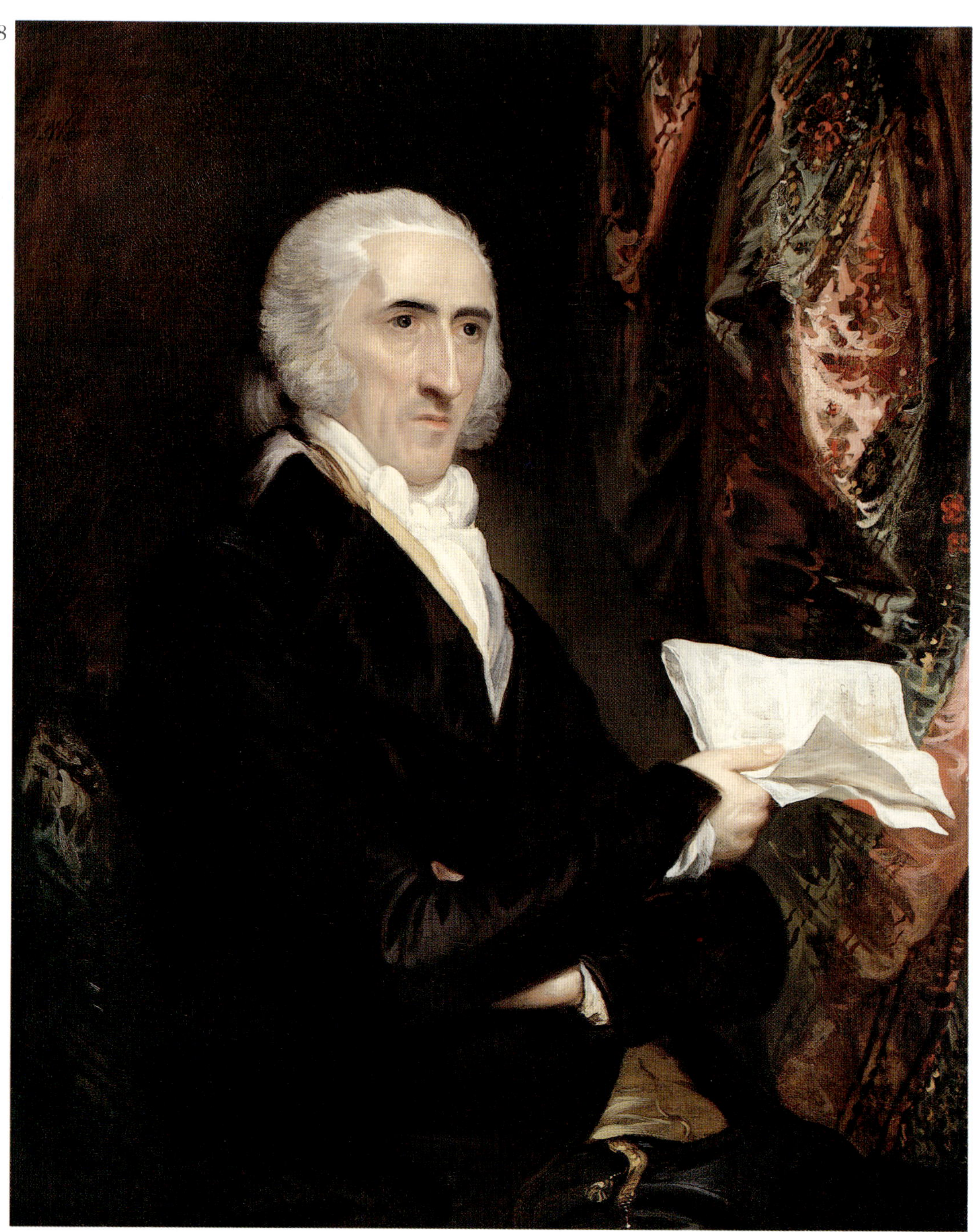

SIR BENJAMIN WEST (1738–1820)

8. *Portrait of Dr. Enoch Edwards*, 1795
   Oil on canvas, 36 x 28 in. (91.4 x 71.1 cm)
   Gift of Herbert L. Pratt, '95
   P1938.1

Following the death of Reynolds in 1792, Benjamin West
succeeded to his post as president of the Royal Academy,
an honor he retained with but one, brief interruption
(1805–6) until his own death in 1820. To have been so
elevated by his peers was a credit as much to his industry
and perspicacity as to his natural gifts as an artist. Born
near Philadelphia of Quaker parents, West was first active
as a portrait limner in Philadelphia and briefly in New
York. He made his way to Italy and from there to England
where he arrived in 1763. In the course of his three years
spent in Italy, he ventured to Florence, Bologna, and Venice
—all with lasting benefit. Most of all, however, he profited
from living in Rome, with its cadre of native masters and
its international colony of artists and intellectuals. There

West first became involved in notions of history painting, a pursuit that would feature importantly in his future career (see No. 18). Even so, it was as a painter of portraits that West set up shop in London, and he would continue to ply the trade of a "face painter" throughout his active career. On occasion that involvement led to very happy results. One such successful venture is his *Portrait of Dr. Enoch Edwards.*

Awareness of West's extraordinary faculty for managing his professional interests should not distract us from his undoubted personal qualities of warmth and generosity of spirit. He was never anything but a British subject and remained uninvolved in the political affairs of the colonies or the Republic to follow. Over the years he was hospitable to many visitors from his native shores, whether Tory (like Copley) or faithful to the Revolution (like Gilbert Stuart or Charles Willson Peale).

Under the circumstances, it is wholly understandable that other visitors from abroad sought him out on visits to London. One of them was Dr. Enoch Edwards (1751–1802) of Philadelphia, who became West's friend and sat for a portrait in 1795, not long after West became the second president of the Royal Academy. Himself a person of some distinction, both as a surgeon and as a man of political affairs in Pennsylvania, Dr. Edwards was related to West through marriage to a distant cousin of the artist's. Hence, the somewhat intimate, informal quality of the portrayal is to some extent explained. Nevertheless surprising, however, is the freshness of the paint handling itself—one not always to be encountered in West's work, much of which was technically belabored in the artist's preoccupation with his subject matter. Here the Baroque tendencies of his religious subjects undertaken in his later years are impressively adumbrated, especially in the colorful draperies depicted at the upper right. The sparkling freshness of those passages in particular recall the lasting impression West's visit to Venice had left upon his adaptable imagination.

GEORGE BEARE (ACTIVE 1741–1749)

9. *Portrait of an Unknown Lady*, 1748
   Oil on canvas, 50 x 40 in. (127 x 101.6 cm)
   Museum Purchase
   1985.4

The eventual emergence of a native English school of painting was above all due to the efforts of William Hogarth. If he was in a sense the successor to Lely and Kneller in becoming the dominant artistic figure of his era, he was also very unlike them for he often catered to the rising bourgeoisie, not the aristocracy. Nor did Hogarth apply his talents so singly to portraiture. Indeed, capable though he was as a portraitist, Hogarth was most of all devoted to the creation of moralizing genre subjects. In addition, he was deeply concerned with theoretical speculations relating to his role as teacher and publisher of his own, commercially successful engravings. Although a number of that singular master's prints are among the reserves of the Mead Art Museum, we cannot boast a painting by his hand. Given that lack, however, we could do no better than to have recently acquired a fine portrait by Hogarth's lesser known contemporary, George Beare, whose portraits are so close in quality and character to Hogarth's own production as to have been sometimes mistaken for works by Hogarth himself.

Almost nothing is known about Beare as a person, save that he worked in the west of England during the 1740s. The *Portrait of an Unknown Lady*, signed and dated 1748, is an important addition to his recognized oeuvre, which includes thirty works altogether, only a few of them signed or dated. Most are identified with their artist by stylistic attribution alone. And while the names of some of Beare's sitters are known, many of their company share the present anonymity of the respectable lady now housed at Amherst College. Beare's patrons seem to have come from the ranks of the landed gentry or from a mercantile or commercial background. Comfortable though their circumstances clearly were, they thus made no traceable mark upon their times. Still, they share a personable air of countenance, with much of that look of individual dignity and alertness animating Hogarth's portrayals of similar subjects in London.

Beare's *Portrait of an Unknown Lady* has another level

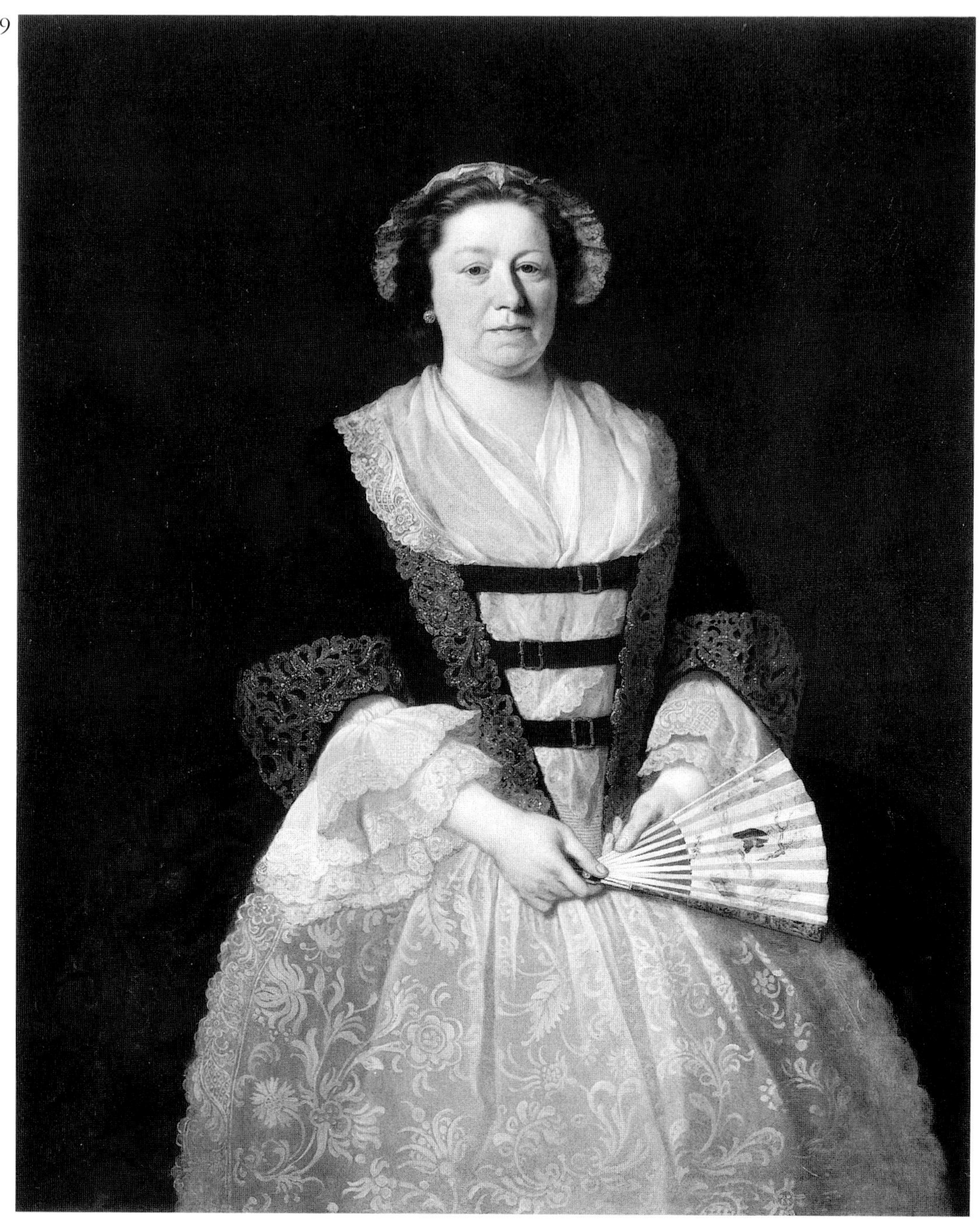

of interest in its present location, for it provides instructive comparisons with portraits by John Singleton Copley (1738–1815) in the Amherst College Collection. Copley's portraits of Benjamin Blackstone, Jr. and Eleanor Phipps Blackstone, ca. 1762–64, date from just over a decade later than the Beare canvas, so that associations between the respective approaches of the two painters are reasonable to posit. Links between artistic practice in England and the beginnings of a colonial school in North America can be historically traced, as various English painters made their way to the New World during the eighteenth century. The transmission of fashions by miscellaneous engravings as well as rarely encountered paintings played a role as well. Beare's handling of details and textures of costume is very attentive, closely akin to Copley's work. At the very least it may be observed that both artists derive from the same artistic roots, however indirectly. And as the output of provincial painters in England comes to be better understood, associations of the sort just proposed may well take on further substance.

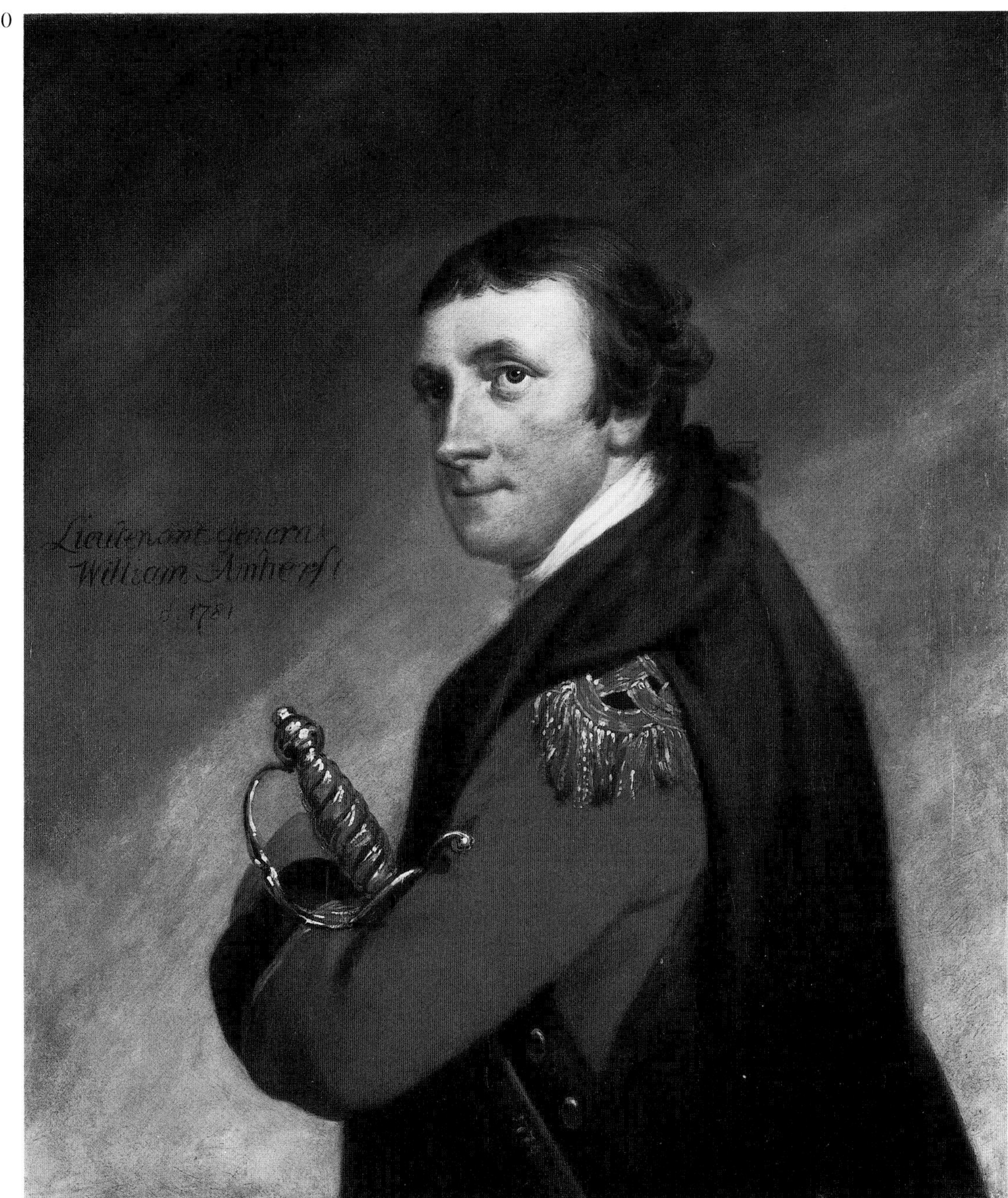

ROBERT EDGE PINE (1742–1790)

10. *Lieutenant General William Amherst*, 1779
    Oil on canvas, 30 x 25 in. (76.2 x 63.5 cm)
    Museum Purchase
    1967.83

It is hardly a compensation to realize that British artists gravitated to the New World, even as certain American masters found their way back to mother England. Probably the best of those to reverse the tide of eastward migration was Robert Edge Pine. Although no match for a Copley or West, he was nevertheless a capable portrait master. He had won a modicum of success in England before his departure for Philadelphia in 1784, once peace had been concluded following the American Revolution. It has been surmised that his motives were at once commercial and ideological. A friend of the famous actor, David Garrick, he displayed an original turn of mind in portraying actors in costume, but his ambitions really were to excel in more serious history painting. Reputedly he wished to specialize in that genre when he was established in the young republic, whose political ideals appear to have appealed to him.

Once in Philadelphia, however, Pine was mainly employed at painting faces, not in major historical projects. Moreover, he had to journey in the southern states much of the time to find sufficient clients, for the local Quakers were as immune to his decorative blandishments as also were the tight-fisted Germans of the city. He nevertheless produced a prodigious amount of work during his brief career in Philadelphia. He died four years after his arrival, reportedly of apoplexy. Shortly thereafter his creditors forced the sale of his house and its contents, which included many prints and a "valuable Collection of Original Paintings" including theatrical subjects by Pine. Their new owner was an entrepreneur named Daniel Bowen, who displayed the collection in Philadelphia, New York, and Boston. Sad to say, in 1803, the building that was used to show the works in Boston went up in smoke and with it, most of

Pine's American works. The surviving evidence of his substantial output in the United States is spotty and almost uniformly inept.

Pine's story is especially sad because works such as this portrait of Lieutenant General William Amherst (1722–1781) show him to have been more than merely a competent artist. His composition shows its maker's fondness for catching his sitter's likeness in a three-quarters view. That formula, which served him well in his depictions of actors, introduces a note of lively informality into his characterization. Inasmuch as William Amherst was born in Bath, as was his bride Elizabeth Patterson, it is quite likely that this portrait was painted there, before Pine departed for London the same year (1779). Given Pine's taste for innovation disclosed in the Amherst portrait and his ventures into theatrical depictions, it is the more to be regretted that his ambitions went unfulfilled.

SIR HENRY RAEBURN (1756–1823)

11. *Portrait of Lieutenant General, The Honorable William Stewart*, ca. 1815–23
Oil on canvas, 30 x 25 in. (76.2 x 63.5 cm)
Bequest of Herbert L. Pratt, '95
1945.15

In Sir Henry Raeburn one encounters a very different personality from the foregoing painters. Unlike Ramsay, who was professionally identified with the English establishment, Raeburn pursued his career almost entirely in Edinburgh. At Reynolds' urging he visited Italy while still a young man (ca. 1785–87), and he eventually became associated with the Royal Academy. Otherwise Raeburn was in essence self-taught, aside from brief experience in a goldsmith's shop while yet a youth and a modicum of practical acquaintance with engraving. It is surprising, therefore, that Raeburn evolved an independent style marked by great boldness of scale and substance of form. Reputedly, he sometimes took

to modeling—which implies an interest in plasticity borne out in the almost tangible quality consistently to be observed in his paintings.

Painted directly on the canvas without any preliminary drawing, his images were defined succinctly and compellingly. They possessed a play of light and shadow once they assumed mature formulation (and that came early in his career). Raeburn's personal use of the classic devices of *chiaroscuro* realism, with the rendition of form stated in bold contrasts of light and shadow, were never subjected to radical change. His results are almost invariably predictable, but that is admittedly a mixed blessing when one is faced by too large a sampling of his production.

By Raeburn's time the Scottish aristocrats and professional people were sufficiently affluent to support an artist of high caliber. Raeburn, in return, was equally possessed of the temperament and talent to suit their needs. His approach was marked by a plainspoken candor that held an obvious appeal to clients brought up in the ethos of pragmatic restraint then prevalent in Scotland. Raeburn's *Portrait*

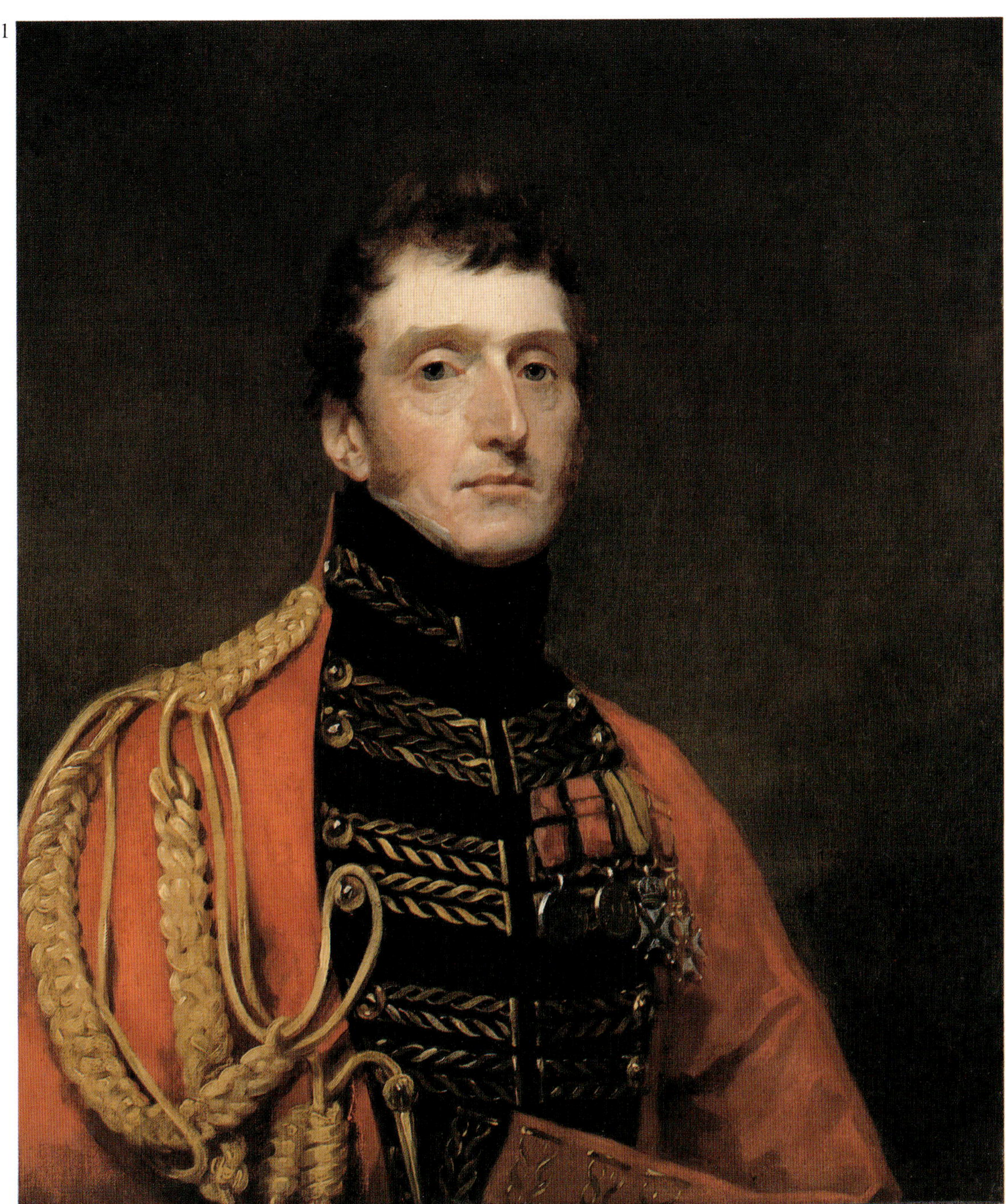

of Lieutenant General, The Honorable William Stewart (alternatively "Stuart") is a fine sample of Raeburn's art, with its firm set of facial features and its brisk handling of surface.

William Stewart (1772–1827) was a man of distinction, a career officer with a long record of arduous military service, much of it in campaigns abroad, and a member of Parliament late in life. Born the second son of the seventh Earl of Galloway, he received his commission as ensign in 1786, at the tender age of twelve. The following year he was promoted to lieutenant, after the fashion of military preferment enjoyed by members of aristocratic families at the time. Many times wounded, Stewart suffered the loss of an arm, most likely in 1812 at the Battle of Waterloo.

Having attained the rank of lieutenant general in 1813, the veteran campaigner appears in that military identity in Raeburn's portrait, which was painted shortly thereafter. Far more than a mere military period piece, the painting evokes something of the presence of a man who kept an informative journal and maintained a personal correspondence with Lord Wellington and Admiral Nelson with both of whom he had served. At Nelson's request, Stewart named his first son Horatio.

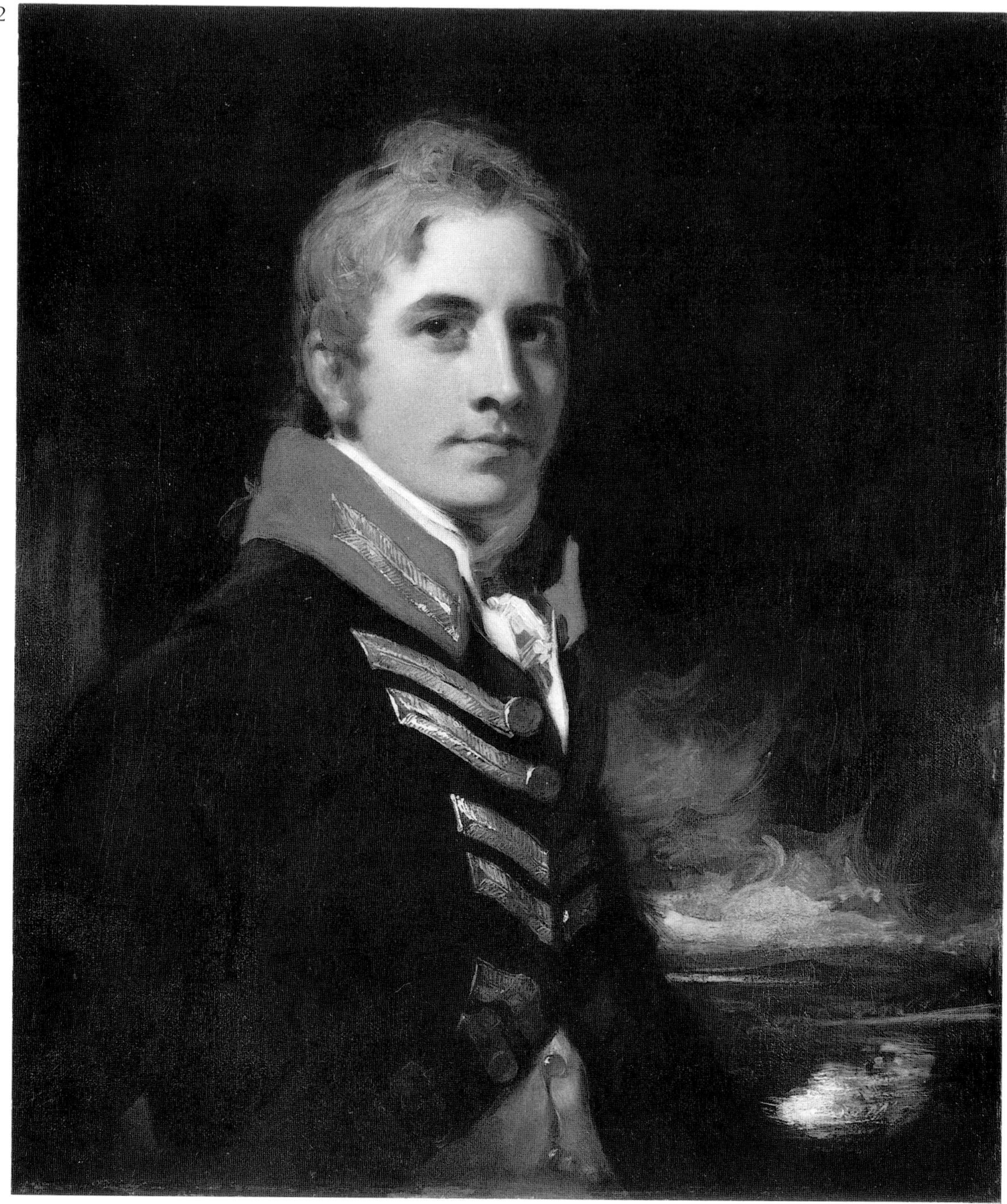

JOHN HOPPNER (1758–1810)

12. *Portrait of William Pitt Amherst*
   Oil on canvas, 30 x 25 in. (76.2 x 63.5 cm)
   Museum Purchase
   1967.81

It is of more than passing interest to compare Raeburn's portrait of General Stewart (No. 11) with John Hoppner's winning likeness of his slightly older contemporary, William Pitt Amherst (1773–1857), shown at an earlier time of life. A product of the Royal Academy school, entered in 1775, Hoppner testifies to the effectiveness of academy training. The artistic values of Reynolds and other leading masters of his generation were perpetuated successfully. Hoppner's blandishments, often regarded as primarily suited to the depiction of women and children, are appropriate here. The young gentleman is shown in an appealingly alert and responsive guise, his face quickened with a look of good humored confidence. Hoppner's capacities for skillful economy and freshness of execution appear at their best in this portrait, making it one of the most engaging of our entire ensemble of Amherst family portraits.

The great vogue Hoppner enjoyed was based upon his capacity to assimilate from his more original predecessors, most notably, Reynolds and Romney. But his flair for felicitous contrivance sufficed for those who clustered about the Prince of Wales, whose official portrait painter he became in 1789. Honors at the Royal Academy were granted only later, however, and not in time for him to enjoy them very long, for Hoppner died at the comparatively early age of fifty-two, in the full flush of his professional success.

William Pitt Amherst, whose given name honored one of his godfathers, was born in Bath under reassuring circumstances of comfort and privilege. The death of his mother Elizabeth Patterson Amherst in 1776, and his father General William Amherst in 1781, left the young boy and his sister Elizabeth in the care of their uncle Lord Jeffery, who remained childless. They were promptly taken to their uncle's country seat, Montreal, to be raised as

his own children. In due course William Pitt was legally adopted by the baron, becoming heir to his title and properties. Subsequently educated at Oxford and culturally groomed on a Grand Tour befitting one of his station, he succeeded to the family title in 1797 after Lord Amherst's death. He also received a Master of Arts degree from Oxford that same year, and a few years later, in 1800, he married the young widow of the Earl of Plymouth. It proved to be an auspicious marital alliance. Gaining the favor of the Prince Regent, later King George IV, the second Baron Amherst was entrusted with many important assignments. One of them permitted him a detour to visit Napoleon, then in exile on St. Helena. Most important, however, was his service in India and Burma, for which he was created Earl Amherst of Arakan and Viscount Holmesdale. His favor at court continued under King William IV.

SIR THOMAS LAWRENCE (1769–1830)

13. *Portrait of Sarah Hickman Amherst*
   Oil on canvas, 30 x 25 in. (76.2 x 63.5 cm)
   Museum Purchase
   1967.82

14. *Portrait of Benjamin West*, ca. 1820–21
   Oil on panel, 28⅞ x 23⅞ in. (73.3 x 60.6 cm)
   Bequest of Herbert L. Pratt, '95
   1964.82

15. *Charles Baring Wall*
   Oil on canvas, 32 x 27 in. (81.3 x 68.6 cm)
   Gift of Dwight W. Morrow, Jr., '33
   1956.9

By any standard of measure, the most gifted of British portrait masters of later generations was Sir Thomas Lawrence, who was third in the impressive line of artists serving as presidents of the Royal Academy. And it is to our good fortune that Lawrence was selected as portraitist of the first wife of William Pitt Amherst, Sarah Hickman. It may not be one of Lawrence's most lavish or important performances

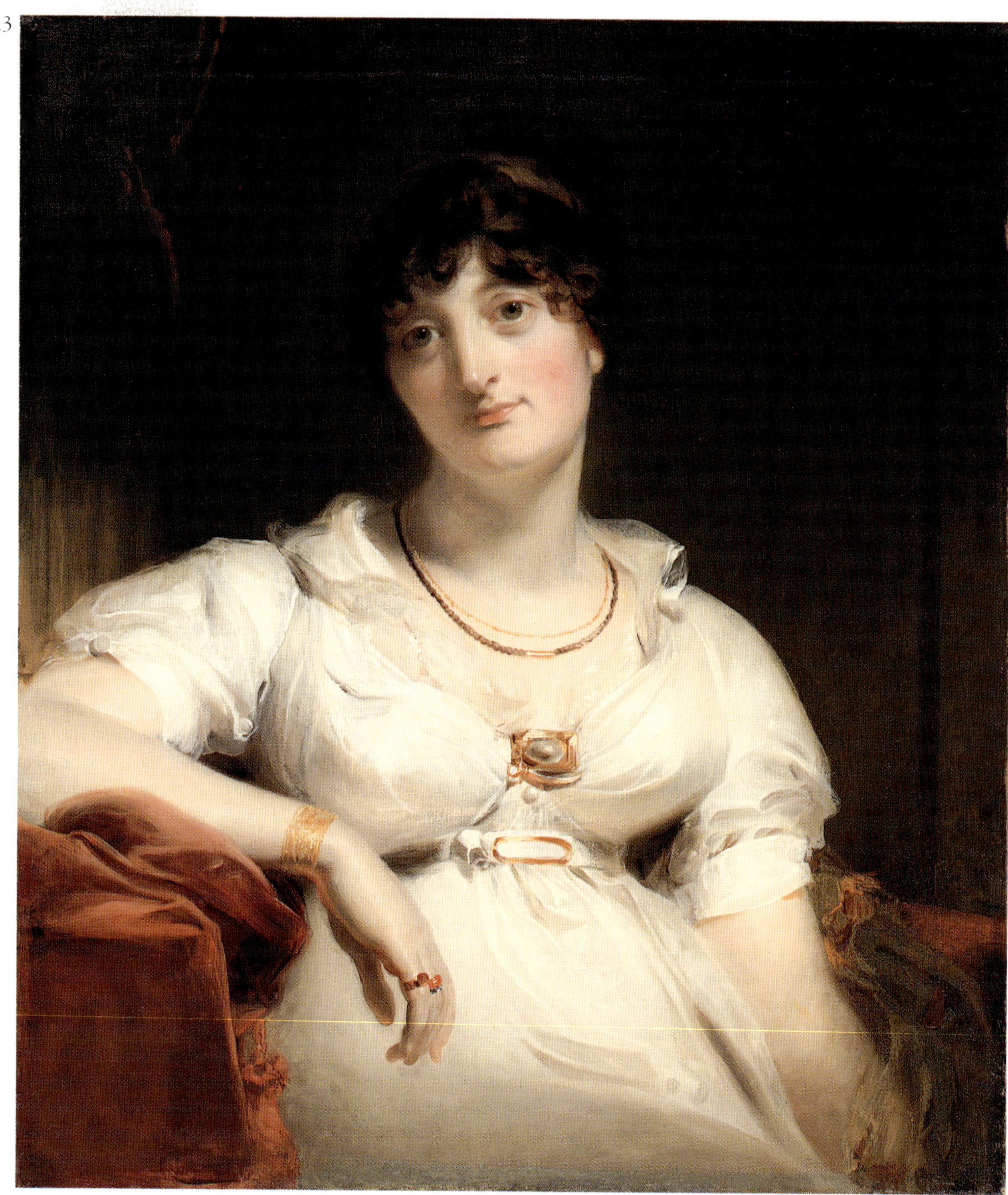

in his dazzling visual registry of British aristocracy, but it is a better than fair demonstration of his brilliant flair. It serves as a fitting companion to Hoppner's urbane portrayal of her husband (No. 12).

To judge by the sitters' appearances, the two portraits seem to have been made at about the same time. Hoppner had enjoyed special favor among those privy to the Prince Regent, as young Amherst was. But Hoppner's death in 1810 left the way unimpeded for the meteoric rise of the phenomenally gifted Lawrence. The latter rose to a status of international reputation unprecedented for a British artist. In 1818 the regent sent him to Aachen and Vienna, to paint the allied victors gathered to conclude the Treaty of Vienna, which brought the Napoleonic Wars to a formal close. While in Vienna he was able to study the masterpieces of Titian and Velásquez in the magnificent Imperial Collection. (Himself a distinguished connoisseur, he formed a collection of old master drawings that has seldom if ever been equaled.) Proceeding from Vienna to Rome, Lawrence painted *Pope Pius VII*, which remains, with his portrait of

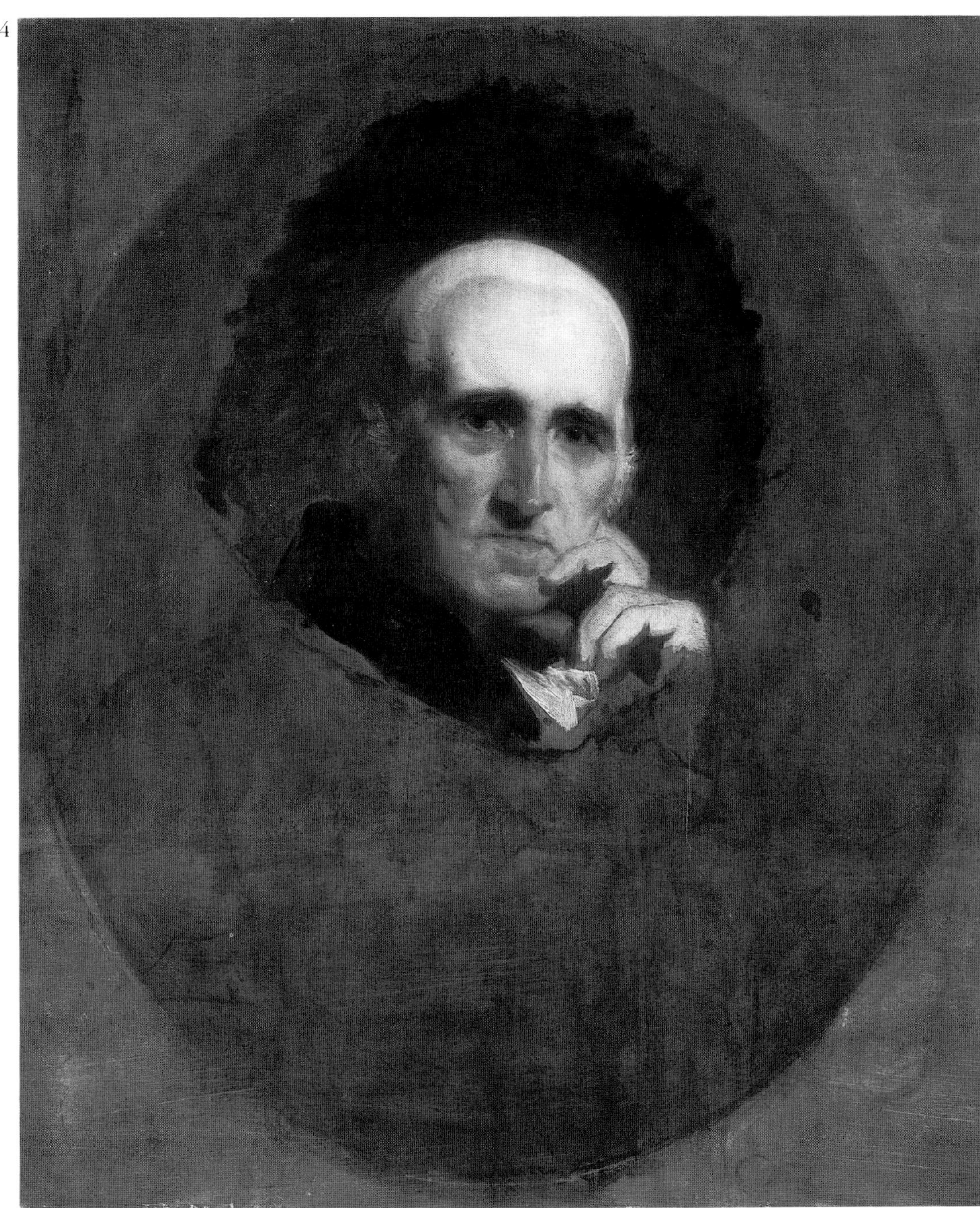

the Archduke Charles done in Vienna, one of his greatest masterpieces.

Upon his return to London in 1820, Lawrence succeeded to the presidency of the Royal Academy, a post left vacant by the death of Benjamin West that year. Lawrence's relationships with West had always been cordial, and the older man's influence, both at court and in the academy, had been helpful to him. It is gratifying to have an artistic record of that association in the form of an oil study of West by Lawrence (No. 14). Once dated around 1794, it was subsequently presumed to portray West at about the same stage of life as he is shown in a full-length portrait of him that Lawrence exhibited at the Royal Academy in 1821 (hence after West's death). It now seems more likely, however, to have been painted around 1811, at which time Lawrence showed another half-length portrait of West (now lost) at the Royal Academy. The set of facial features, hair line, and indications of costume relate closely to the visual evidence of the earlier canvas, which is known from an engraving after the original made by H. Meyer in 1813.

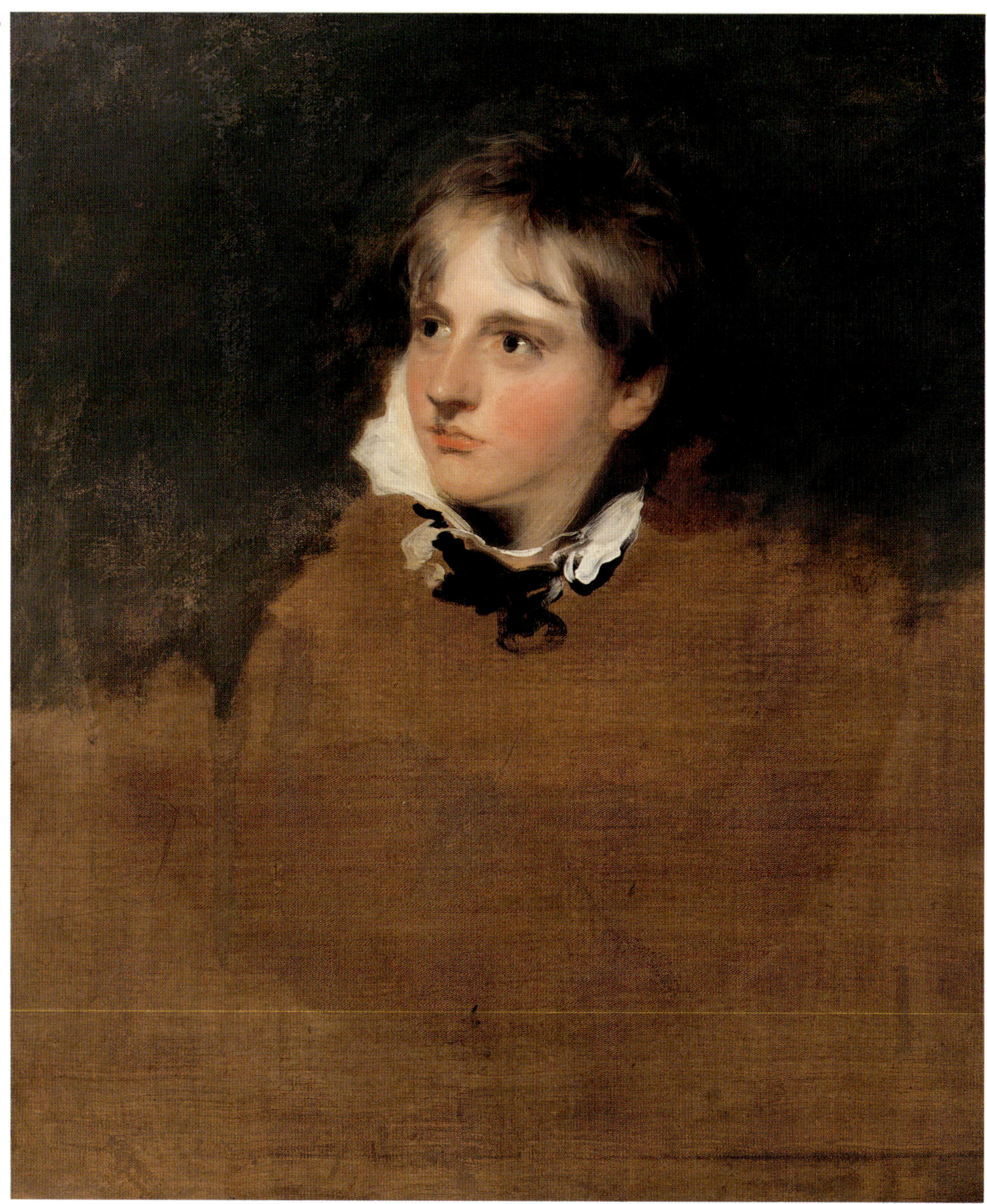

Revealing similar technical procedures but in the depiction of a youthful subject is a second oil study possessed, however, of very contrasting qualities of freshness and charm: *Charles Baring Wall* (No. 15). This superb further glimpse into Lawrence's habits of work in progress isolates that felicitousness of touch that earned him so wide and enduring a reputation as a portraitist *par excellence*.

Lady Amherst was herself an accomplished person—sufficiently so that her own biography is now in preparation. Her years spent in India while her husband was governor general afforded her an opportunity to study the flora and fauna of that exotic environment. Certain flowering trees are now known by her name, as is an especially handsome variety of pheasant (*Chrysolophus amherstiae*), introduced from India into the coverts of England by Lady Amherst. Her interest in the decorative arts is also memorialized in a form of chinaware that bears her name. Her elaborate dessert service, unfortunately too delicate to travel with the exhibition, is now in the Amherst College Collection.

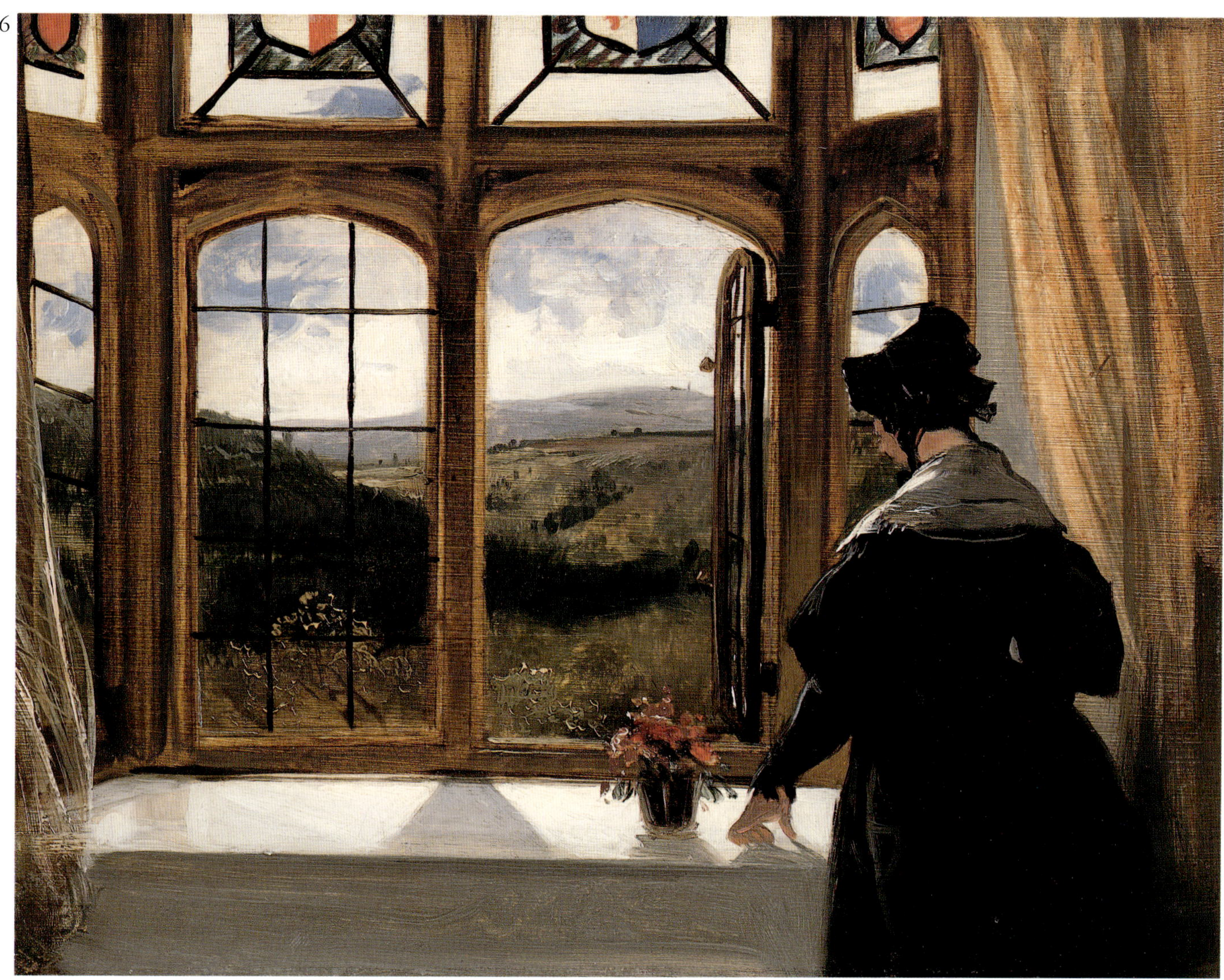

SIR EDWIN HENRY LANDSEER (1802–1873)

16. *The Duchess of Bedford*, 1829–30)
Oil on canvas, 10⅛ x 12⅛ in. (25.7 x 30.8 cm)
Museum Purchase
1978.112

Lawrence's untimely death at the age of sixty, in 1830, in effect marked a cadence in the Classic Age of portraiture in Britain, even though the practice of painting portraits continued to thrive, if on rather different terms. It was not until the advent of John Singer Sargent (1856–1925) on the international scene that Lawrence's true successor would appear. Meanwhile many other capable artists would accept the portrait artist's role, some of them performng with great distinction. Of course, expectations of them were modified increasingly as the age of Victoria's rule (to commence in 1837) entered its many phases. And more and more, the tastes of the rising bourgeoisie are encoun-

tered as part of the cultural milieu of those times. In the process, the role of the Royal Academy was relieved of its quasi-official status as patronage, both royal and public, took on more personal shadings of preference and value judgment.

One of the beneficiaries of the new emphasis that evolved, as innate British affection for narration triumphed over the more exalted pretensions of the Grand Manner, was Sir Edwin Landseer. Son of John Landseer, a well-known engraver, the aspiring young artist was trained at the Royal Academy in 1816, first shown at the British Institute in 1824, and was made a full member of the academy at an early age in 1831. Known both in his own day and ours primarily as an animalier, Landseer's frequent endowment of his birds and beasts with qualities of mock-human sentiment, aroused an almost universal enthusiasm in Victorian times only to be matched by an equally resolute disparagement among those of "modern" persuasions in the post-Victorian era. Now, after that long hiatus of serious attention to Landseer's work, those superbly rendered transcriptions of natural fact (and Landseer's descriptive prowess *was* remarkable) are attracting critical reappraisal. What is often overlooked, however, is that Landseer was also a portraitist of human subjects on occasion, with a display of painterly skills, particularly in his sketches, rivaling Lawrence in his own domain.

Hardly a "portrait" in the usual sense of the word but nevertheless a variation within that category is a charming oil sketch of an interior with the Duchess of Bedford. This is reputedly a replica of a larger version of the subject which was owned by the Duke of Bedford (present whereabouts unknown). Landseer's precious little scene is appropriately possessed of qualities of visual scale that vastly exceed the actual physical size of the picture. Reportedly, Landseer and the second Duchess of Bedford (1781–1853) enjoyed a long and intimate relationship, despite the fact

that the noblewoman was his senior by some twenty years. His several other representations of the lady portray her in characteristically active roles—on horseback, at a reception, or fashionably dressed for a ball. Since this depiction shows her in a subdued situation and attired in a matronly black, it may date from the time of the death of her husband in 1839, and not as it may otherwise be inferred, from an earlier period, when Landseer was a frequent visitor to the Bedford household at Endsleigh, near Milton Abbey in Devon. However, an old inscription on the back of the academy board on which the picture is painted identifies the setting as Woburn Abbey. Questions of the actual locale aside, there can be no doubt of the painter's fluency of touch or of the conviction with which he summarizes a wealth of visual information, as he shows the duchess gazing from her elevated station upon the spreading landscape that surrounds the family seat.

JAMES SANT (1820–1916)

17. *Light Thrown on a Dark Passage*
   Oil on canvas, 36 x 30 in. (91.4 x 76.2 cm)
   Museum Purchase
   1985.31

As has been mentioned before, what might be called a "domestic" tone came to be widely favored in Victorian Britain. To be sure, the inclusion of direct likenesses in representations of historical moments had become an established mode, one that had been widely adopted throughout Europe, as large acreages of historical "machines" eloquently

testify. And the tradition of the "conversation piece" which had been nurtured in eighteenth-century Britain remained a stock-in-trade for many professional practitioners. The borderlines between strict portrait representation and the depiction of familiar, anecdotal situations was therefore apt to remain indistinct. Such is the case with portraits of the Royal Family by favored artists, including the prolific painter James Sant, who rose to the station of portrait painter of Queen Victoria, an honor bestowed in 1872. He showed his mettle early in a large group portrait, *The 7th Earl of Cardigan Relating the Story of the Cavalry Charge of Balaclava to Prince Consort and the Royal Children of Windsor*

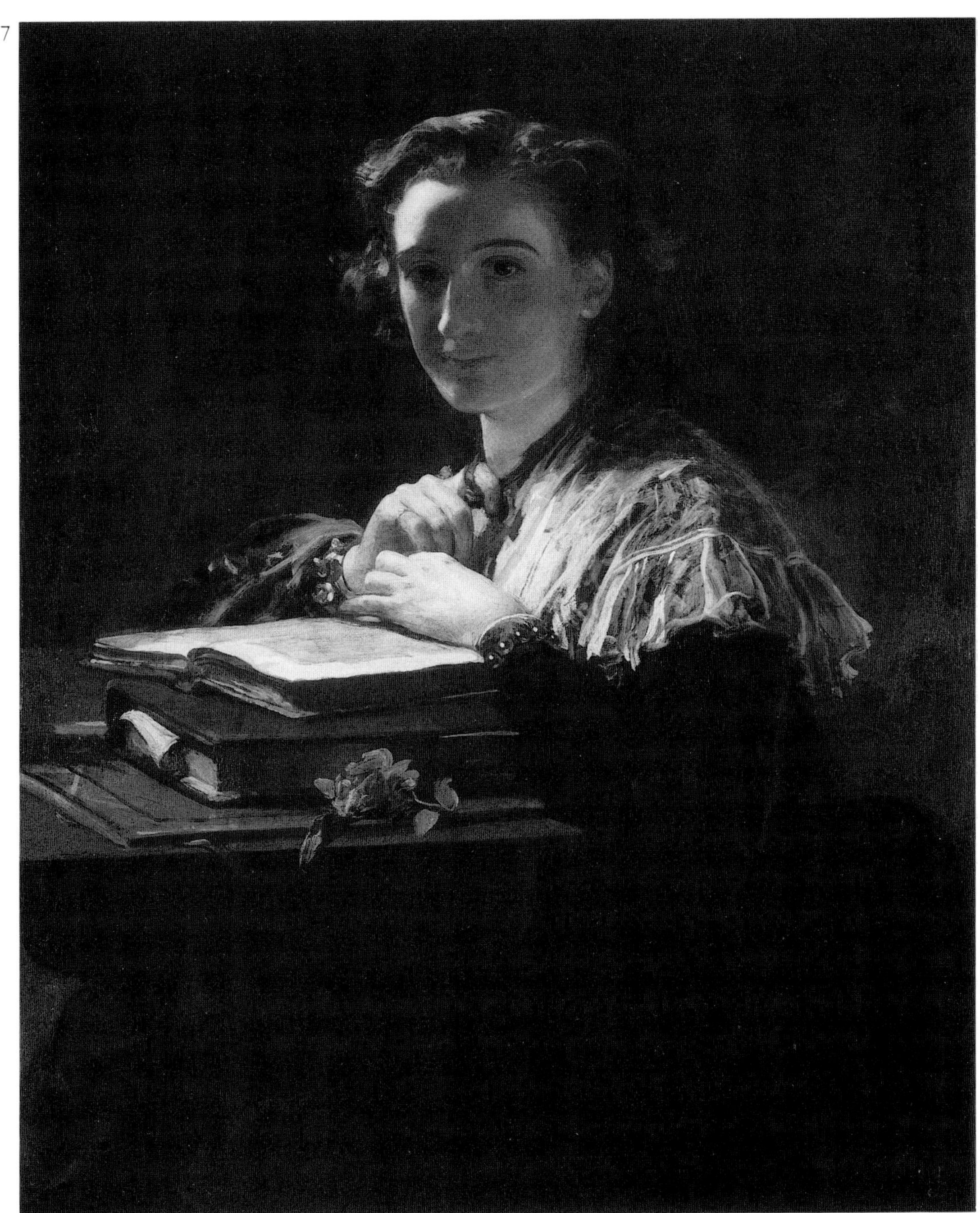

(1854). The freer, more painterly manner of his mature years is to be admired in such well-known canvases as *The Schoolmaster's Daughter*. The latter canvas was presented as Sant's diploma painting following his election as a full member of the Royal Academy in 1869. It was shown at the academy in 1871 and remains in the collection of that institution.

A smaller, wholly informal portrayal by Sant of an attractive, but unidentifed sitter was recently purchased for the Amherst College Collection. Titled *Light Thrown on a Dark Passage*, it is an especially appealing example of the melding of the portrait and genre traditions in its period. At the same time, it beautifully exemplifies the sensitivity to individual, personal identity that was cultivated by artists of Sant's class and the technical prowess they could regularly summon to their tasks. It is thus a fitting complement to the other Victorian works in the collection, as well as to echoes of the same tastes for reticent, but strong feminine presences in the oeuvre of such American counterparts as Eastman Johnson (1824–1906), in his beautiful portrait of Edwina Booth (1885), also in the Mead Art Museum.

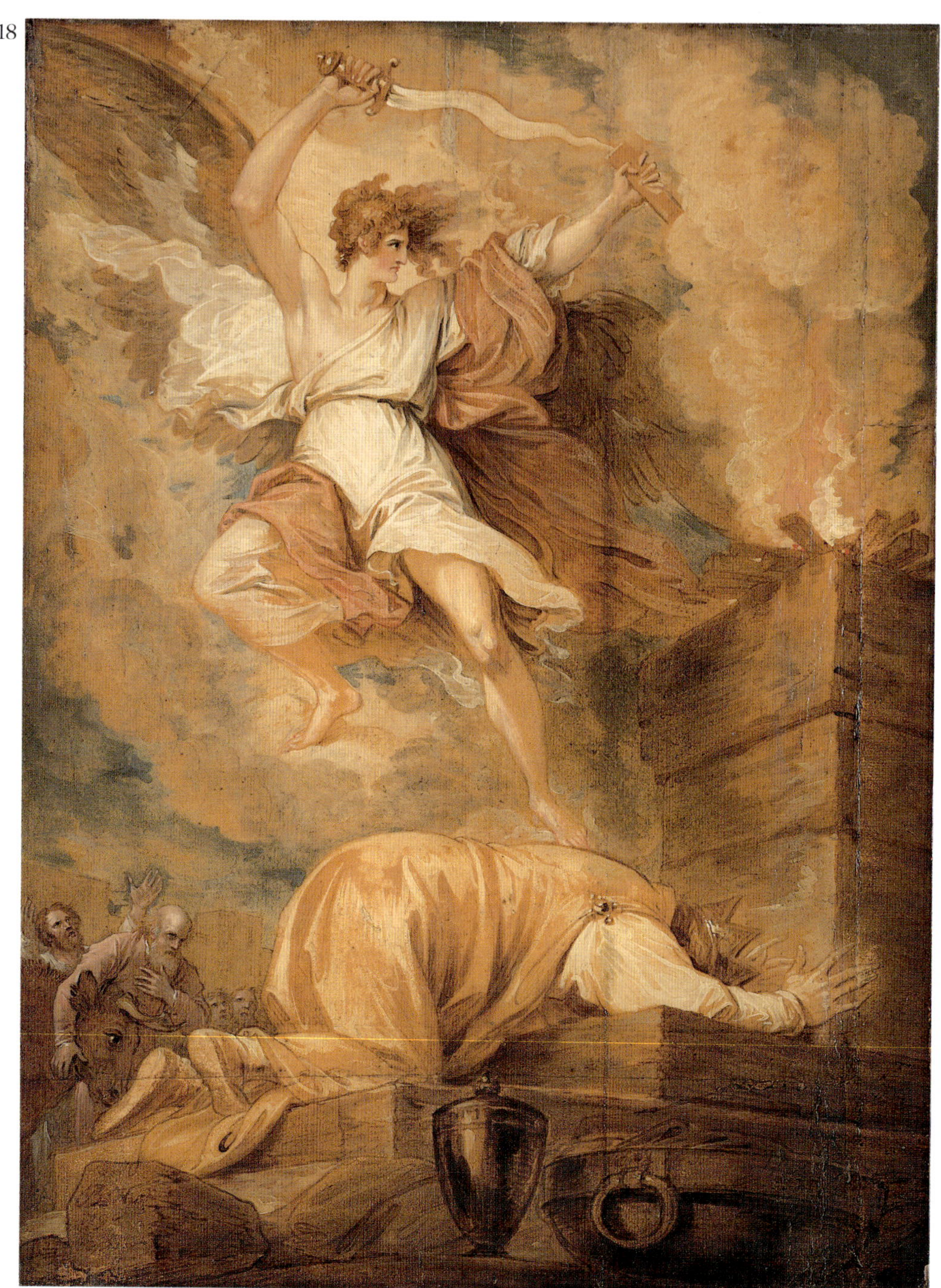

SIR BENJAMIN WEST (1738-1820)

18. *David Prostrate, whilst the Destroying Angel Sheathes the Sword*, 1798
Oil on paper mounted on panel, 31 x 22 in.
(91.4 x 71.1 cm)
Museum Purchase
1950.23

Benjamin West's precocity in venturing into novelties of style and subject have already been remarked upon with regard to his *Portrait of Dr. Enoch Edwards* (No. 8). That characteristic of his personality has exercised countervailing effects upon his reputation as an artist. Surprising ventures into modes so contrasting as Neoclassicism and the Baroque may as readily be taken as signs of either bold invention or inner contradiction signaling a lack of true creative core.

West's powers of accommodation may well be documented
in a picture now in the Amherst College Collection, but
not included in the present exhibition, the attribution of
which is still open to dispute. Representing a classical
episode, *Coriolanus Yields to his Mother's Appeal* bears West's
signature and a date of 1792. This canvas thus exemplifies
the emergent Neoclassicism of the earlier eighteenth-
century Italian painters. Interest of the kind appeared full-
blown in West's starling *Agrippina Landing at Brindisium
with the Ashes of Germanicus*. This painting was commissioned by the Archbishop of York after West had exhibited
two narrative pictures in 1764 at the Society of Arts. The
archbishop introduced West to King George III, and soon
the painter had earned the support of the Crown.

Efforts to attribute the *Coriolanus* to an earlier, Italian
master such as Agostino Masucci (d. 1758) remain inconclusive; nor does it make sense to conclude that it is either
an earlier work purchased by West and signed by him or a
facile copy made by West after an earlier model. Questions
about West's origins as an artist still remain to be answered.

It is clear, however, that West's changes of manner
were a factor in the look of modernity that so many observers
imputed to his subjects. Indeed, that susceptibility to
suggestion from diverse sources does anticipate the varia-
bility of approach assumed by artists of much later,

"modern" times. West's own willingness to venture along
new paths—or at least, unusual ones in the British context—are observable in such pathfinding undertakings as
his *Death of General Wolfe* (1771) or the religious subjects to
which he turned toward the end of the eighteenth century.
Among them our *David Prostrate, whilst the Destroying Angel
Sheathes the Sword* is a fine example.

West's more painterly and Romantic inclinations of
those years are vigorously embodied in this painting. And
here again, he was exceedingly precocious, not only within
the English milieu, but also in the larger, European sense.
In its bold freedom of conception and suggestive painterly
handling, West's conception harks back to Baroque traditions that had been widely discredited in the flush of
contrasting Neoclassical enthusiasms. The scene shows
David repentent at the altar in the effort to spare Jerusalem
from the destruction of an angry Lord (2 Sam. 24:16–25).
Perhaps done in preparation for a larger picture of much
the same description, exhibited in 1800, this composition
signifies a rising popularity of biblical subjects at the time.
It also reminds us of the eminent artist's irrepressible
responsiveness to the call of opportunity—a susceptibility
that surely was a touchstone to his remarkable versatility
as a performer.

ANGELICA KAUFFMANN (1741–1807)

19. *The Return of Telemachus*, ca. 1770–80
   Oil on canvas, 46 x 56 in. (116.8 x 142.2 cm)
   Museum Purchase
   1984.91

Critical opinions may differ as to the creative caliber of
Angelica Kauffmann's work or the durability of her contribution to the history of art in Britain, but it is generally
agreed that her involvement with the Royal Academy as a
founding member and her associations with British colleagues and patrons constitute a most interesting episode
in developments of the period. Born in the small Swiss
municipality of Chur, Kauffmann moved to Italy while
still quite young. By 1763 she had settled in Rome, then
the liveliest intellectual capital of Europe, with its numerous foreign colonies, not least of all, the British. A close
friend and portraitist of her countryman, the Neoclassical

theorist J. J. Winckelmann (1717–1768), she soon realized
her personal variant upon that point of view—a set of
style that changed little in the course of her career.

A versatile person, with musical and literary interests
and ingratiating linguistic skills, she made friends among
the British residents of Rome and eventually, in 1766,
traveled to London. She had exhibited there the year before
at the Free Society of Artists. Quickly gaining favor with
Reynolds and the Swiss-born Henry Fuseli (1741–1825),
she was one of only two women invited to join the group
who formed the Royal Academy. The other was Mary
Moser about whom little is now known. In 1782, Kauffmann returned to Rome in the company of her new
husband, an Italian painter, Antonio Zucchi (1726–1795)
Although she continued to exhibit at the Royal Academy
and contributed works to the famous Shakespeare Gallery
run by John Boydell (1719–1804), Kauffmann spent the
rest of her years in Rome.

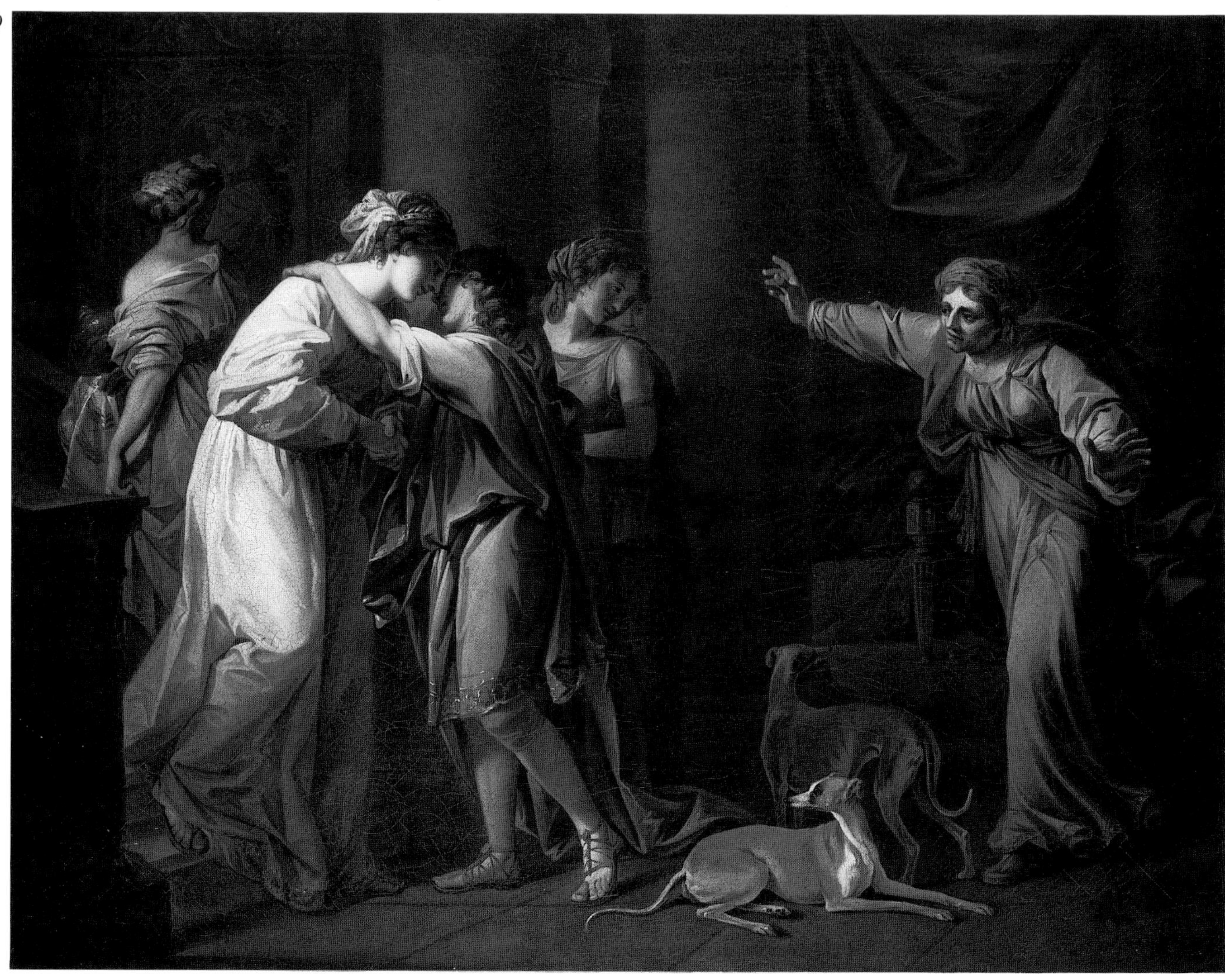

The Return of Telemachus, one of Kauffmann's four entries in the first exhibition at the Royal Academy in 1769, was based on a theme from Homer's *Odyssey*. Her staging of this episode closely follows Homer's narrative (*Odyssey* 7). Telemachus returns to the household of his mother, Penelope, after a long search for his father, Odysseus. Penelope is shown embracing her son, while his old nurse, Eurycleia, approaches excitedly. Viewers of Kauffmann's time, steeped as they were in both biblical and classical lore, were prepared to link classical and Christian meanings in dramatic events such as this, wherein Penelope might assume some of the burden of the Virgin Mary's grief and ennoblement in suffering. And by the same token, the wandering of Telemachus bore resemblances to the story of the Prodigal Son, with its overtones of redemption through love. In that penchant for conflating levels of moral content in moments charged with emotion, but governed by stoic restraint, Kauffmann exemplifies the preachments of Neoclassical theory, with its heroic virtue. She was to return often to Homer for inspiration on future occasions.

The Amherst College canvas is one of several closely related versions of this scene, so one must assume that her composition enjoyed a certain favor. Despite the endearments of her personality, her interpretations of classical subjects did not escape cavil as being over-idealized, prizing grace more than truth. She did, however, help implant the growing taste for Neoclassicism nurtured above all in Rome —tastes shared with Benjamin West, among others. And her talent as a decorator was much appreciated by architects, particularly the brothers Adam, who employed her on numerous occasions to ornament their elegant interiors. In that role above all is her historical contribution most appreciated. For her contemporaries, her compositions were widely popularized by a number of printmakers.

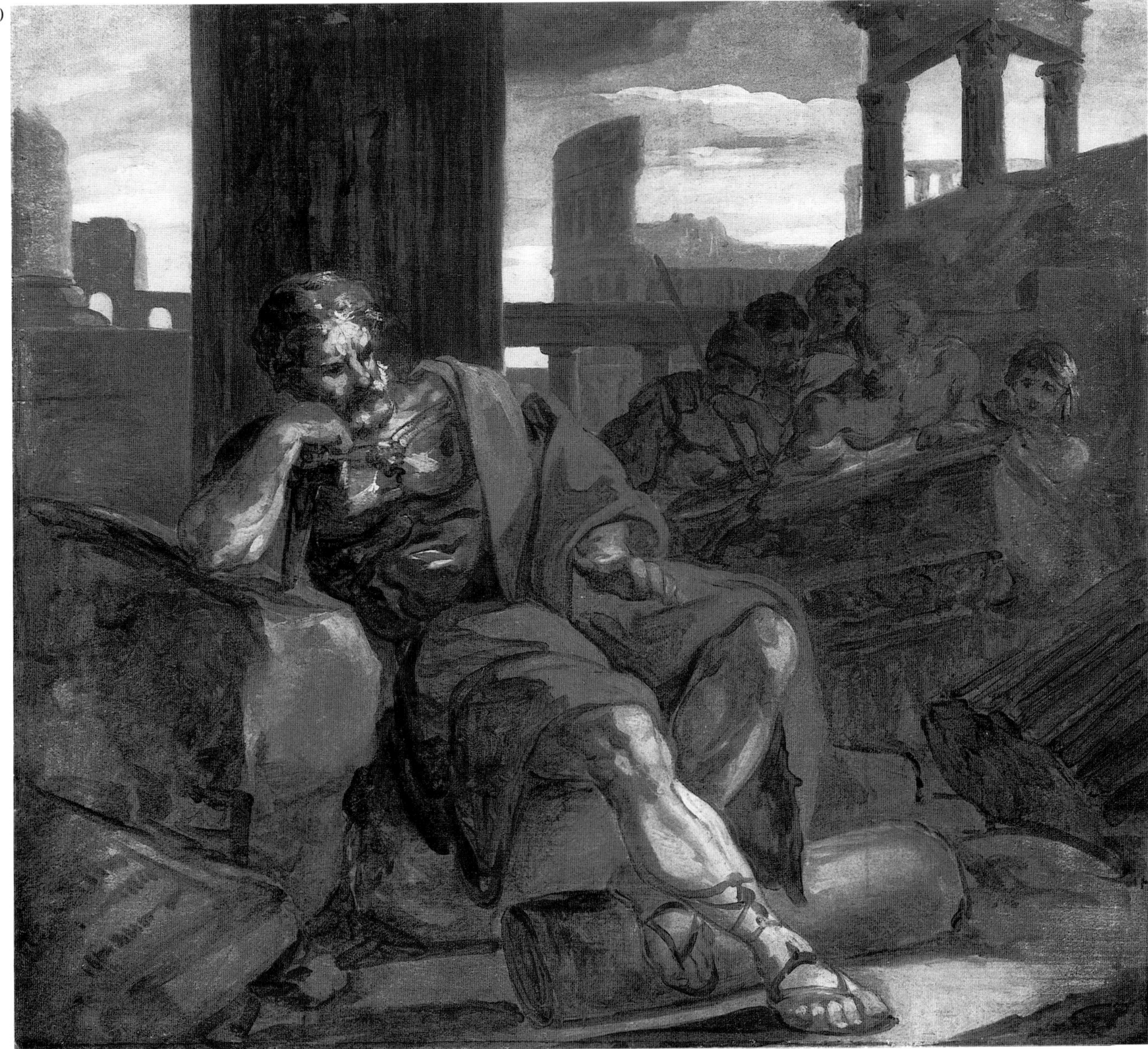

THOMAS BARKER OF BATH (1769–1847)

20. *Marius*, ca. 1790–93
  Oil on paper laid on canvas, 20 x 18 in. (50.8 x 45.7 cm)
  Museum Purchase
  1984.15

The classical associations which formed an important part of history painting are impressively attested in a remarkable oil study by Thomas Barker recently acquired for the collection. Called "Barker of Bath" to avoid confusion with another artist of the same name, Barker's considerable reputation in his own day derived mainly from his ability to compose stylish genre scenes and "fancy pictures." He was also admired for his skills as a landscapist. A versatile fellow, however, Barker equally turned his hand on occasion to painting portraits or subjects from religion or history. Although his career was centered at Bath, he exhibited with some frequency in London, both at the British Institution and the Royal Academy. In addition his name was known from lithographic reproductions of his drawings and from transfer copies of his rustic personages that appeared as appliqués on ceramic articles or fabrics. (Motifs from Hogarth's works were subjected to the same kind of commercial appropriation.)

Barker's story is interesting and relates directly to the attribution of the present picture. His father had gravitated from his preparations for a law career to become an impoverished animal painter, moving from Pontypool in Wales to Bath. His son's precocity attracted the attentions of a wealthy coachmaker of the city, who underwrote the boy's education and employed him to make copies from works in his collection of old master paintings. Later, that generous patron advanced the money for young Barker to spend an extended period of further study in Italy, whence he departed at age twenty-one, in 1890. By the time of his return to England four years later, his benefactor had suffered bankruptcy, but by then Barker was prepared to undertake an independent career and for a time was quite prosperous. His spendthrift ways, however, eventually reduced him to financially straightened circumstances during his later years.

During his halcyon days in Rome, Barker became intimately acquainted with the classical topography of Latium. He also formed a taste for the Gothic themes of grottoes and menacing *banditti* which had been popularized by Salvator Rosa and other Continental artists who contributed to the rising tide of the picturesque. Barker is said to have made sketches of the kind during his stay there. Moreover, the technique of the Amherst picture which may be one of those trial pieces is considered consistent with other works securely documented as by Barker.

Research on the subject matter itself remains somewhat inconclusive, however, for the elderly man in this composition is of an iconographical type used to portray the Emperor Justinian's general Belisarius. In later legend, Belisarius was reduced to the state of a blind beggar, chanced upon and suddenly recognized by a veteran of his former command. Alternatively, the theme Barker shows could be that of Marius meditating amongst the ruins of Carthage, a subject that also had some currency at that period. If so, the spectators would be intrusive. In either case, the looming outlines of the Roman Colosseum would be appropriate only as a generalized reference to antiquity.

While the precise nature and identity of the subject must for the time being remain uncertain, there is no uncertainty whatsoever about the power of the artist's conception. Though small in compass, his sketch is imbued with a quality of monumental scale appropriate to its picturesque message about the mortal desserts of power and ambition. It is thus a moral *exemplum* in the tradition of commentaries on the vanity of human existence.

Sir George Hayter (1792–1871)

21. *Family Portrait With Two Children*, 1857
   Oil on canvas, 24 x 20 in. (61 x 50.8 cm)
   Museum Purchase
   1975.73

Long the victims of modern critical disrepute, the favorite painters of the Victorian age have once again come to be accepted—if perhaps without the heady enthusiasm of that former age. Given the vast productivity of that era the holdings of the Mead Art Museum are indeed modest in number and scope. Still, they do afford more than a glimpse of the larger picture, with its special savors that are so indelibly detectable in the art of other Western nations of the time—not least of all, contemporaneous preferences in the United States. It is now widely agreed that, especially in the early years of Victoria's reign, the natively Germanic tastes of her beloved consort, Prince Albert, affected prevailing standards in his adopted land. But they found so highly compatible a climate there that they seem a wholly natural outgrowth of indigenous factors. Most notable among them perhaps was a virtually absolute entrenchment of bourgeois standards in a land where the new economic and political institutions of modern industrialist society had first taken classic shape. Among other traits fostered by those cultural conditions was a delight in dissimilation which rivaled, but in no way imitated, the mock heroics of earlier, Rococo invention. Hence, in an age of unapologetic involvement in exploitation, artistic refuge could be

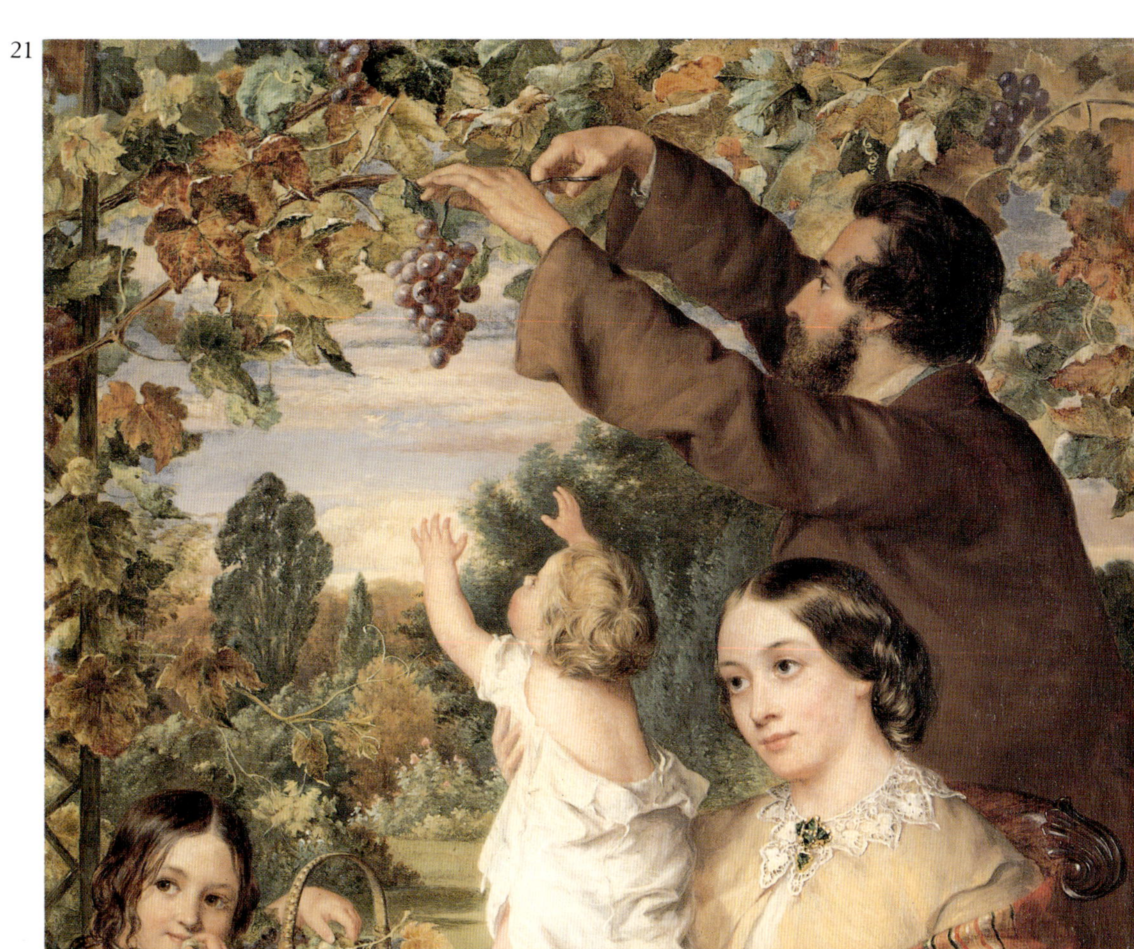

found in carefully nurtured moral conceits which centered above all on the image of innocence and domesticity.

Surely this is the message of *Family Portrait With Two Children* by Sir George Hayter, a favorite of the queen. Hayter here turns to subjects of far less than royal social rank whom he elevates to a quasi-religious status, for his is essentially a paraphrase of the traditional Holy Family. One could hardly imagine a more patent compression of the virtues of domesticity than are encapsulated in this sympathetic depiction of Hayter's unidentifiable bourgeois sitters. He thus extends the traditions of Reynolds (as in

his famous *The Age of Innocence*), wherein a specific subject is graced with a larger, symbolic frame of reference. Needless to say, the darker side of the moral universe was also cast in contemporary terms by other Victorian artists, in an extension of Hogarth's moralizing genre, but so far there is no image of fallen virtue or other solemn messages of the time in the repertory of the Mead collection. At least this sample of the sunnier side of the Victorian coin suffices. In its crisp forms and blond tonalities, with their heightened local colorations, an attractive aspect of the High Victorian mode is nicely summarized.

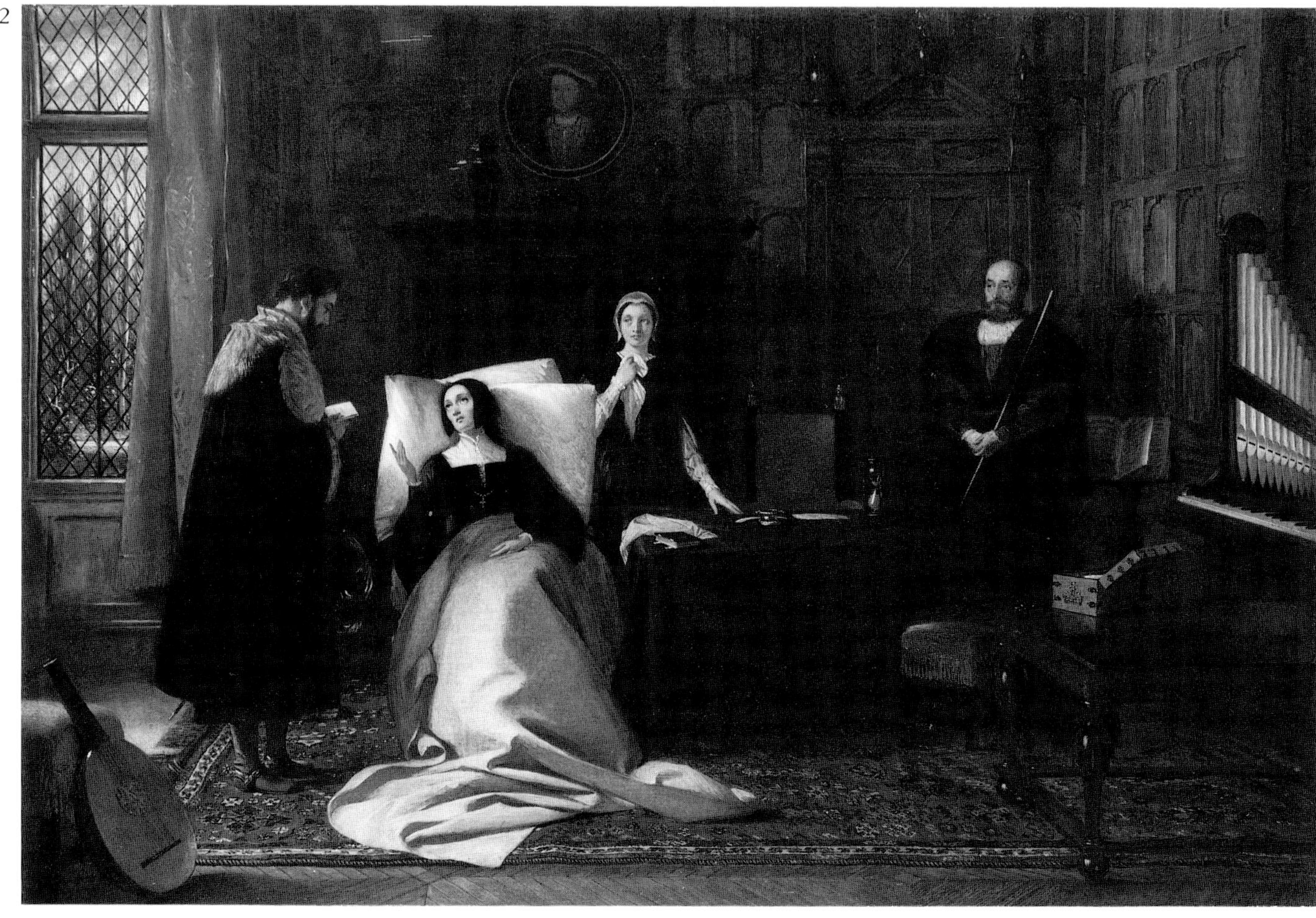

CHARLES ROBERT LESLIE (1794–1859)

22. *Queen Catherine of Aragon's Interview with Capucius, Henry VIII's Ambassador, at Kimbolton*
Oil on canvas, 24 x 32 in. (61 x 81.3 cm)
Museum Purchase
1979.72

Although Leslie spent his childhood in Philadelphia, he was actually born in London, and in 1811, he returned there for art lessons. Save for a brief term as drawing master at West Point in New York (1833–34), he remained in England thereafter. Upon arriving in London, Leslie entered the Royal Academy classes, where he studied with Reynolds and the American-born Washington Allston (1779–1842), who was then in London for an extended period of residence. Leslie's further associations of the time, including a close acquaintance with Washington Irving, are no doubt indicative of those literary leanings which would continue to color Leslie's choice of subjects for paintings. Aside from his popular illustrations of *Don Quixote*, he turned frequently to Shakespeare, Goldsmith, and Molière for theatrical situations in which his gift for sum-

marizing memorable scenes could be exercised to best advantage. Leslie's success in handling this genre earned him both public acceptance and professional recognition at the Royal Academy, where he was elevated to the status of a full member in 1826. Leslie also made a significant contribution—and one that is probably more widely recognized than his art—in publishing a sympathetic and informative biography of his good friend, John Constable. Though an incomparably greater artist, the latter incidentally never rose to a comparable level of acceptance at the Royal Academy: Constable remained only an associate member, presumably as a stubborn rebuke to his single-minded devotion to the lesser art of landscape painting.

Paintings of Shakespearean themes had been well established by Leslie's time. The print publisher and entrepreneur, John Boydell, did much to entrench their popularity by virtue of his Shakespeare Gallery (begun 1786), for which some 150 pictures were eventually provided by over thirty artists, including Henry Fuseli (1741–1825) and other well-known masters of the day. Taking a page from Hogarth's book, Boydell counted upon realizing his ultimate profit mainly from engravings made after his accumulating stock of Shakespearean subjects. Not all of the canvases resulting from his enterprise were of artistically high quality, but the venture did have the historical importance of providing a context of public awareness that encouraged finer efforts at history painting culminating in the Romantic period already taking shape.

Leslie is known to have turned to subjects from Shakespeare's *Henry VIII* five times during his career—once, in 1826, for his diploma picture for exhibition at the Royal Academy. The Amherst canvas was featured at the academy exhibition of 1850. It had been commissioned by an engineer named Isumbard Kingdom Brunel as a companion piece to a scene from *Henry VIII* (act 1, scene 4) which Leslie had painted for Brunel the year before. Both canvases were ordered as part of a series of Shakespearean subjects that Brunel planned to install in a special room. Unlike Leslie's usual wont to portray a lively and humorous side of the Bard's plots, he here turns to a more sober moment set in Queen Catherine's apartment, as she awaits death. Though fallen from the favor of the king (represented in a tondo portrait above the fireplace) the queen receives the emperor's ambassador, Capucius, expressing her forgiveness of the king. Still true to her faith, but isolated in a foreign court, she faces the denouement of her cruel destiny with stoic dignity.

THOMAS FRANCIS DICKSEE (1819–1895)

23. *Ophelia*, 1875
   Oil on canvas, 37 x 24¾ in. (94 x 62.9 cm)
   Museum Purchase
   1961.4

Theatrical and literary subjects continued to enjoy a vogue among painters and patrons of a later generation, as may be seen in a somewhat traditionally composed but nevertheless touching interpretation of *Ophelia*, by Sir Thomas Francis Dicksee. Unlike the adventuresome famous interpretation by John Everett Millais (1829–1896) of Shakespeare's pathetic personage, who is shown in death, floating in the water, Dicksee's Ophelia appears in the last, fated moments of her brief, unhappy life. Pale and drawn of facial feature and dressed in bridal white with a fillet of flowers about her hair, Dicksee's maiden sits dejectedly on

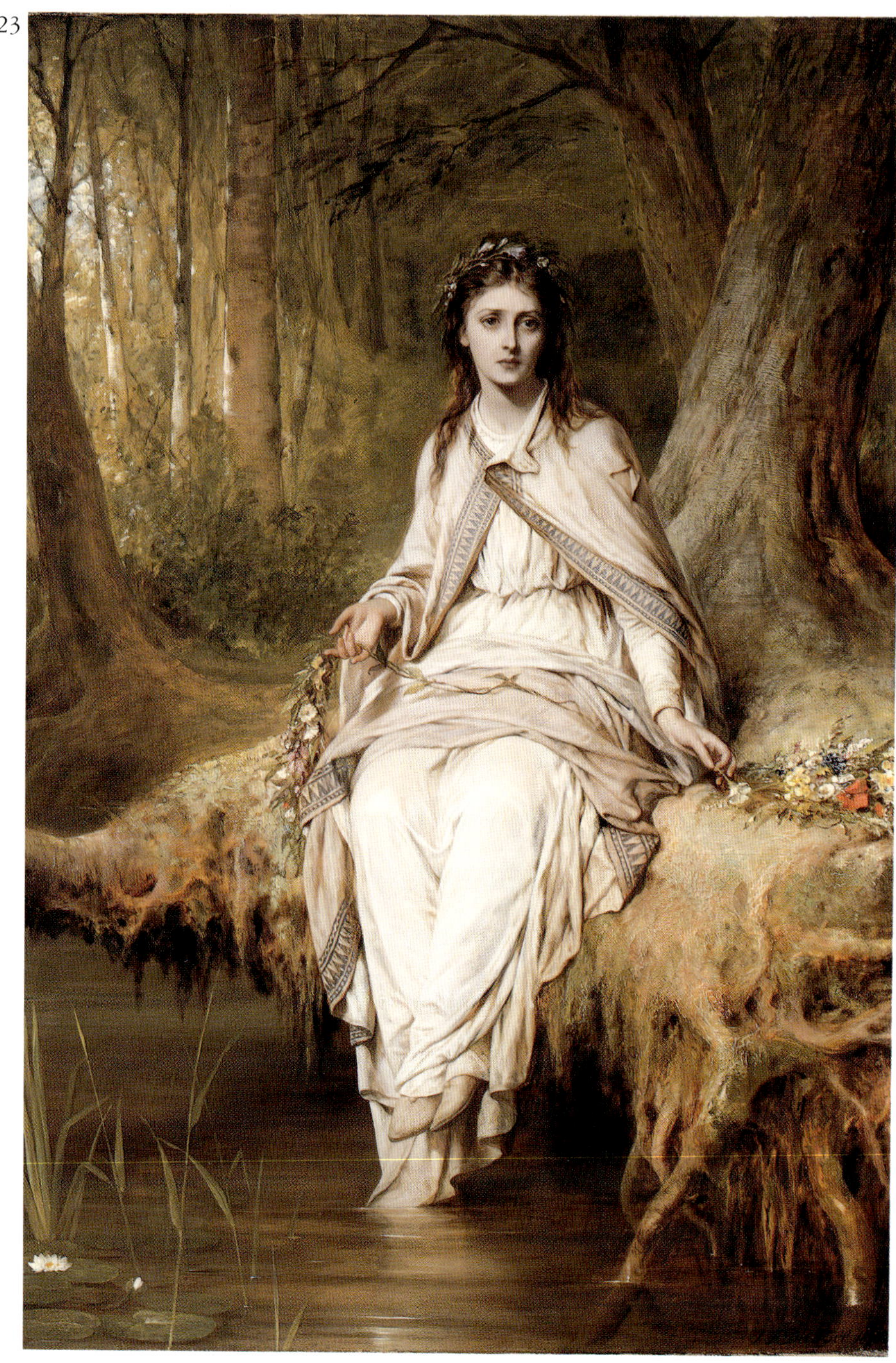

a woodland bank at the side of the stream in which she would find her mortal end. The flowers she holds or that lie nearby, in their own fragile and fleeting beauty, serve only to stress, not relieve, the sense of Ophelia's fatal plight. She is thus isolated as the victim of the plot, not incorporated as a tragic heroine, as for example, Queen Catherine of Aaragon appears in Leslie's earlier depiction of another Shakespearean theme. Leslie's interpretation stands for the more formal, historically oriented staging sought in the first half of the nineteenth-century by the British School.

Dicksee's isolation of the personal and individual marks a special, more intimate focus that belongs to the high Victorian ethos, wherein the boundaries between sentiment and sentimentality are, however, often put in jeopardy. It is a credit to Dicksee's judgment that he has avoided the bathos that scenes of the sort often elicited in the hands of a less tactful artist. Dicksee's *Ophelia* thus illustrates the qualities that earned him an honorable place in the ranks of those who followed the artists of the Pre-Raphaelite movement.

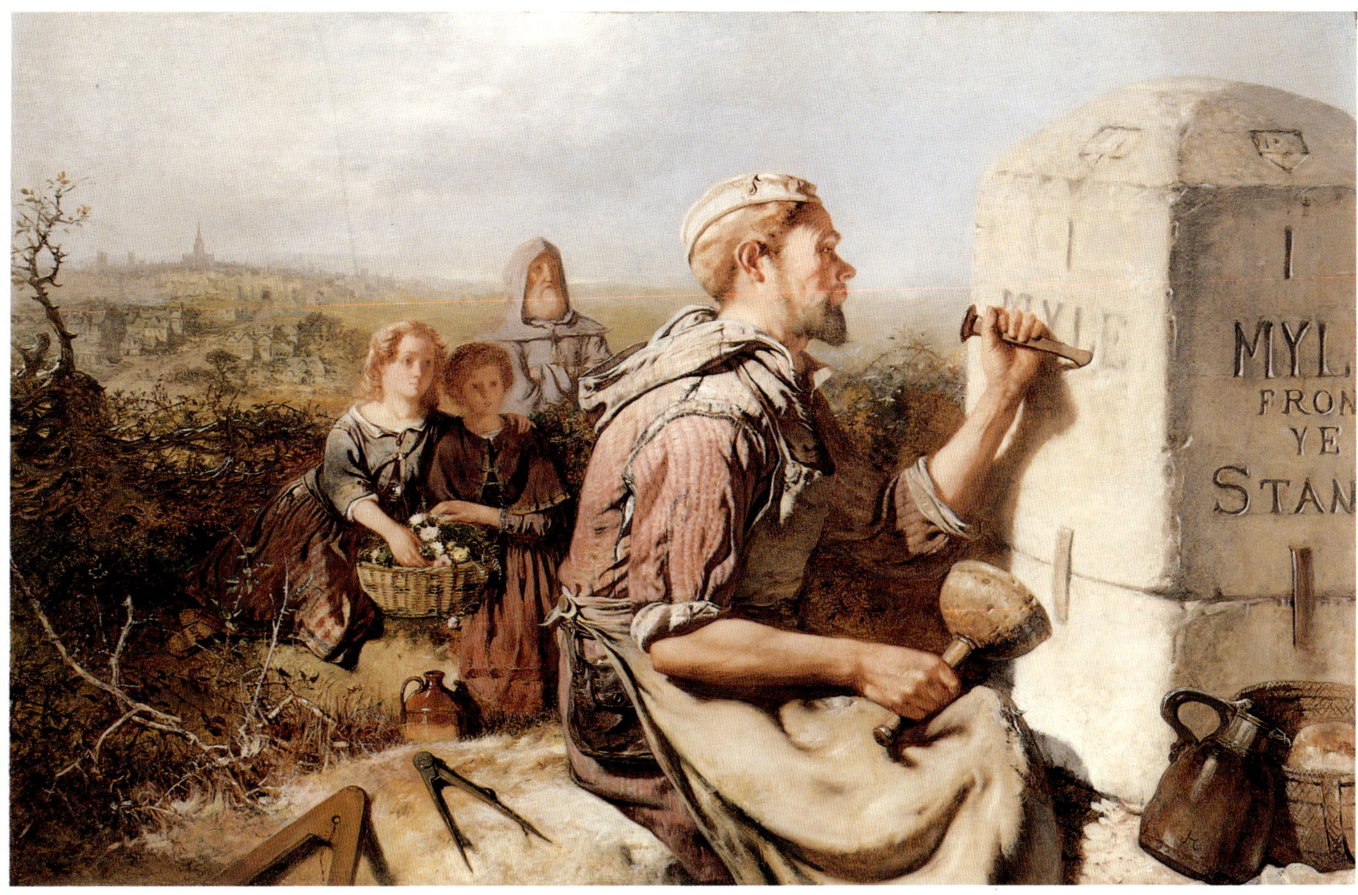

JOHN RITCHIE (ACTIVE 1858–1875)

24. *The Stone Mason*
   Oil on canvas, 20 x 30 in. (50.8 x 76.2 cm)
   Museum Purchase
   1979.72

Scenes from everyday life had a natural appeal for the newly expanded art public of Victorian Britain, and by mid-century some artists created unprecedented popular sensations with the showing of their work. One of the pioneers in establishing elaborate genre pictures aimed at the rising taste for literal description was William Powell Frith (1819–1909) whose *Life at the Seaside (Ramsgate Sands)* and *Derby Day* remain masterpieces of their kind. In these works, the artist's precocious use of photographic documentation is clearly evident. If not quite in Frith's class, but related in approach, is a genre painting acquired for the Mead Art Museum by a little known, but very capable artist, John Ritchie. His large complex painting, *A Summer Day in Hyde Park*, forms a worthy pendant to Frith's *Life at the Seaside*, which was exhibited at the Royal Academy in 1854 and may well have inspired Ritchie's undertaking of a related subject. Ritchie's depiction of the Serpentine in Hyde Park was shown at the British Institution in 1858,

the year it was completed. His more characteristic products were costume pictures depicting genre situations of earlier periods.

Elements of past and present merge in Ritchie's *Stone Mason* in which the dignity of work is expressed. Unlike Frith, who affected a noncommittal stance devoid of the moral and didactic overtones that had come to be common, Ritchie here strikes a quasi-religious note in the inclusion of the two young onlookers, with their hint of the future, and of a monkish companion, who seems to speak of tradition and the past. Apparently the scene is set near Stamford in Lincolnshire looking down from the hill toward London. But for all the specific suggestion of the locale and more especially, in the plainspoken visage of the workman, the narrative message is veiled. In a far less monumental way, Ritchie's roadside worker is an English counterpart to the images of Courbet or Millet, in which the dignity of labor and, sometimes, its human costs are personified. Such overtones of social awareness implicit in Ritchie's canvas were not uncommon in the repertory of Victorian artists, and the poignancy of modern human existence was often a theme, as in such masterpieces of the day as Ford Maddox Brown's famous commentary, *The Last of England*.

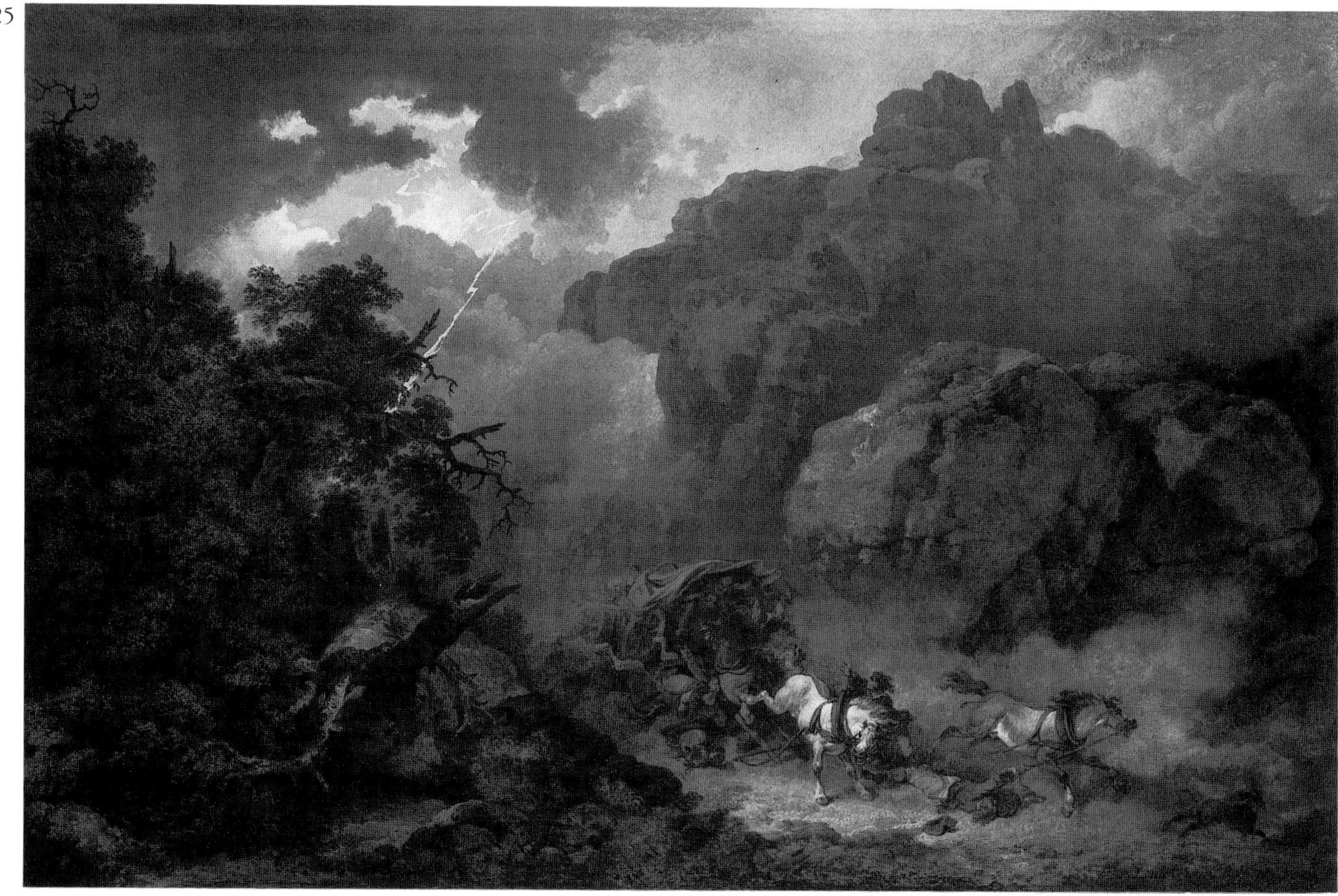

PHILIPPE JACQUES DE LOUTHERBOURG (1740–1812)

25. *Landscape With Carriage in a Storm*, 1804
Oil on canvas, 28⅜ x 41½ in. (72 x 105.4 cm)
Museum Purchase in honor of Susan Dwight Bliss
1974.30

Descended from a family of painters in Basel, Loutherbourg
was born in Strasbourg and educated in the Protestant
school there before going to Paris with Carle Van Loo
(1705–1765). He continued his studies with a battle painter
who had come to Paris, and in 1763, his *Cavalry Combat*
was accepted for his debut at the French Royal Academy. It
attracted favorable attention—not least of all, from the
influential savant, Denis Diderot. By 1767, Loutherbourg
was a full member of the academy and had come to enjoy
considerable success as an artist. But his domestic situation
was less auspicious. In 1771 he deserted his wife and
several children, to seek safe haven in London.

Thanks to an opportune letter of introduction from a
mutual friend at the Opera Comique, he gained favor with
the famous actor David Garrick, who became Loutherbourg's first advocate in London. He did portraits of Garrick
in famous roles and for a time, he painted scenographic
decor for the Drury Lane theater. In a related vein, he also
confected his *Eidophusikon*, a kind of panorama with figures
and landscape that moved mechanically. That theatrical
tour de force attracted the keen interest of Gainsborough
when it was put on private exhibition in 1781. The year
before, Loutherbourg had been admitted to the ranks of
the Royal Academy. Intellectually restless and with a taste
for the unusual, Loutherbourg played host for a time to the
scandalous adventurer, Allessandro Cagliostro (1743–1795)
after his release from the Bastille. For a time Loutherbourg
took lessons in the occult from Cagliostro, but he soon
returned to the more gainful pursuit of landscape and
battle paintings in which he excelled. Honored in 1780
with membership in the Royal Academy, he was a conspicuous exhibitor at the academy. He gained added visibility
by holding special showings of important pieces, which he
organized for financial profit, after the practice of other
artists of the period.

Loutherbourg's *Landscape with Carriage in a Storm*, exhibited at the Royal Academy in 1804, richly embodies the evocative power that its artist could summon on occasion. It summarizes the complex aesthetic forces to which he was responsive. The cult of the picturesque so favored in England had assimilated the Continental traditions of such painters as Salvator Rosa (1615–1673), in their fixation on the irregularities of nature as inspiring strong emotion in the viewer. By extension, Burke's concept of the sublime and the beautiful is also portended here, in its spectacle of the awesome power of nature with all its capacity to strike terror.

Scenes of disasters—whether on land or sea—were abundantly conjured by eighteenth-century masters among whom Claude-Joseph Vernet (1714–1789) and Allessandro Magnasco (1667–1749) are significant, in their efforts to strike a numbing awe in the heart of the spectator. The assimilable Loutherbourg was not only alert to these and other strands of interest, but was also adept at threading them into his own, personal warp of expression. Here, in his *Landscape with Carriage in a Storm*, he pulls out all the stops, as the presence of man and beasts is made insignificant and totally vulnerable to the eruptive, cataclysmic power of natural forces. It is understandable that, in an age acutely susceptible to emotional provocations of the picturesque and the sublime, younger artists including Turner, would—as they did—respond enthusiastically to Loutherbourg's art.

GEORGE MORLAND (1763–1804)

26. *Landscape*, 1798
> Oil on canvas, 19½ x 28 in. (49.5 x 63.5 cm)
> Gift of the children of Elizabeth C. and
> Dwight W. Morrow, '95
> 1955.459

The pastoral side of the picturesque may be appreciated in George Morland's *Landscape*. While actually derived no less traceably from extant conventions that evolved internationally from time-honored models, superficially at least, Morland's views are credited with having a recognizably "English" look, compared with Loutherbourg's obviously theatrical contrivances. Be that as it may, Morland's works were popular in their day and much imitated—often badly.

His promise had been recognized early by his father, a painter of sorts, who "articled" his precocious son as his own apprentice, to help repair or even forge Dutch masterworks. From childhood on, Morland was therefore schooled in the practice of the old masters, however oppressed he may have been in the process of acquiring that expertise. Once freed from filial servitude, he adopted an unheard of degree of independence in thenceforth painting only subjects of his own choosing and selling them only indirectly. He thus traded one form of exploitation for another; dealers preyed upon his continual need for money as a result of his habitual mismanagement of his personal affairs.

In spite of all this, Morland's work attained a popular following, largely from the circulation of skillfully executed, reproductive prints. Many of his subjects were translated

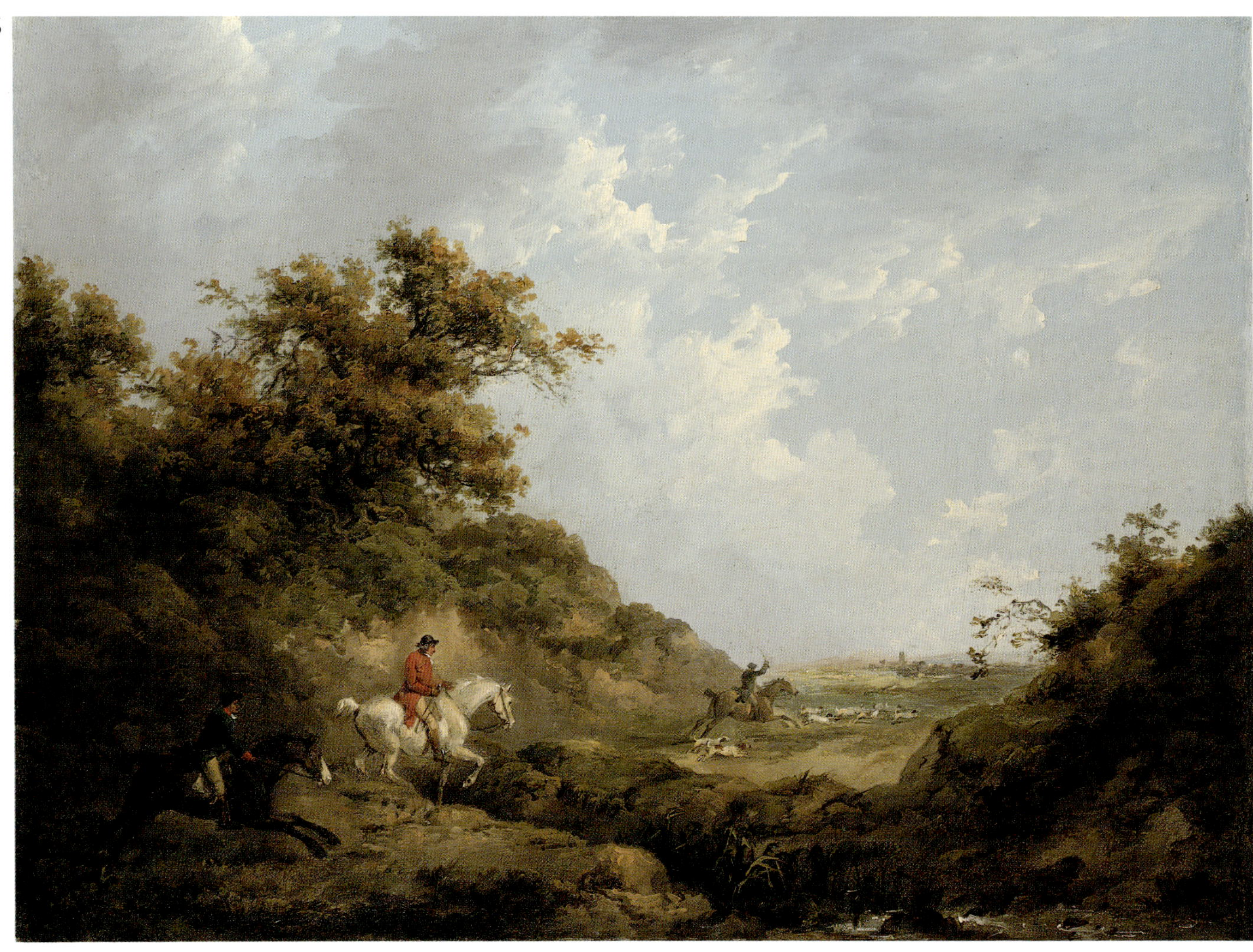

into mezzotint engravings by his capable brother-in-law, James Ward.

Morland's early subjects treated genre situations in which personages recruited from the upper bourgeoisie are cast in little moral dramas in which virtue is rewarded: Morland ingratiatingly reversed the coin of Hogarth's powerful but negatively couched admonitions against vice. In his later years, however, Morland adopted a new repertory, and in the 1790s he abandoned those middle-class parables in favor of an interest in the picturesque, as it was to be discerned in the little incidents of rustic life. Glimpses into gypsy ways, the fortunes of the road experienced by other itinerants, or scenes of the hunt became his subjects. In many respects they reflect interests that took shape elsewhere, most importantly, in the French Rococo or the early works of Goya. Antecedents of all this are, of course, to be found much earlier, especially in the bandit-ridden landscapes of Salvator Rosa. At the same time this side of Morland's production links the naturalistic tendencies of

the Dutch and of Gainsborough with the Romantic inclinations of the dawning nineteenth century.

Morland's *Landscape* in the Mead Art Museum represents the later stages of his art and hence shows him at the height of his accomplishment. His very dating on the face of the canvas (which occurs but infrequently in his work and mostly at this period) has been taken as a favorable sign of a demonstrable concern on his part for asserting quality in an *oeuvre* that overall includes too many works of slovenly character. His interest in the so-called cottage form of the picturesque here takes the form of the charming contours of a countryside that may be plausibly accepted as English, despite the patent exercise of conventions that he inherited from tradition—conventions that would moreover long survive him. Still, in the freshness of his color and vivacity of his detail, Morland here testifies to a touch with nature that allies him with those who were to turn ever more enthusiastically to an art based on response to direct observation of the natural world.

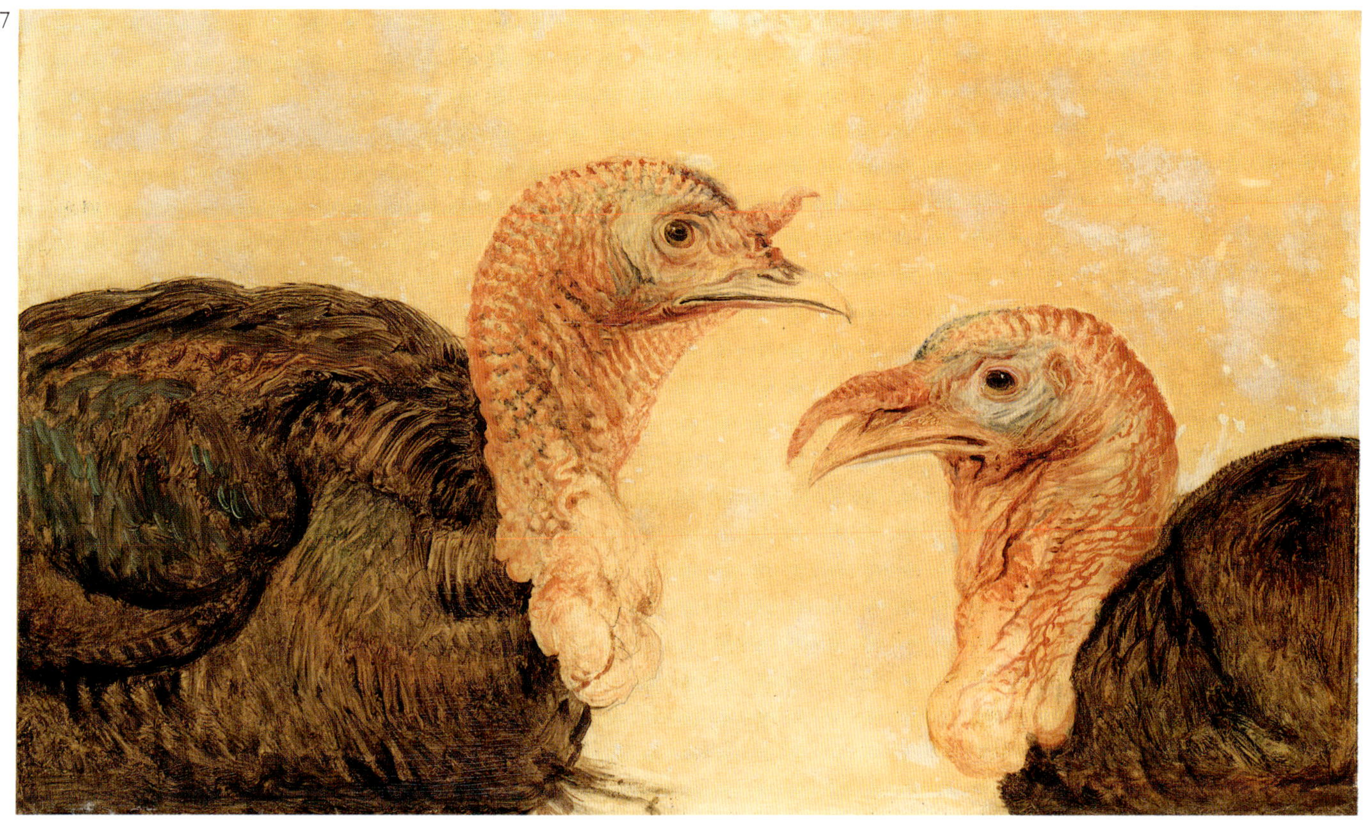

JAMES R. A. WARD (1769–1859)

27. *Two Turkeys*
   Oil on paper, 17½ x 10½ in. (44.5 x 26.7 cm)
   Museum Purchase
   1979.71

Falling outside the categories that apply to the present exhibition is James Ward's portrayal of *Two Turkeys*. Neither landscape nor history picture, it perhaps most closely pertains to the art of portraiture—if in an unusual way. Were Landseer, George Stubbs (1724–1806), and the other animaliers represented by related works, the story would be otherwise, of course. And tokens of that special genre do at least appear in the form of prints after Landseer. At any rate, modest though it is and isolated from most of its neighboring exhibits, Ward's vivid little piece provides a touchstone to other developments in the eighteenth and nineteenth centuries, for it refers to honorable traditions that tell us much about the intellectual as well as the artistic climate of the age.

　　Born into a humble, working-class family, Ward served an apprenticeship to an engraver and quickly rose to the distinction of being named mezzotint engraver to the Prince

of Wales. Thereafter attracted to painting, he first studied with George Morland, who had married Ward's sister Anne. Ambitions for ultimate recognition at the Royal Academy led Ward to abandon engraving. He turned instead to painting "portraits" of favored livestock, specimens for prosperous landowners. His *Two Turkeys* belongs to that phase of his career, which culminated in such grandiose compositions as *Fighting Bulls With a View of St. Donat's Castle in the Background*, a major effort inspired by Rubens' *Chateau Steen*, which Ward had studied in Benjamin West's studio. Strong echoes of that response to Rubens' art are to be recognized also in Ward's turkeys, with their fresh color and fluid paint handling.

　　Ward's attention to the animal world links the accomplishment of his great predecessor, George Stubbs, and his successor, Sir Edwin Landseer. Imbued with the spirit of enlightened inquiry, Stubbs had gone so far as to investigate the anatomy of the horse and the other creatures he represented, and to publish on the results of his studies. Ward was not so scientifically inclined—nor was Landseer, for that matter—but Ward was at least the inheritor of that pragmatic faith in direct observation that was particularly cultivated in the Age of Enlightenment. In addition, he was one of many of his own generation to take close notice of the visual consequences of the new practices of breeding of the time. For that reason, animal fanciers—whether of horses, dogs, cattle, or fowl—took pleasure in the look of their stock, and animal "portraits" came to abound. Pride of ownership was far from new; one recalls, for example, the abundance of Dutch Baroque pictures recording favorite animals. With the refinement of classifications through careful study, wild creatures as well came to be better known. (Audubon's were among many publications of the time that were responsive to widely shared interests in natural history.) In respects such as these, Ward's exotic imports from North America (the wild turkey was Ben Franklin's favored bird) recall issues of greater significance than may at first blush seem to be the case.

Ward went on to complete other ambitious works, chief among them, his famous *Gordale Scar, Yorkshire* (1811–15), now in the Tate Gallery. But his later career did not progress smoothly, despite his hard work and ambition or his ventures into other subject matter, including history painting.

28

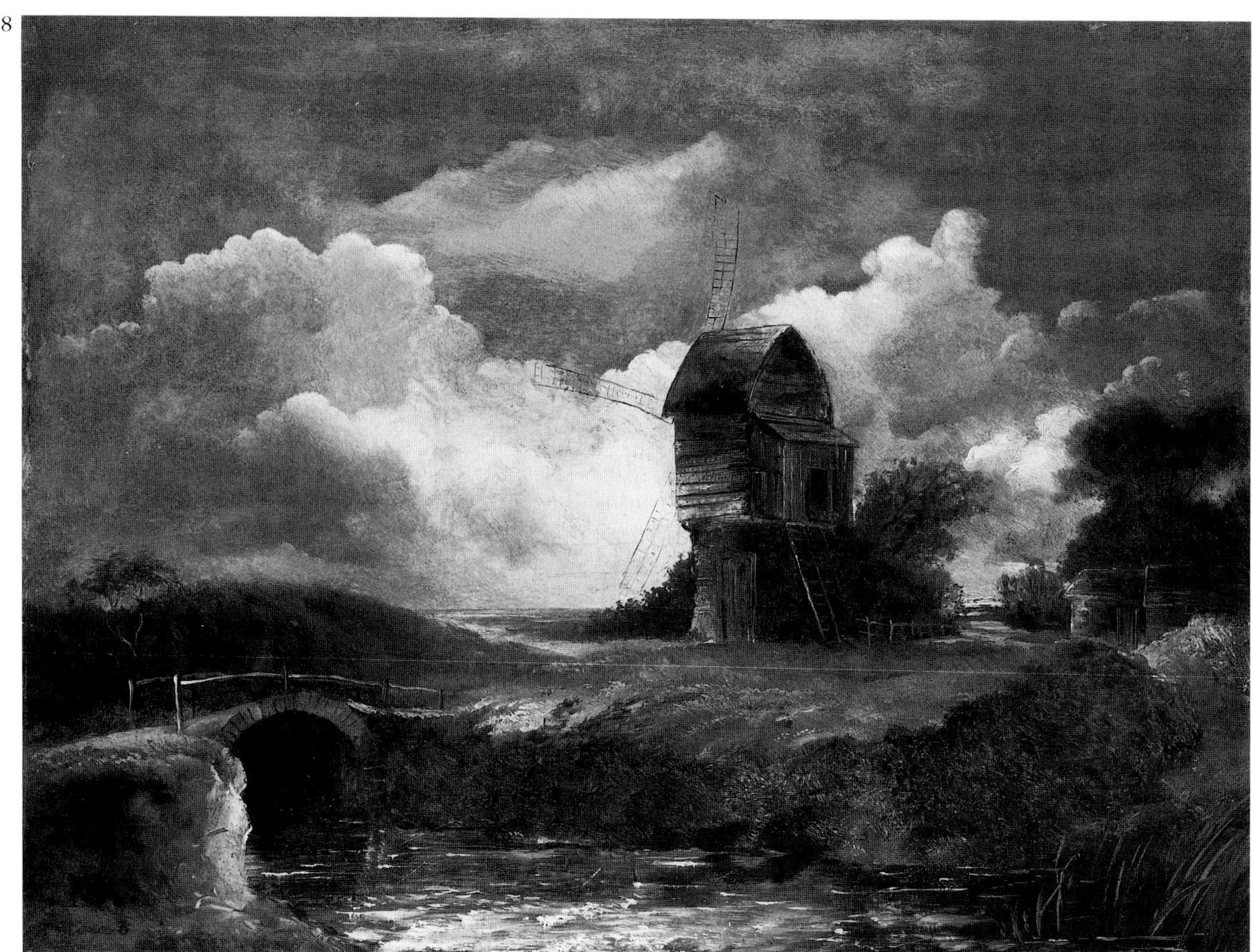

DAVID COX (1783–1859)

28. *A Sussex Windmill*
   Oil on board, 13¼ x 17¾ in. (33.7 x 45.1 cm)
   Gift of Calvin K. Arter
   1960.102

Born near Birmingham, the son of a blacksmith, David Cox was briefly apprenticed to a local miniature painter, and there found employment painting stage scenery for a local theatrical company. After four years experience at that craft, Cox moved to London in 1804, with the ambition to become a watercolorist. Apart from some lessons with John Varley, one of the early specialists in that medium,

Cox had the benefit of almost no formal training. Undaunted by his comparative lack of formal background, he succeeded in placing works in exhibitions at the Royal Academy from 1805 to 1808, and in 1813 he gained election to the Old Water Colour Society. By the time of his death in 1859, Cox had exhibited some 849 watercolors at the society.

Like many other artists of his time and since, Cox was dependent for his livelihood on income from teaching. In addition, he published several books of instruction. For some years he lived in Hereford, where he was employed as a drawing master at Miss Croucher's Academy of Drawing, but in 1827 he moved back to London. In 1841, he gave up teaching altogether and retired to Birmingham and a life devoted solely to painting. Although he made three short trips abroad—to the Low Countries in 1826, Paris in 1829, and the French coast in 1832—Cox was mainly attracted to the countryside of Britain. In later years he spent summers in Bettws-y-Coed, where he was lured by the picturesque beauty of the Welsh moors of that rugged part of the country.

Although Cox's reputation is primarily associated with his work as a watercolorist, he was also accomplished in the use of oils. In some respects analogies with Constable may be detected in Cox's avoidance of the commonplace of the picturesque mode in favor of a more intuitive response to the observable conditions of place, time, and weather. Freed in his personal efforts from the preachments of the classroom, Cox gave rein to an undisguised enjoyment of the natural world. And one suspects that his youthful experiences with creating effects of scenographic suggestion lingered with him as he framed the views of his mature years. Indeed, there is something theatrical—hence quintessentially picturesque—in his scene of the rustic mill and bridge. It succeeds in conveying a sense of fresh and unencumbered experience of some humble rural landmarks the artist had chanced upon in his wanderings.

JOHN MARTIN (1789–1854)

29. *Salamacis and Hermaphroditis*, ca. 1814
    Oil on canvas, 17 x 23½ in. (43.2 x 59.7 cm)
    Museum Purchase
    1976.67

If David Cox may be said to represent the rustic implications of the picturesque, John Martin embodies a more grandiose notion of its meaning. One of a family of eccentrics, Martin's contribution is permeated with the energies of Romantic individualism, and it has been said that upon Loutherbourg's death in 1812, Martin succeeded him as a master of the fantastic. But he brought to that idiom a technique of vitrious polish and stylized precision developed in his employment, just before, as a commercial glass painter. At the same time he also shared much with the visionary spirit of William Blake (1757–1827) and Henry Fuseli (1741–1825). However, Martin differed fundamentally from those older contemporaries in shunning their emphasis upon large-scale figures. Characteristically, his figures are kept small within landscape settings of virtually cosmic proportion and evocative power in their own right. Like Blake and Fuseli he was far from naive or untutored. A healthy store of knowledge and sophistication fed his extraordinary imaginings: he was tutored in artistic matters. He had been exposed to prints after Claude Lorraine, Salvator Rosa, and other famous masters, in the collection of an immigrant Italian painter, Bonifaci Musso, who had somehow found his way to Newcastle at a time when Martin, still a youth, was apprenticed to a coach painter of that city. Having had access to the Italian's treasures, Martin was disposed from an early age to satisfy his yearnings for the sublime basically in terms of landscape situations —grandiose vistas which he often chose to embellish with elaborate architectural inventions.

From the time of his debut at the Royal Academy in 1811, Martin won praise in some circles as a worthy rival to Turner. Martin's penchant for composing awesome, luminous panoramas obviously calculated to trigger the viewer's experience of sublimity, invited vaunting comparisons of that sort. Partly by reason of their uninhibited excess, however, Martin's reputation faded far more seriously than Turner's, and his efforts remained unappreciated until

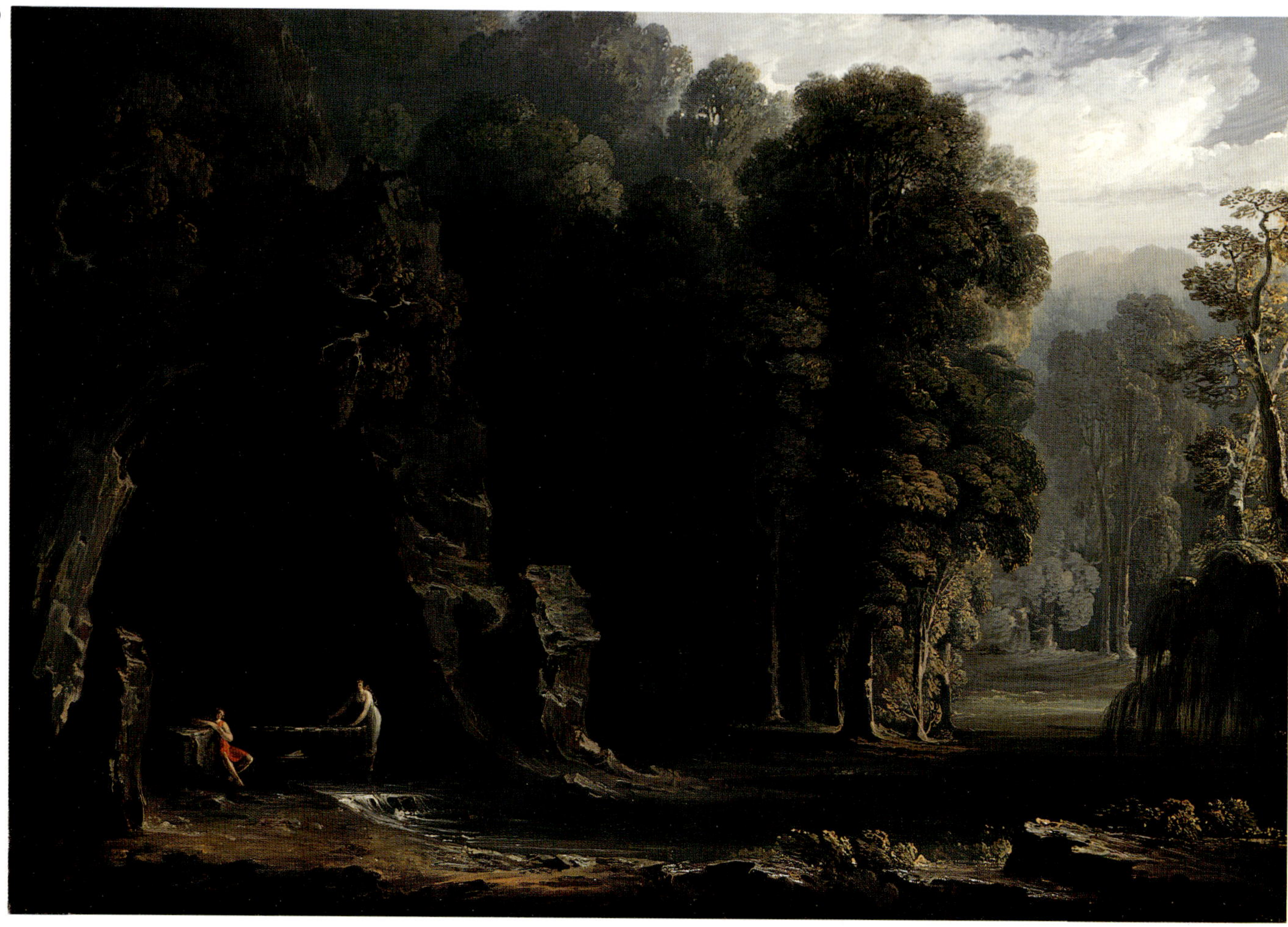

quite recently. Fortunately, in *Salamacis and Hermaphroditis*, a rather early and comparatively restrained example of his work, his gifts may be appreciated in a rare, but characteristic form. A larger version of the same subject (now lost) was exhibited at the British Institution in 1814.

The imagery of Martin's mature works was primarily Christian in origin but given a distinctively mystical, visionary turn of expression. In this canvas, however, Martin turned to Ovid's *Metamorphosis*—a time-honored source of artistic inspiration. The scene is set in an imaginary Caria, where lived a water nymph named Salamacis. The passionate maiden became enamored of the surpassingly handsome young son of Hermes and Aphrodite, who bore their compounded name, Hermaphroditis. To the nymph's frustration, the innocent youth spurned her advances, but when he bathed in the waters of Salamacis' spring, her prayer to the gods to be forever united with him was answered by their being combined as a single person, fused in sexual characteristics. In answer to Hermaphroditis' protest to his parents upon this transformation, they willed all men who bathed in Salamacis' spring from then on to be deprived of their masculinity.

For some reason the curious image of Hermaphroditis gained popular favor in Hellenistic times—no doubt for erotic reasons. It is rather rare in later periods. Although Martin's adoption of this theme is unexplained, it is possible that its appeal lay in its contrariety—in the mystical fusion of male and female forces in a fashion so contradictory to the insistent separation of the sexes in the Christian traditions.

Speculation about Martin's motives aside, his conception of the scene bears a striking resemblance to the first scene in the series *The Voyages of Life*, by Thomas Cole (1801–1848), in which the sustaining waters of life issue from a dark cave, like that in Martin's picture. The two artists were introduced to each other in 1829 by C. R. Leslie, on the occasion of Cole's visit to Europe and return to England, which he had left as a child when his parents emigrated to America. Cole had already shown the influence of prints by Martin that he had come across. Later, Martin's imprint on his conceptions is most appreciable, as may also be seen in such other works by Cole as *The Course of Empire* and *The Architect's Dream*. Indeed, in that sense, Martin's own inheritors are to be found less in England than in the Hudson River School.

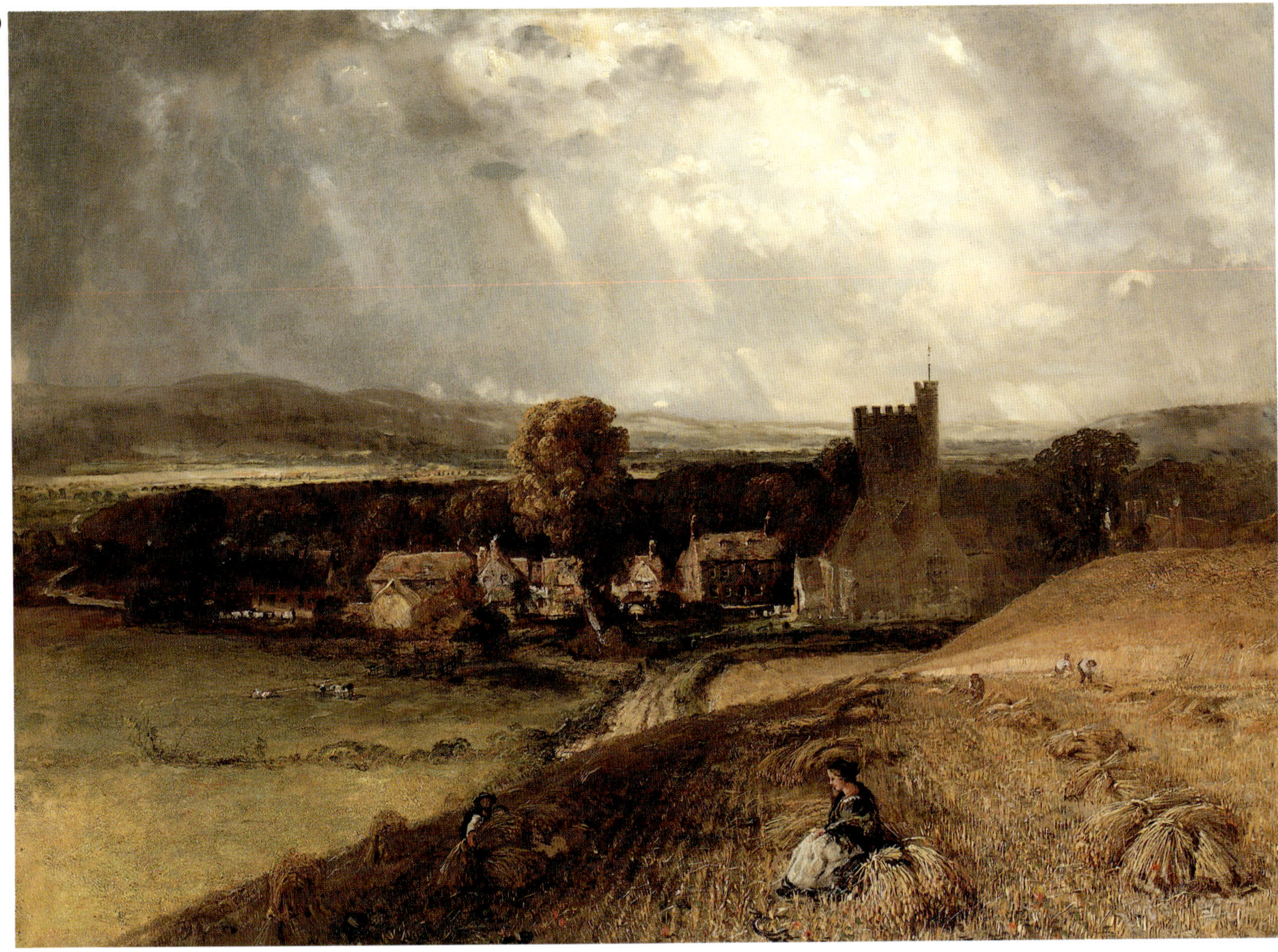

JOHN LINNELL (1792–1882)

30. *Landscape*
   Oil on canvas, 19½ x 26½ in. (49.5 x 67.3 cm)
   Gift of Calvin K. Arter
   1960.110

31. *On The Surrey Hills*
   Oil on board, 7⅛ x 8⁷/₁₀ in. (18.1 x 22.1 cm)
   Gift of Prof. Arthur H. Baxter
   P 1937.2

Although he was a prolific painter and continued his work until he died at age ninety, John Linnell is best known to posterity for his patronage of William Blake. The two met in 1818. It was Linnell who commissioned the *Book of Job* illustrations and who outlined the second set of the water-color illustrations for Blake to color. He also commissioned Blake's famous illustrations of Dante's *Divine Comedy*. It was he who introduced Blake to his future son-in-law, Samuel Palmer (1805–1881)—an acquaintance that was not without consequence for Palmer's own, very admirable art.

All this would suggest a person of generous impulses and kindly disposition. Such was hardly the case. Converted to the Baptist sect in 1812, Linnell became a fanatic in his religious beliefs. Quarrelsome and miserly, yet prolific as a painter of a wide range of subjects, at age sixty Linnell retired from residence in London and Hampstead to a new home in Surrey, where he lorded over his extended family and painted the surrounding countryside for yet another thirty years. The two paintings in the present exhibition relate to that phase of his prolonged career.

Linnell had not been born to the prosperity he experienced in those later years. His father was a framemaker who earned extra cash by selling pictures and prints. With his eye for business, Mr. Linnell put his still-adolescent son to the task of copying works by Morland for sale at his shop in Bloomsbury. In 1805 the son took up the study of watercolors with John Varley. He continued his training thereafter at the Royal Academy and for a time was employed by Dr. Thomas Monroe to work as a student-copyist in his famous academy at Adelphi Terrace.

It was at Monroe's establishment that many another

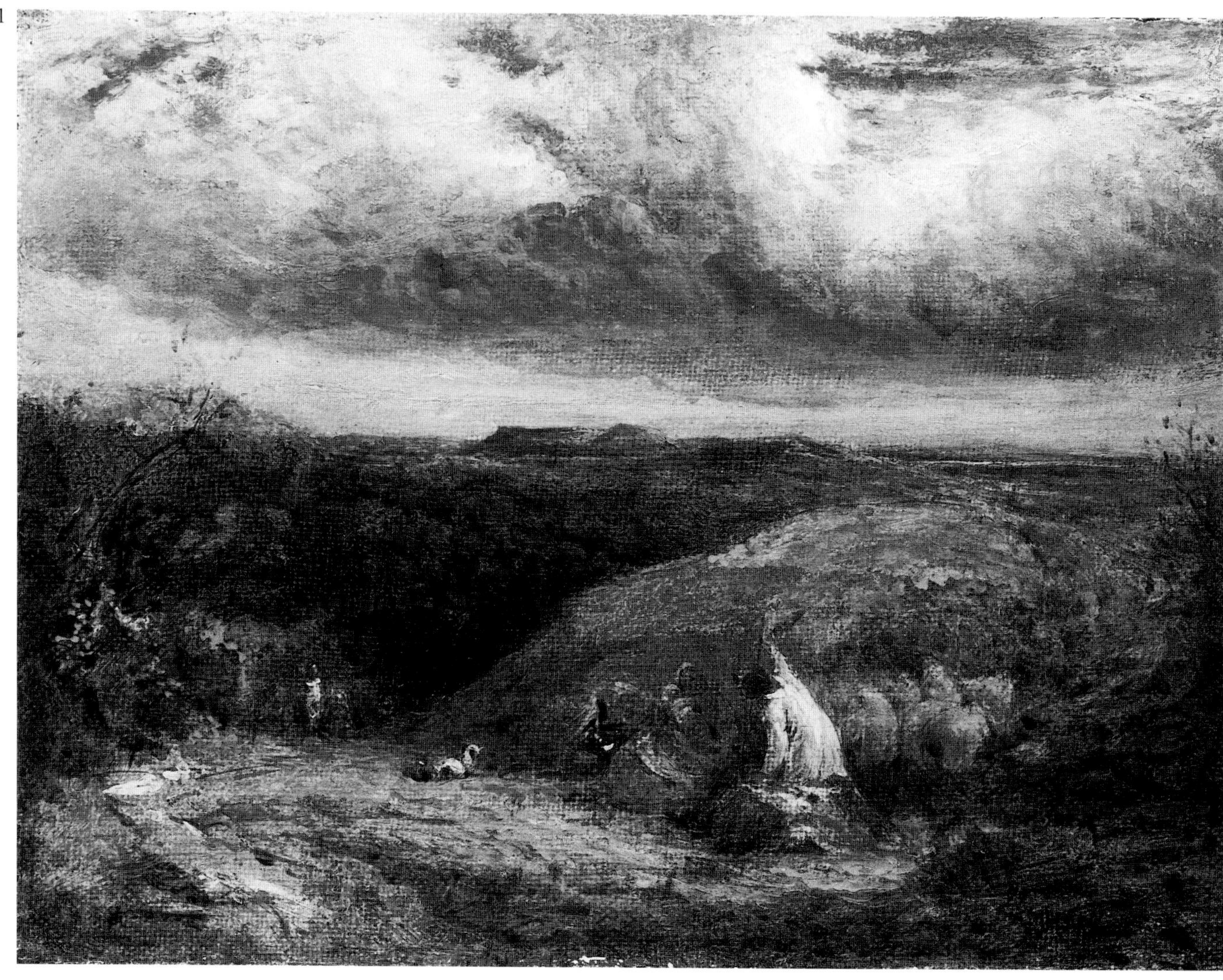

promising young artist—not least of all, Turner—gained valuable background in watercolor painting. Linnell had already exhibited at the Royal Academy in 1807, and two years earlier, at the remarkable age of thirteen, he had been accepted as a member of the Old Water Colour Society. Despite that early recognition, however, he never gained admission to the Royal Academy, to which he regularly presented himself as a candidate for a period of twenty years, beginning in 1821. When at last he was invited to join that august organization some years later, he declined. By then he had no need of institutional approval, and he continued to nurse resentment against John Constable, whom he blamed for his long history of rejection at the academy.

The two paintings shown here represent the softer style Linnell adopted in his period at Surrey, when he turned from the portraiture that had been his mainstay, to the landscape subjects that abounded in the countryside around his house at Redhill. Preferring to paint what he called "aspects of nature," not special landmarks of the region, he dealt in a somewhat generalized way with effects of time and season. His *Landscape*, for example, constitutes a virtual essay in a quiescent mode of the picturesque tradition, as the human silence within a grand sweep of nature contrasts with the visual activity of changing meteorological events. Yet there is a basically schematic pattern here in the banded alterations of light and dark, not the sense of unpredictable, volatile change one encounters in Constable's manipulations of similar elements. Linnell seems motivated to reflect upon the recurrent, virtually classic—even generic—aspects of nature, rather than to record the specific, individual look of a given place and time as Constable did so superbly. In his own way, Linnell thus advances a view of nature as a lyrical and perpetual setting for human existence.

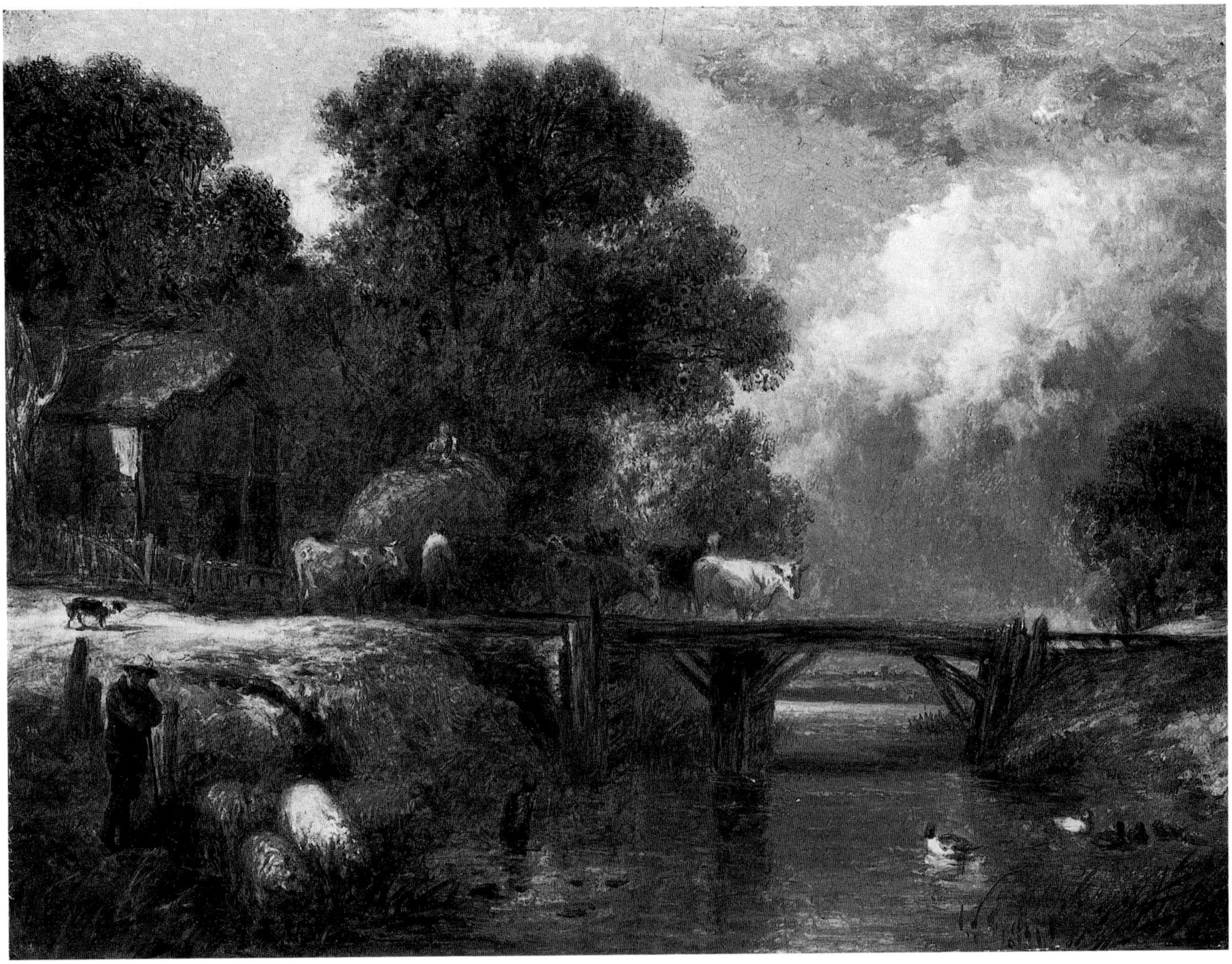

ATTRIBUTED TO FREDERICK W. WATTS,
(1800–1862)

32. *Landscape With Cattle*
   Oil on paper mounted on board, approx. 9¼ x 7¼ in.
   (23.5 x 18.4 cm)
   Gift or Mr. and Mrs. Robert L. Leeds, '51
   1975.84

In the lack of a painting by John Constable one can do no better than to present a subject comparable to his by a minor artist who was strongly influenced by him, Frederick Willam Watts. The small *Landscape with Cattle* can be securely attributed to Watts, for it bears the marks typical of that artist's rural form of the picturesque—one that is totally in accord with the much publicized plea by William Gilpin (1724–1804) for recognition of the special beauties of English scenery, with its irregularities of shape and

tantalizing variety of atmospheric effect. Clearly, Watts was strongly affected by Constable's view of landscape art with its lush transcription of the transient effects of a moody nature "always in motion—always in harmony." Younger than Constable, Watts apparently lived in Hampstead, where Constable also worked. He is not mentioned in Constable's voluminous papers—whether from inadvertance or deliberate neglect cannot be said. It is fair to say that Constable was not prone to be generous toward those he might regard as competitors.

Resemblances of Watts' paintings to Constable's were much criticized at the time. What is more, Watts' posthumous reputation also suffered from inferences that his efforts were merely imitative, or even intended to deceive. Viewed from a greater temporal distance, however, Watts emerges as a minor, but authentic landscape artist who followed the same paths as Constable, but with detectably individual artistic purposes. Attracted to much the same subject matter as Constable was, he explores the quiet meadows, rivers, and locks of the countryside—if rather less boldly, yet with what seems to have been a genuine interest in the scenic character. At his best, Watts thus provided a sympathetic prolongation of the initiatives so brilliantly announced in John Constable's art. In the present context, our little painting by Watts nicely complements the mezzotint by David Lucas (No. 52) which also recalls Constable's genius, though in a quite different way.

ROBERT GIBB THE ELDER (1801–1837)

33. *Fonthill Abbey*, 1826
   Oil on canvas, 11½ x 15¾ in. (29.2 x 40 cm)
   Museum Purchase
   1953.62

Little is known of the author of this accomplished rendition of Fonthill Abbey save that he was born in Aberdeen, died quite young, and fathered a son of the same name who followed in his footsteps in the practice of art. Clearly, the elder Gibb had the benefit of sound professional training, for his control of the perspective of the complicated structure is expert, and the paint is handled with an appreciation for its capacity to render convincing effects of light and shadow that reinforce the conviction of the drawing. All this is the product of well-honed skills developed from the Italian Renaissance onward. In the eighteenth century those devices of topographical landscape painting were employed with masterly comprehension by such painters as Canaletto (1697–1768) and his nephew Bernardo Bellotto (1720–1780), whose works were exceedingly popular throughout Europe, not least of all, among British patrons (Canaletto worked in England from 1746 to 1755). Gibb's *Fonthill Abbey* is in that respect a minor but worthy manifestation of that tradition which had attained—quite understand-ably—immense importance as a form of artistic expression.

At quite another level, Gibb's little canvas has added interest in its subject, for Fonthill Abbey was an exercise in the sublime and the picturesque actualized—temporarily at least—in architectural terms. By the time this painting was executed, in 1826, the soaring, 260-foot-high tower, based in design, but not structural integrity, upon the stupendous spire of Ely Cathedral, was gone. It had collapsed of its own weight the year before, but its brief presence had already made a mark upon the awareness of

the age. A book describing William Beckford's meglomaniac undertaking, *Delineations of Fonthill and its Abbey*, had been published by one John Rutter in 1823. By that time, Beckford had already abandoned the gigantic residence where he had lived reclusively for many years following the death of his young wife: it was sold to a rich gunpowder manufacturer named John Farquhar. Today, there is little to mark the place where the building once stood, but further work on its brief existence is in order, for its story involved other personalities discussed in these pages.

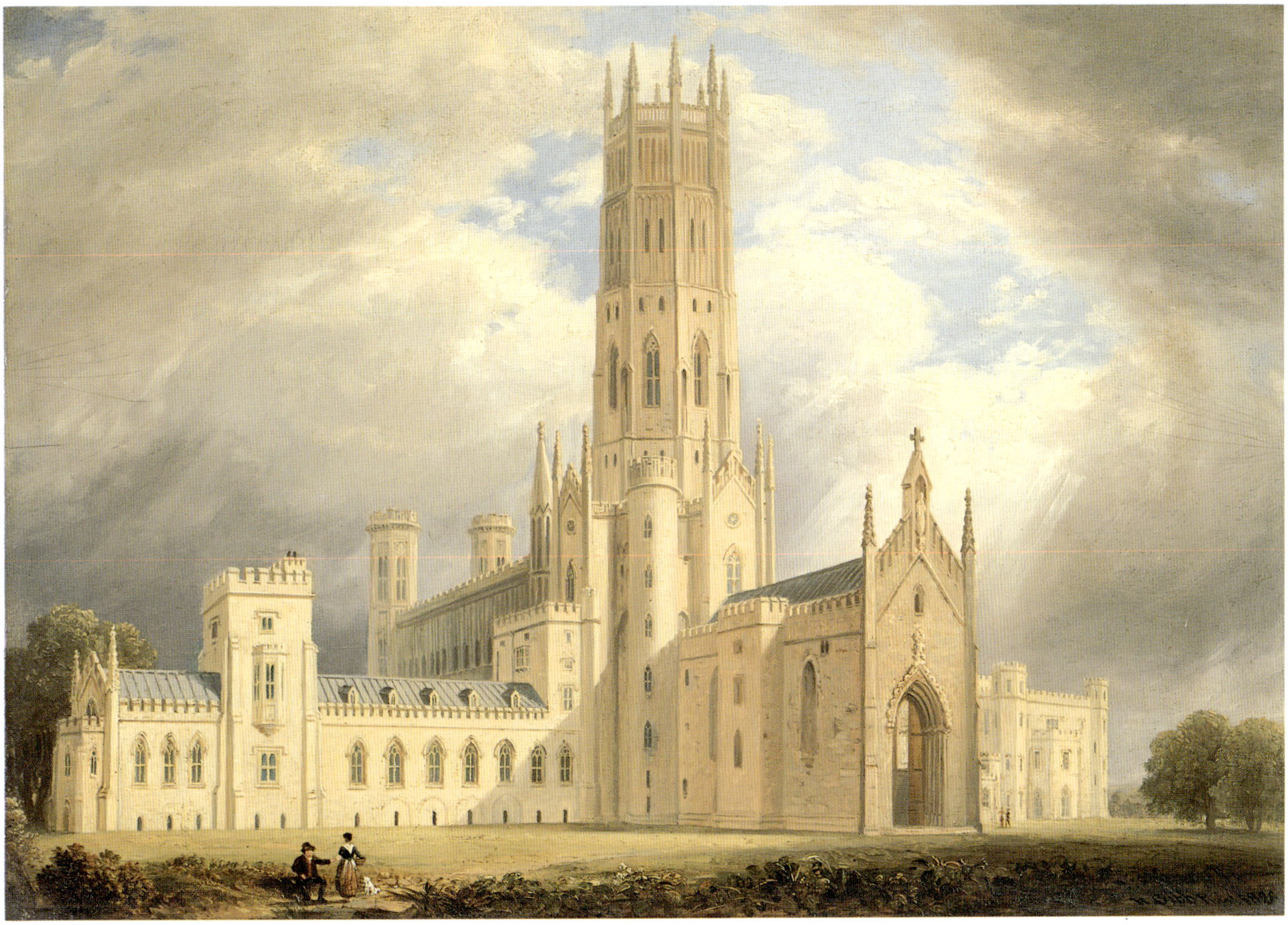

Left independently wealthy at an early age, Beckford employed Loutherbourg to propose designs for renovations of the Palladian mansion he had inherited at Fonthill. He wished to commemorate his twenty-first birthday. That same year, the gifted heir to vast sugar plantations in Jamaica also published *Vathek*, a bizarre, "oriental" tale written in French. He had that text—now regarded as a masterpiece of its aberrant literary order—professionally translated into English. Beckford studied architecture with the noted Sir William Chambers (1723–1796), and

Alexander Cousins was his drawing master. He was by any definition, a person of parts.

With his flair for indulging his whims, regardless of cost, Beckford had hired Turner to paint his ideal "abbey," which had been built to his designs by the adaptable James Wyatt (1746–1873). By then, this structure, originally conceived as an insubstantial "folly," had assumed gargantuan (hence, sublime) proportions, even in its never completed state. To be sure, its first tower had blown down and was replaced. New wings extending some four hundred feet in length had been added, and a vast, walled park had been developed as a paradise reborn, to protect Beckford's mirage of lath and plaster from unwanted intrusions of the modern world. John Martin had been summoned by Beckford (who recognized the soul-mate in him) to portray his creation. In 1819, Beckford had thrice visited the British Institution, to admire Martin's "sublime" *Fall of Babylon*. In return, Martin's published drawings of Fonthill Abbey preserve some notion of that lost wonder and its aura at the time of his visit.

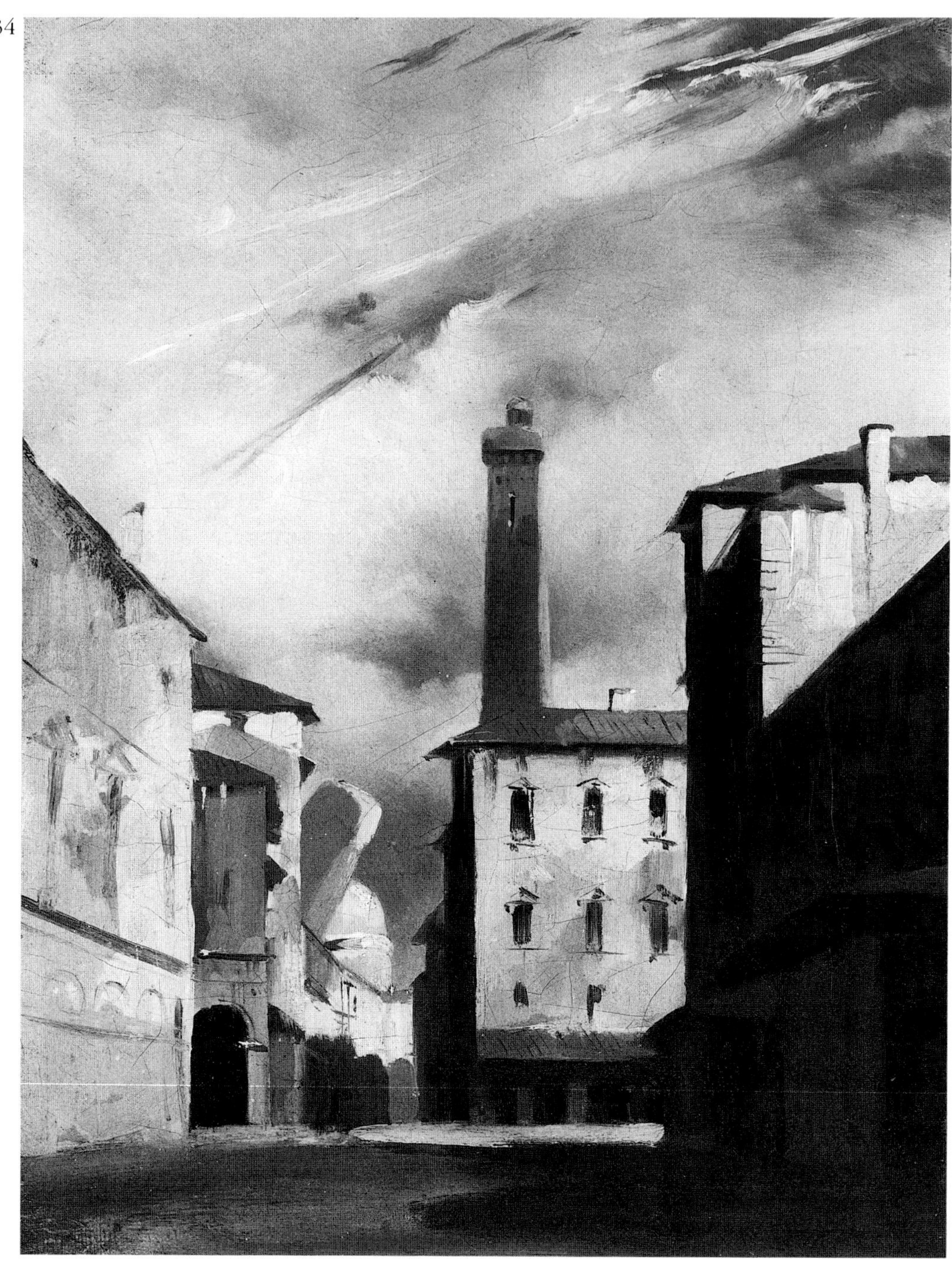

Attributed to THOMAS SHOTTER BOYS (1803–1874)

34. *Viewing a Piazza in Bologna, with Leaning
    Tower in Distance,* 1830s
    Oil on canvas, 12¾ x 9½ in. (32.4 x 24.1 cm)
    Museum Purchase
    1987.4

Apart from Turner, the most brilliant advocate of the topographical tradition of Canaletto and Pannini in British art was Richard Parkes Bonington (1802–1828). In his brief but happy career, Bonington made a glowing impression upon his colleagues in France as well as in England. His friend Delacroix later recalled him as having "a talent that knew no dawn." And his seemingly effortless felicity of touch, whether in oils, watercolors, or the graphic mediums, inspired the admiration of all those who knew him. Widely traveled, he compiled a splendid array of views "taken" in various parts. One of them, a superb watercolor now in the great Wallace Collection, London, shows the same piazza in Bologna as our small cityscape probably painted by Thomas Shotter Boys.

Quite understandably, Bonington attracted a certain

following, among them, his close contemporary, Thomas Shotter Boys (1803–1874). In all likelihood this view of Bologna is by Boys; it reveals the degree to which he approximated the qualities of Bonington's style in the works of his earlier years, one of which this seems to be. Following his apprenticeship to a London engraver named George Cooke (1781–1834), Boys found his way to Paris and came under the spell of Bonington, who was much in evidence in Paris at the time. Like his countryman, Boys worked in watercolor as well as engraving and lithography. Indeed, he would soon after contribute significantly to the technical evolution of lithography for he is credited with the pioneer development of chromolithography around 1837. That innovation was publicized in his illustrated volumes, *Picturesque Architecture in Paris, Ghent, Antwerp, Rouen, Etc.* (1839) and *Original Views of London* (1842). For whatever reasons, Boys' career declined sadly after the 1840s, and toward the end, he was forced to eke out a living by assisting architects and other, lesser artists in the performance of menial finishing and background work.

Given its closeness to the Bonington idiom, the view of Bologna would appear to have been painted in the early 1830s, when the influence of Bonington's example remained fresh in Boys' own works. In it the viewer may appreciate the qualities of practiced spontaneity cultivated by those who worked in the after-image of that gifted exemplar of what the French dubbed—not without admiration—"the Anglo-Venetian mode." Another of their number, James Holland (1800–1870), has also been proposed as a possible author of the present work. Although Bonington had died before Holland arrived in Paris in 1831, his works of the 1830s also reveal a keen appreciation of the former's art. For the moment, however, Boys remains the most convincing candidate for the attribution. Despite the exaggeration of the angle of one of the famous leaning towers of that venerable university city, this elegantly painted little view recalls the wealth of touristic attractions that to this day lure visitors to that special corner of Italy.

EDWARD LEAR (1812–1888)

35. *Pentedatilo,* 1851
    Oil on canvas, 55 x 37 in. (139.7 x 94 cm)
    Museum Purchase
    1968.15

In landscape painting, the ideological equivalent of Reynolds' Grand Manner was given noblest shape in the art of Turner, with his genius for isolating the sublime. Other masters of Romantic landscape, such as Loutherbourg and Martin, sought in their own ways to accommodate to Burke's injunction that artists should inspire awe and terror in the mind of their viewers by projecting an overwhelming sense of Nature's majesty and might. That tradition was upheld with great distinction in the oils painted by Edward Lear in his early maturity. He would later turn almost exclusively to the watercolor medium and would substantially revise his purposes—though not totally redirect it, to be sure —under the influence of William Holman Hunt (1827– 1910) and the Pre-Raphaelites. Lear's watercolor, *Olive Trees in the Garden of Gethsemane* (No. 40) reflects the shifts of emphasis in his subsequent works.

In the period of his concentration upon large-sized landscapes painted in oil, however, he showed greater continuity with the tonalities and painterly techniques of earlier tradition. This corpus dates almost entirely from the years 1840–53. After showing at the academy in 1852, Lear had been dissatisfied with the look of his work, particularly with regard to his drawing. In spite of his age, he enrolled in the academy classes and took up study with the much younger Hunt. Thenceforth, changes occurred in his approach, if by no means a repudiation of his life-long search for the picturesque.

The youngest of twenty-one children, ill-favored of health and personal appearance, but abundantly endowed with wit and artistic talents, Lear set out on his own at an early age. While still an adolescent he gained employment in the gardens of the Zoological Society, and at age eighteen, he had published a book, *Family of the Psittacidae* (1831) with illustrations done after his ornothological drawings, among the first done in England. While employed at making drawings in the menagerie of the 13th Earl of Derby (1832–36), he wrote his famous nonsense verses for his patron's grandchildren. By the time the first volume of those extraordinary verses was published, in 1846, Lear had given up permanent residence in England and set out on a life of wandering that took him as far off as India and Ceylon—a voluntary (though not absolute) exile that would only come to a close with his death on the Italian Riviera, at San Remo, at age seventy-six.

Lear's paripatetic life had begun in 1837, the year Victoria came to the throne. (Lear was off in Italy at the time, on his first journey abroad.) Afflicted with poor eyesight and a frail constitution—he was prone to frequent epileptic seizures—Lear had braved the hardships and hazards of primitive conditions to amass his thousands of on-the-spot drawings and watercolors. All this was experienced not without complaint, but with forebearance.

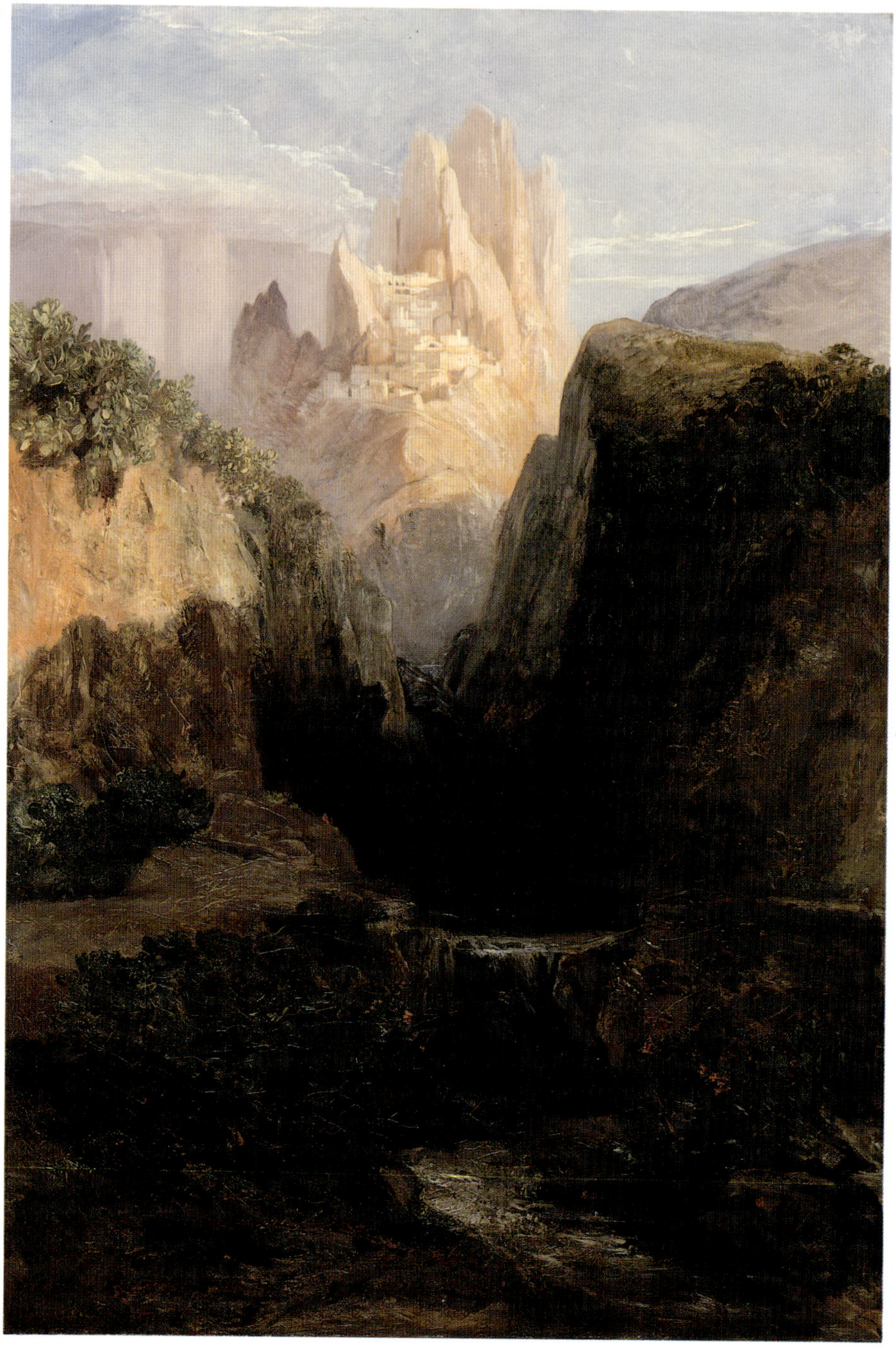

In 1841, the first of his seven travel volumes appeared, *Views of Rome and Its Environs*. The canvas now in Mead relates to a later journey (1847–48), which took him to Calabria. His description of the place is studded with reminders of the powerful Romantic urges that galvanized his will to experience yet another of the strange destinations that lured him on his almost endless search for picturesque novelties.

A brief extract from Lear's *Journals of a Landscape Painter in Southern Calabria and the Kingdom of Naples* dramatically conveys the satisfactions of his experience of Pentedatilo:

The appearance of Pentedatilo is perfectly magical, and repays whatever trouble the effort to reach it may so far have cost. Wild spires of stone shoot up into the air, barren and clearly defined, in the form (as its name implies) of a gigantic hand against the sky, and in the crevices and holes of this fearfully savage pyramid the houses of Pentedatilo are wedged, while darkness and terror brood over all the abyss around this the strangest of human abodes.

2. Watercolor

Watercolor is one of the most ancient of all artistic mediums, having been employed with technical variations throughout the civilized world from the dawn of history. The development and widespread adoption of oil paint, however, led to a comparative neglect of watercolor painting during the Renaissance and Baroque periods. To be sure, such major masters as Dürer had found watercolor techniques advantageous for making records of their travels or accumulating visual documentary references which might serve in composing works of a more elaborate, formal nature. The practicality of an aqueous medium as a quick-drying vehicle for rendering all manner of image—whether in the most summary and fleeting of suggestion or in painstaking detail—was not lost on those historical masters. Their watercolor studies were, however, apt to be regarded more as a branch of drawing than as independent artistic creations. Hence, while the toned drawings produced by such artists as Adrian van Ostade (1610–1685) were sold as works of art in their own right and were admired accordingly, they were not the mainstay of their makers' livelihood or reputation. A renewed interest in watercolor as a medium of specialists, to be valued for its own qualities and standards, was a comparatively modern phenomenon. Above all that revival took on momentum in eighteenth- and early nineteenth-century Britain.

While the collection at Amherst College does not yet boast representation of the greatest British practitioners in the watercolor medium—Turner, Bonington, and Constable are notably missing—it does offer a variety of examples by noteworthy artists in which the evolution of its use over the years may be appreciated. It is ironic that the rising popularity of watercolor painting should have centered in Britain just when the Royal Academy was entering its most flourishing years. The academy's strict heirarchy of values in subject matter, with an insistence upon for-

mal performance in oil painting, automatically cast watercolor into a distinctly minor role in the system of values. (The case was much the same with the graphic processes, which were regarded as innately reproductive, not creative in nature.) Accordingly, those artists who specialized in that cadet branch of watercolor representation were inspired to institute their own, independent societies, such as the Royal Society of Painters in Water Colour. They thus set a pattern of claims to professional autonomy which would long persist in the English-speaking world, within which nagging "ambiguities" of status and artistic purpose nevertheless also survived.

Those theoretical and historical questions aside, however, watercolor enjoys the special appeal of its inherent virtues of economy. Most often used for comparatively small works, it has characteristically involved light and portable materials, so that conditions of execution were flexible. Elaborate studio provisions were unnecessary, and the option of working under informal conditions, whether indoors or out-of-doors, was often advantageous. That ease of working directly from the subject in nature had significant implications for the future. At the same time, the aspirant to a mastery of painting in watercolor was freed from the traditional need for lengthy apprenticeship in the technically more complex, formally demanding mediums.

Many amateurs were in due course attracted to the practice of watercolor painting—often with some distinction—even as the drawing master came to play a conspicuous role in the education of those who were considered well-brought-up. While British gentlewomen were surprisingly scarce in the initial ranks of watercolorists, by the latter part of the nineteenth century they too were attracted in great numbers to this form of personal cultivation. Particularly in the early phases of this development, some degree of accomplishment in representation was encouraged amongst the swelling ranks of the Crown's military

and naval officers or of civil servants, as skills of the kind relevant to their promotion of imperial interests. In that context of conveying topological or other documentary information, watercolor images satisfied practical as well as vicarious fascinations of the dawning modern age, long before—and long after—the invention of the camera.

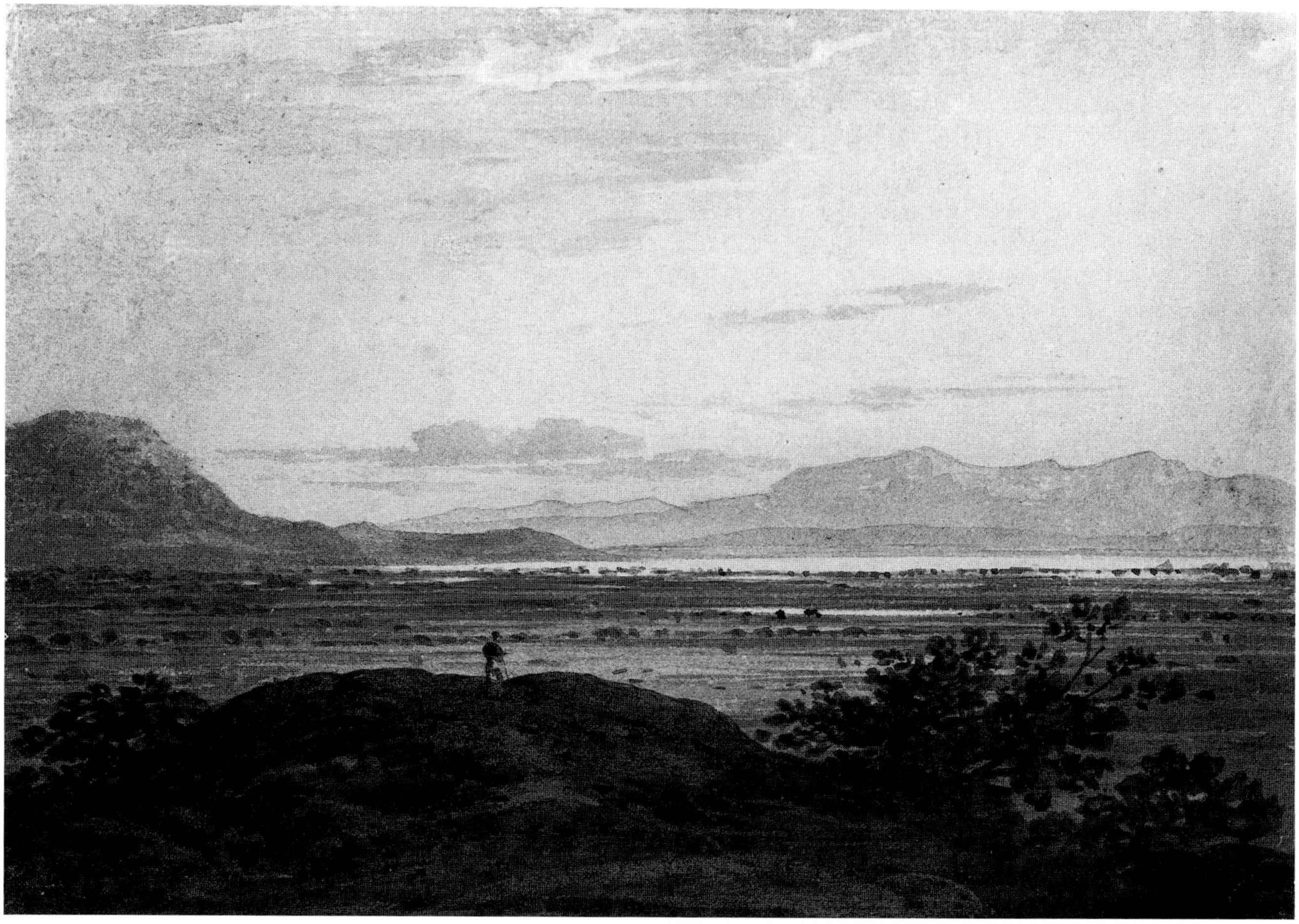

For the collector, watercolors held the great attraction of being intimate, informal, and often graced with the special qualities of freshness the medium invites. Being small and easily handled, as well as traditionally less costly than oils, they came to be favored by a clientele that included connoisseurs of highly cultivated tastes. Among them the early London collector, Dr. Thomas Monroe, is of especial importance. As a watercolorist of some competence in his own right, Monroe was also an enterprising collector. Indeed, "the good doctor's" activities as a dilettante extended well beyond his patronage of such budding

artists as Thomas Girtin, Joseph Mallord William Turner, and John Varley—the last of whom is represented in the present exhibition. Monroe's now famous "academy" housed at his residence, No. 8 Adelphi Terrace, was thus a seedbed for young talent, where master examples could be studied and copied under his tutelage. Thanks to the efforts of enthusiasts such as Dr. Monroe, watercolorists came to be "as plentiful as blackberries" during the early years of the past century, when societies devoted to the special interests of the watercolorist were founded.

Although the body of works at the Mead Art Museum illustrating the emergence of this characteristic tradition of British art remains comparatively small, it is nevertheless sufficiently broad in range and distinguished in artistic quality to illustrate the broad lines of that development. An annotated review of the finest and most characteristic of their number follows.

John Varley (1778–1842)

36. *The Plains of Marathon*
   Watercolor, 5 x 7¼ in. (12.7 x 18.4 cm)
   Museum Purchase with funds from the
   William K. Allison '20 Memorial Fund
   1985.22

John Varley was one of the most prolific early advocates of watercolor and a major protagonist of the rising interest in that medium. He was essentially self-taught, aside from brief tutelage as an assistant at a school of a minor artist, Joseph Charles Barrow (active 1789–1820). Around 1797–98 he accompanied Barrow on a trip to Peterborough, which inspired his first exhibit at the Royal Academy, in 1798. Around 1800 Varley gained further visibility as a protégé of Dr. Monroe, and while a member of Monroe's circle, he was for a time influenced by Thomas Girtin (1775–1802). Soon Varley himself came to enjoy the role of teacher. His many pupils over the years included John Linnell, Samuel Palmer, David Cox, Copley Fielding, William Mulready, Turner of Oxford, and William Holman Hunt. The seriousness of his devotion to teaching is attested in his *Treatise on the Principles of Landscape Drawing* (1816–21) and *Pictorial Treatise on the Art of Drawing in Perspective* (1821). Also given to mysticism, Varley remained a close friend of William Blake's from the time of their meeting in 1819, until the latter's death in 1827. That side of his interests was

commemorated by the publication in 1828 of *A Treatise in Zodiacal Physiognomy.*

During Varley's long career he evolved a succession of manners which are detectable to connoisseurs of his work, but no special expertise is required to recognize his consistent concern for the innate properties of his chosen medium, with its capacities for overlapping transparent washes of color. *The Plains of Marathon*, recently acquired for the Amherst College Collection, cannot be precisely dated but would appear to relate to his later efforts. Though sometimes criticized as repetitive in technique and less direct in spirit, Varley's works of these years are nevertheless often distinguished, as here, by a richly atmospheric mood and an attractive resonance of subtly nuanced color.

While Varley traveled extensively in Britain, especially in Wales, he never visited Greece. It may therefore be assumed that this "view" derived from some intermediate topographic source such as a sketch brought back by some acquaintance from a trip abroad. In his later years Varley seems to have consulted such second-hand sources of thematic inspiration more and more frequently as an alternative to direct observation of natural fact. Accordingly, works of that phase of his career are often of interest more as compositional exercises of a generalized character than as topographic subjects with specific associations. In them he returned tirelessly to the exercise of his powers as a master of the watercolor medium.

David Cox (1783–1859)

37. *View Near Bettws-y-Coed, Wales*, 1844
   Watercolor, 10 x 13¾ in. (25.4 x 34.9 cm)
   Gift of Professor Arthur H. Baxter
   PWC 1937.2

Son of a Birmingham blacksmith, David Cox had little education, apart from brief training with a local drawing master, Joseph Barber (1757–1811). A stint as a toymaker's apprentice and work as a scene painter followed, after which he departed for London, in 1804. There he worked as a stage painter, draftsman, and drawing master. In that last pursuit, he taught at several respected institutions and tutored privately. He retired from teaching altogether in 1841 and to his native Birmingham, where he worked independently as an artist. Despite his relative lack of pro-

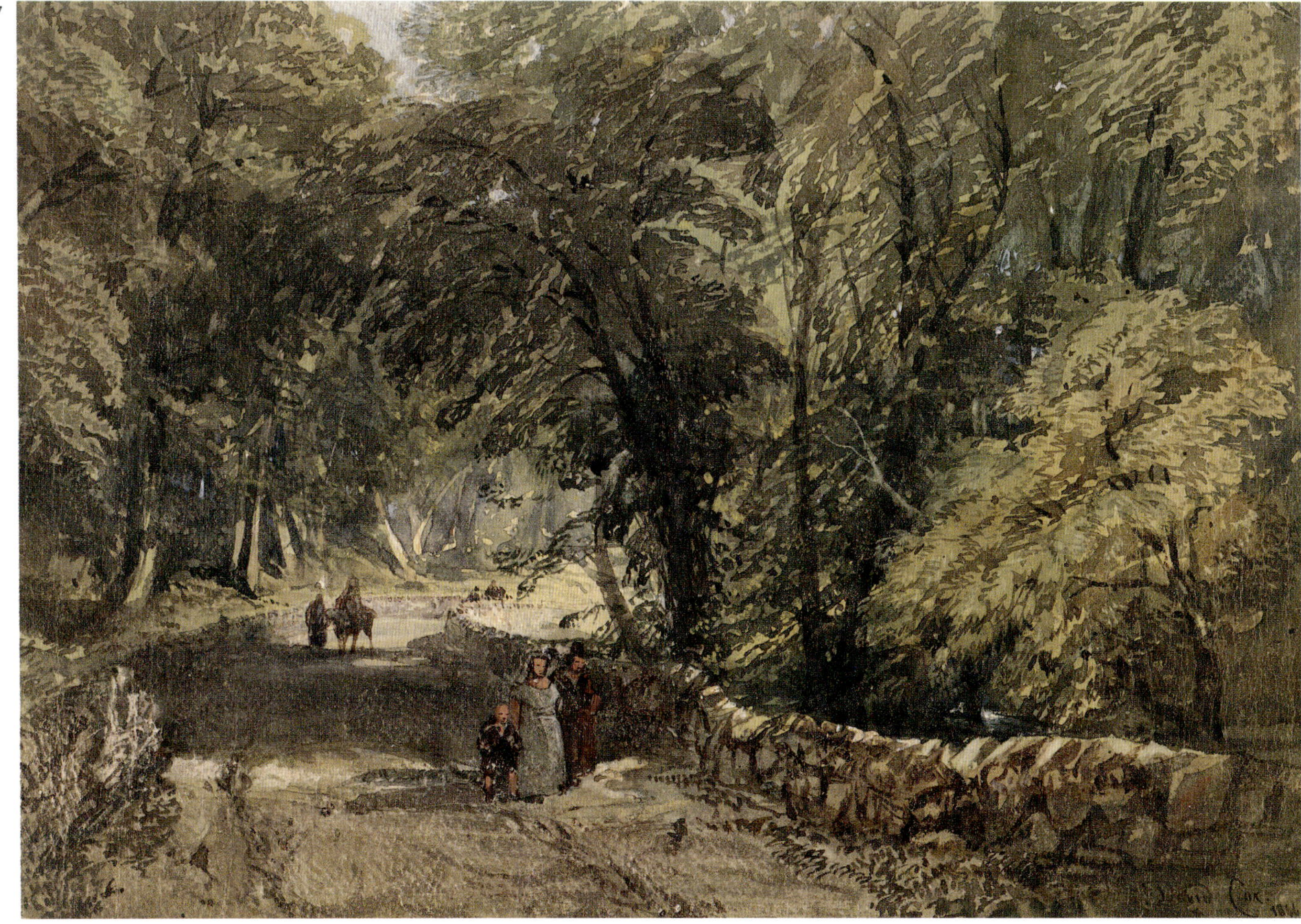

fessional background, Cox placed works in exhibitions of the Association of Artists in Watercolours from 1809 to 1812 and served as president of that organization in 1810. When the group disbanded in 1812, Cox earned a place in the (Old) Society of Painters in Watercolour and remained a full member when that association was reorganized in 1820. By the time of his death in 1859, Cox had shown some 849 watercolors in exhibitions sponsored by the society. His activities as a teacher led, moreover, to the publication of several manuals: *Treatise on Landscape Painting and Effect in Watercolour* (1814), *Progressive Lessons on Landscape for Young Beginners* (1816), *A Series of Progressive Lessons* (ca. 1816), and *The Young Artist's Companion* (1825).

In his use of the watercolor medium, Cox was above all indebted to John Varley, with whom he studied for a time in the 1870s, but whose example he had already followed both in technique and thematically, in exploring the rugged beauties of the Welsh countryside. During his middle and late years, Cox was especially attracted to subjects drawn from North Wales, centering on Bettws-y-Coed. In them he indulged his increasing confidence in a bold, fresh manner, in which his eventual fondness for the effects afforded by the use of rough-textured papers prepared especially for him in Dundee, thenceforth known to the trade as "Cox paper."

Stylistically, Cox underwent several stages of development, evolving gradually from a virtually monochromatic phase to the use of more pronounced, though always restricted color. The breadth of handling in *View Near Bettws-y-Coed* relates to his last period, when his brushwork became increasingly impressionistic. Cox is also represented in the present exhibition by a lively landscape in oils, in which his spontaneity may be admired in his handling of that other medium of expression.

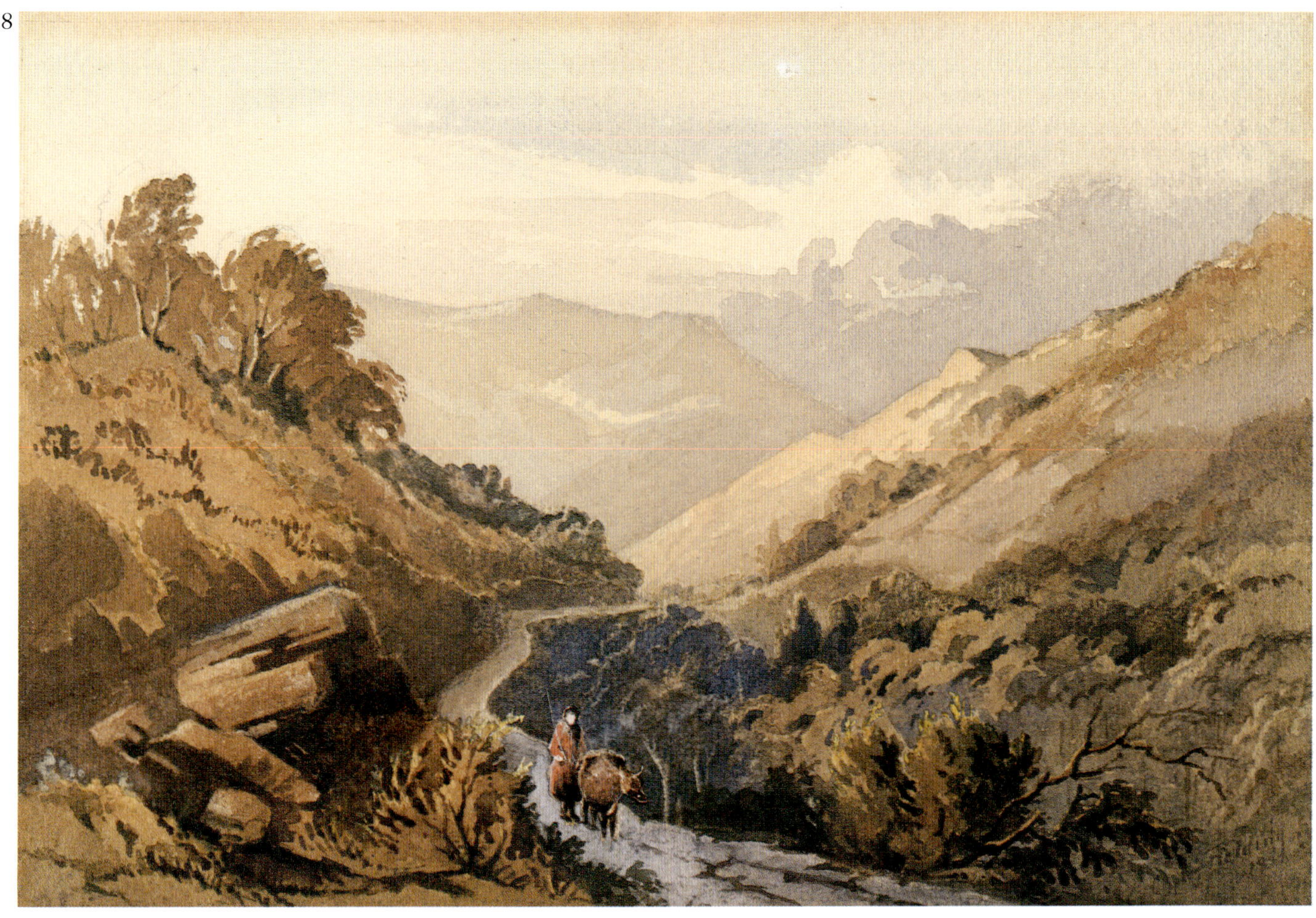

ANTHONY VAN DYKE COPLEY FIELDING
(1787–1855)

38. *Landscape and Figures—Ireland*, 1811
   Watercolor, 6½ x 9½ in. (16.5 x 24.1 cm)
   Gift of Professor Arthur H. Baxter
   PWC 1937.10

The best known of a family of minor but capable artists, Copley Fielding was a productive and widely recognized specialist in watercolor painting and a drawing master of fashionable repute. After initial study with his father, Nathan Theodore Fielding (1775–1818), he continued his training under John Varley. He began exhibiting with the Royal Society of Painters in Watercolours and continued that association for most of his career. In 1813 he became secretary of the society, and from 1831 to 1855, he served as president. Although he was also competent at oil painting and showed at the Royal Academy from 1811 to 1842, those canvases—all landscapes and architectural subjects —totaled but seventeen in number. By contrast he sometimes submitted as many as fifty entries a year to the Royal Society of Watercolours exhibitions.

Copley Fielding and his brother Thales (also a watercolorist) were among Eugène Delacroix's favorite companions during a prolonged visit to London in 1825, and it was largely through the Fieldings that Delacroix gained a command of "English" watercolor techniques which were later to gain widespread favor on the Continent. The brilliant but short-lived Richard Parkes Bonington (1802–1828) was another member of that congenial circle. Copley Fielding was one of the first British artists to benefit from the cultural rapprochement between Britain and France during the postwar years of the Bourbon Restoration, and along with Bonington and Constable, he won a medal at the

Paris Salon of 1824. Unlike his brother Thales, however, he never traveled abroad, and Italian subjects that occur in his work, as they sometimes do, derive from the preliminary renditions of others.

Copley Fielding's accomplishments as a watercolorist may be appreciated in *Landscape and Figures—Ireland*, one of two attractive examples of his art in the collection in the Mead Art Museum. Although it is an early specimen of his talent, it nevertheless typifies the qualities that earned him popularity for the effects of craggy, atmospheric landscape he came to favor, whether in Scotland, Wales, or the north of England. These and his other scenes of Sussex Downs or his seascapes won him the enthusiasm of no less a contemporary critic than John Ruskin, who praised the "flashing freedom" and conviction of his depictions.

GEORGE RICHMOND (1809–1896)

39. *Portrait of a Lady*, 1833
   Watercolor and mixed media, 13 x 10 in. (33 x 25.4 cm)
   Bequest of Shirley Orr Stillson
   1976.47

George Richmond was the son of a lesser miniaturist, Thomas Richmond. At age fifteen he enrolled as a student at the Royal Academy Schools, where he joined the class of Henry Fuseli (1741–1825). There he became the fast friend of fellow students, Samuel Palmer (1805–1881) and Edward Calvert (1799–1883). Through them he became an intimate of the circle of William Blake (1757–1827) in the years just before Blake's death in 1827 and was present at Blake's home at Shoreham on that sad occasion. As a member of Palmer's coterie, Richmond possessed youthful, mystical enthusiasms, based on Blake's teachings. Despite their youth, the group called themselves "The Ancients," honoring their common fascination with the works of those "ancient" painters and poets, such as Virgil and Milton, whose memories Blake himself had so admired.

Richmond was soon forced to sacrifice service to those interests in favor of the practical issue of earning a livelihood. This he did by painting portrait miniatures. He still was practicing in that vein when he went to Paris for study in 1828. Around 1831, he began to work at a somewhat larger size, with an eye to the suitability of his watercolor portrait subjects for reproduction as engravings. He prospered in his chosen line of specialization and eventually, from 1846 onward, worked in oil as well as his accustomed mediums of watercolor, chalk, and crayon. Elected an associate of the Royal Academy in 1856, he was accorded full membership in 1866.

Richmond's *Portrait of a Lady* is a fine early example

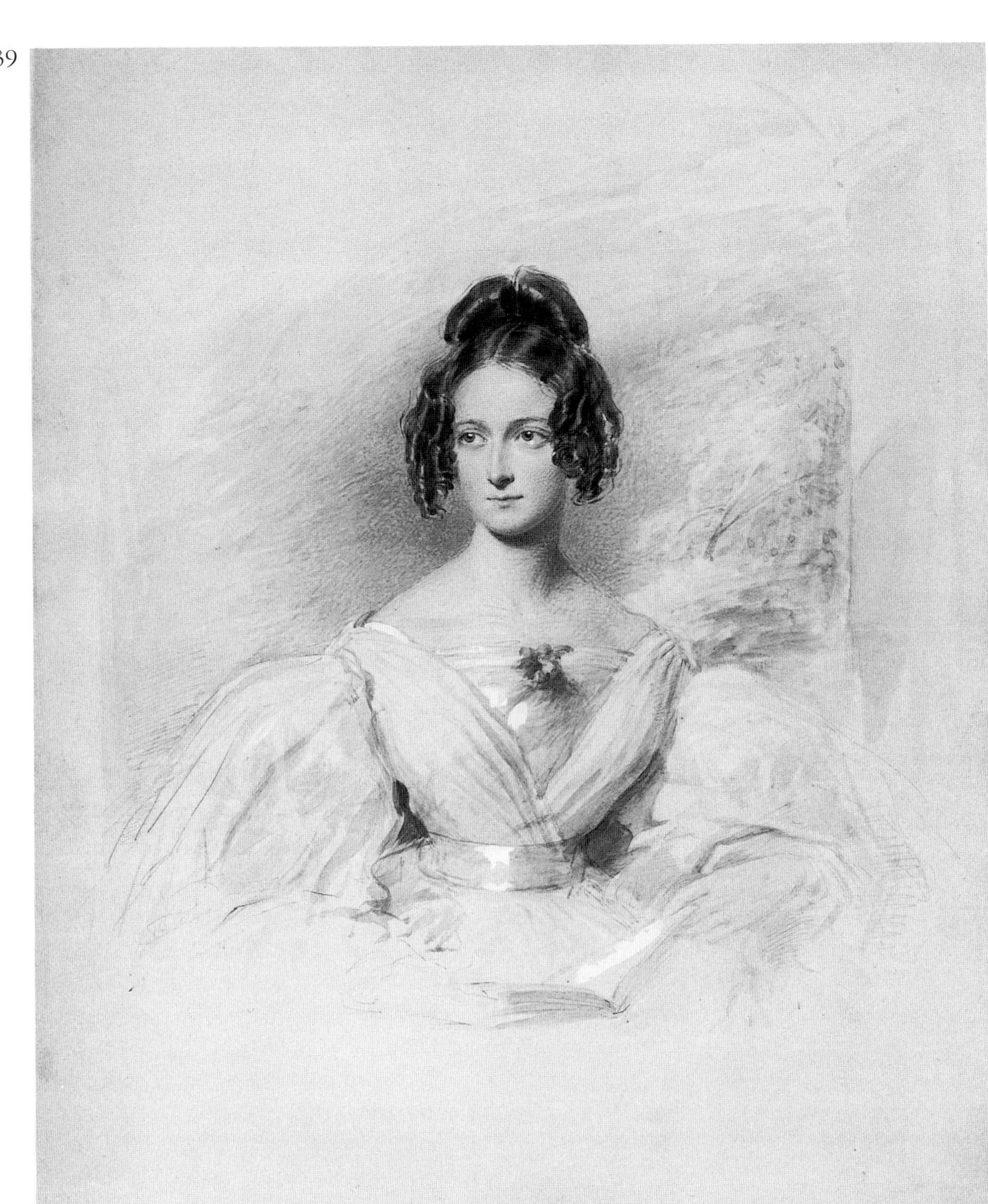

of his art from the period just following his abandonment of miniature scale in favor of a slightly enlarged, watercolor format. The delicacy of his handling unmistakably recalls the niceties of touch essential to his metier as a miniaturist. The small accentuations in opaque "body color," such as the flowers at the neckline or the other decorative features of costume are indicated with the practiced skill of a master craftsman: they are at once precise and free.

The characterization of the lady herself is consistent with those formal attributes, not least of all the delicately nuanced tonalities of color which prevail. Altogether they at once present the features of an attractive individual and the ideal image of young womanhood given the attributes of purity and self-possession prized at the dawn of the Victorian era. However different that sensibility might be from those that pertain in our own or intervening ages, the modern viewer can but admire Richmond's capacity to reflect it. His *Portrait of a Lady* thus epitomizes its maker's reported ideal of portraiture as "the truth lovingly told." For such ingratiating qualities as the foregoing, Richmond has come to be accounted the outstanding portraitist in watercolor of his day.

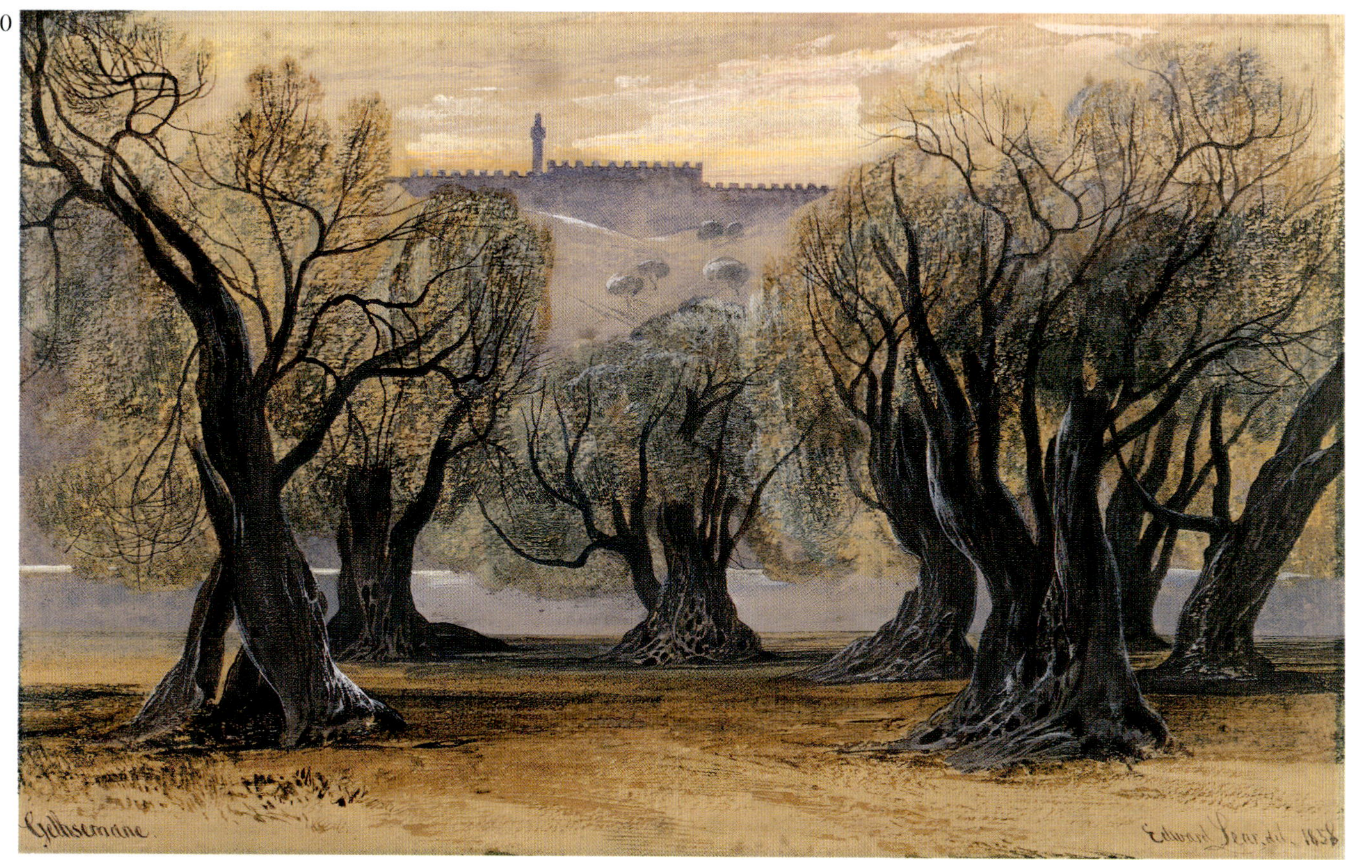

EDWARD LEAR (1812–1888)

40. *Olive Trees in the Garden of Gethsemane*
  Watercolor, 6½ x 20½ in. (16.5 x 51.4 cm)
  Museum Purchase
  1951.138

Now more famous as the great master of nonsense verse, Lear sustained a lifelong career as a professional artist. Benefitting as a child from some instruction by Thomas Hartley Cromek (1809–1873), Lear gained a livelihood making colored drawings for zoological publications, mainly those devoted to the study of birds. That enterprise was first undertaken in 1831, as an employee of the Zoological Gardens and then continued at Knowsley, where he was employed by the Earl of Derby from 1832 to 1836. With his eyesight impaired by the strain of those minute tasks, he eventually turned to the less optically exacting genre of landscape representation, and though physically frail in health, he committed his energies to periods of ambitious foreign travel in pursuit of fresh subjects. His wanderlust took him through the Balkans, the Holy Land, Egypt, and North Africa. In 1848, he first toured Greece, Albania, and Malta, and by 1849 he had made his way to Egypt. From 1855 to 1855, he wintered in Corfu and visited London, Greece, and the Holy Land in the summertimes.

Eventually, in the years 1873 to 1875, he ventured as far as India and Ceylon. He last saw England in 1880, before making his final move from Cannes to San Remo, where he died. He left a massive inventory of over ten thousand drawings and watercolors, most of them dated and elaborately annotated.

Lear's "topographies" were drawn in pencil directly from the site. They usually bear color notes and other information which served as *aides-memoire* for reworking in sepia-toned pen-and-ink with color washes—tasks reserved for winter evenings. *Olive Trees in the Garden of Gesthemane* reveals the more carefully developed elaboration in that process that sometimes was undertaken. Especially in the more tightly finished efforts the influence of William Holman Hunt (1829–1910) is strong. Upon his return to England after a visit to Egypt in 1849, Lear had enrolled for a time in the Royal Academy Schools and at that time came under Hunt's influence. Hunt's remarkable precision of execution would seem to have inspired Lear's more closely worked surfaces in this view, and the heightened coloristic intensities cultivated by Hunt also occur. Lear's little watercolor thus affords an instructive contrast with his canvas, *Pentedatilo*, (No. 35) which is conceived in the darker tonalities that had traditionally pertained in British painting before the shift of taste for a brighter palette of the Pre-Raphaelites and many of their contemporaries.

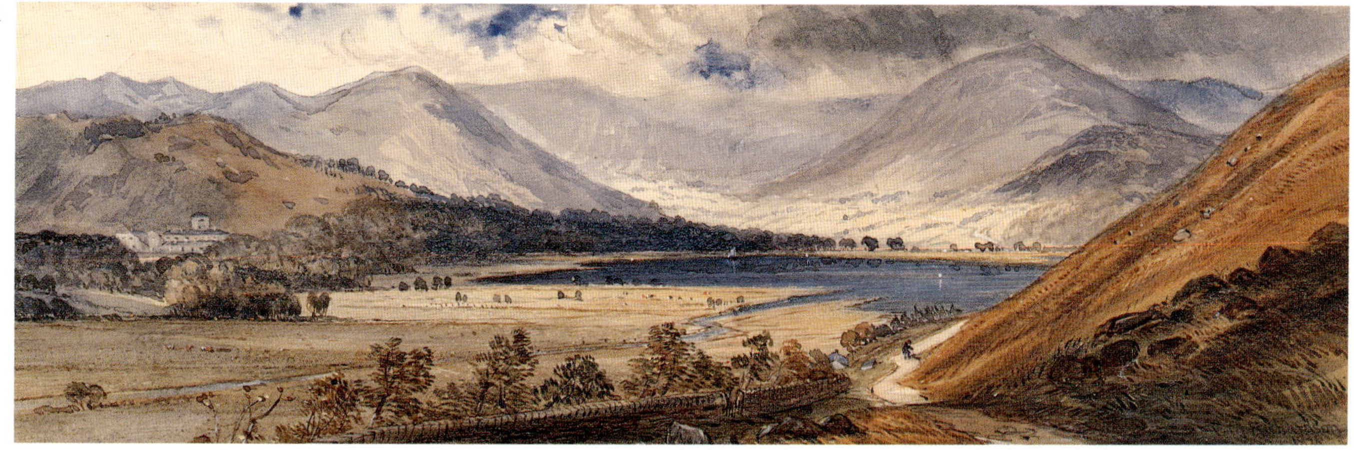

THOMAS MILES RICHARDSON (1813–1890)

41. *View at Scaw Fell*, 1876
Watercolor, 4½ x 13¼ in. (11.4 x 33.7 cm)
Gift of Professor Arthur H. Baxter
PWC 1937.8

Son and pupil of the well-known watercolorist, Thomas Miles Richardson Senior (1784–1848), the younger Richardson also came to be associated primarily with the practice of watercolor painting. Following his initial work with his father in their native Newcastle, he settled in London in 1845. By then he already enjoyed a secure reputation in the capital, however, where he exhibited at the Royal Academy from 1837 to 1848. He was also a prominent contributor to exhibitions at the Old Water-Colour Society and the British Institution. Elected an associate of the Royal Water Colour Society in 1843, he became a full member in 1851.

Richardson came to be widely known for his production of Scottish landscapes where grazing cattle sometimes provide enlivening, local notes. Later he turned to Switzerland and Italy for inspiration, choosing terrain that suited his preference for panoramic views, frequently assuming elongated, lateral formats. Richardson's technique is apt to be conservative compared to the more spontaneous modes of handling which increasingly came into fashion, and he has sometimes been criticized for overworking his surfaces in satisfying his desire for close observation of natural detail.

View at Scaw Fell included in the present exhibition is characteristically rendered in carefully reworked tones of color, touched with admixtures of opaque white. Despite its dependence upon techniques that were coming to seem old-fashioned in the eyes of the contemporaneous practice of watercolor painting, Richardson's scene nevertheless exudes a sense of the quiet satisfactions enjoyed by visitors of his era to the picturesque locales of the lakes and mountains dear to the hearts of Victorian vacationers.

HERCULES BRABAZON (1821–1906)

42. *View of Murano*
Watercolor, 9¾ x 13 in. (24.8 x 33 cm)
Gift of Mrs. C. N. Bliss
1949.28

A prolific and gifted watercolorist, Hercules Brabazon was an example of the British tradition of accomplished amateurism and love of travel. Born in Paris, he pursued his formal studies first at Harrow and then in Geneva before

enrolling at Trinity College, Cambridge, where he read in mathematics. It was only after then that he turned to the serious study of watercolor, which he learned largely through copying earlier British masters of that medium, especially Cox and Turner. His artistic leanings were then indulged by a three-year period of study in Rome, where in 1847 he worked with James T. D'Egville (ca. 1806–1880) and for a time with Alfred Downing Fripp (1822–1895), after the latter's arrival in Rome in 1850. Apart from the direct influences of those mentors, Brabazon came to be an ar-

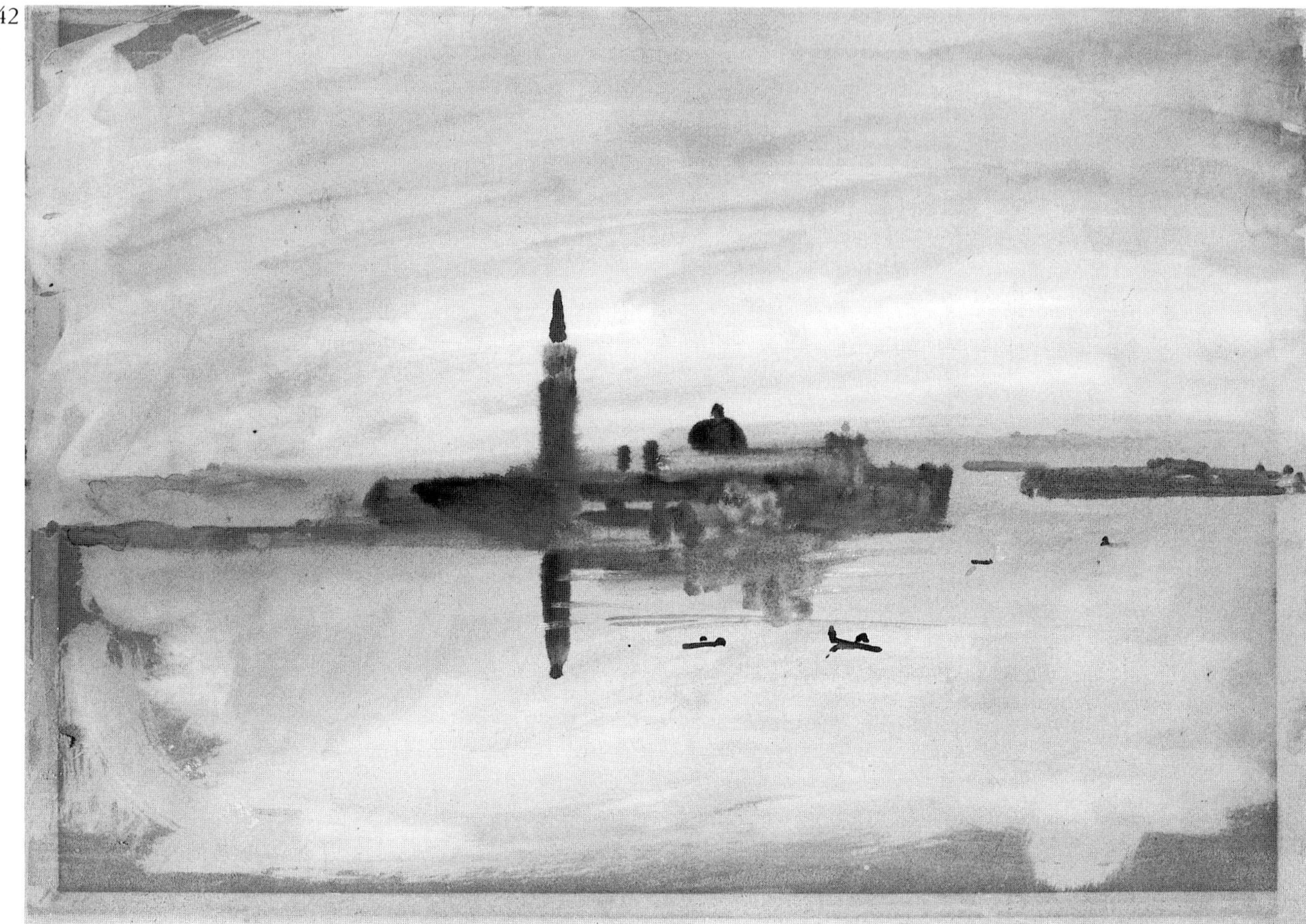

dent admirer of John Ruskin's drawings and of Turner's developed, impressionistically suggestive manner. Overtones of the latter source of inspiration in particular are evident in Brabazon's fully characteristic works with their broadly fluid washes of tone and spontaneous quality of execution, in which bold accentuations of color give focus to otherwise elusively graded expanses of tone. Accomplished though he was, and voluminously productive, Brabazon rarely showed his work and was reluctant to sell. Finally, in 1891 he gave in to the urgings of Sargent and other artist friends and consented to an exhibition of his works at the Goupil Gallery, London. That professional debut, delayed until the age of seventy, was an outstanding success, and thenceforth he enjoyed special recognition as an exemplar of the modern movement of the time.

Blessed with the means to do so from the proceeds of his extensive estates in England and Ireland, Brabazon indulged his love of travel, spending his summers in England and winters in France, Italy, Germany, or Spain. His itinerary was extended after 1867 to include Egypt and other areas of North Africa, and in 1870 he ventured as far as India. His predilection for the experience of foreign travel is vividly recalled in his many vibrant sketches. Brabazon's affection for skillfully manipulated "wet" washes of "body color" is often recalled in the watercolors of John Singer Sargent, who greatly admired the older man's work and was visibly affected by it. *View of Murano* demonstrates Brabazon's preferences and his skillful technique.

Roger Fry (1866–1934)

43. *The Brickfield in Italy*
   Watercolor, 13 x 19½ in. (33 x 24.1 cm)
   Museum Purchase
   1985.5

To some extent heir to longstanding British traditions of travel and artistic accomplishment as proper pursuits of the well bred, Fry turned to serious study in the visual arts following his own student years at King's College, Cam-

bridge, where he earned a degree in science. Despite his ambitions as a creative artist which then took shape, Fry's posthumous reputation, like Lear's, came to rest mainly with his literary contribution, where he stands beside Ruskin as a leading figure in art criticism in the English language.

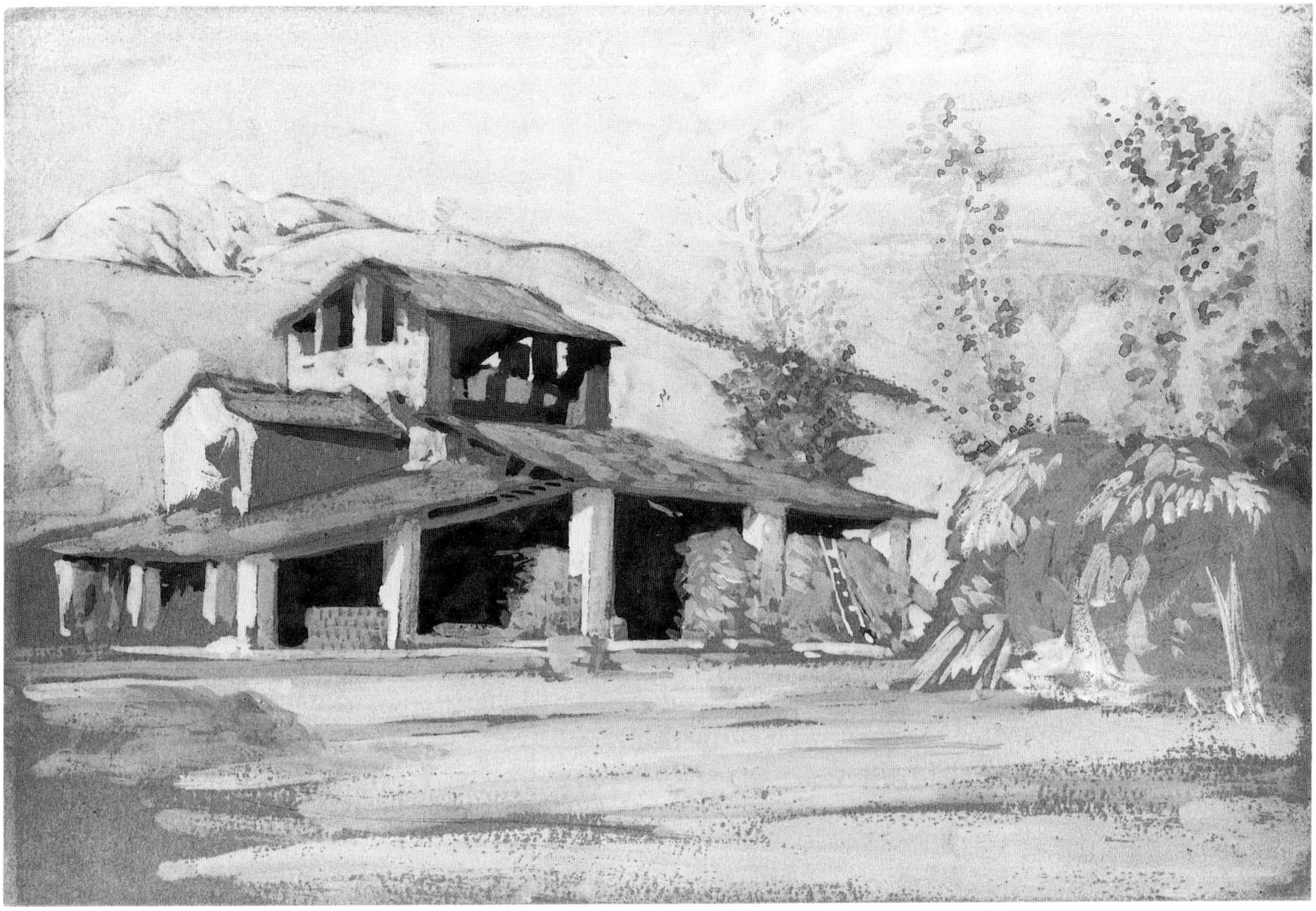

What is less popularly recognized, however, is the fact that throughout his life Fry remained an active painter, faithfully devoted to the pursuit of his creative ambitions. The finely cultivated sensibilities that may be detected in the artistic products of his hand confirm the distinguished qualities of mind and spirit that inspired Fry's performance as a critic of such enormous distinction.

The Brickfield in Italy was recently purchased for the Amherst College Collection as a reminder of Fry's not inconsiderable accomplishment as a practicing artist. Firmly constructed in its pictorial order, it exemplifies a concern for clarity that closely relates to its maker's later decision to found the Omega Workshop in 1913, where the same principles might be applied to the production of avant-garde, utilitarian objects.

Like other members of the so-called Bloomsbury group of artists—among them, Duncan Grant and Vanessa Bell—Fry remained, however, surprisingly conservative in his adaptations from the Post-Impressionist and Fauve idioms he so ardently advocated in his mature criticism. In *The Brickfield in Italy*, however, those attributes do not pertain. The work appears to date to the 1890s, when Fry twice visited Italy (1891, 1894), both to study works by the Italian masters and to paint. It is consistent in character with the offerings then to be seen at the New English Art Club, where Fry began to show in 1894. It demonstrates a frequent manner of the period: relatively flat, decorative, translucent washes, with accents in "body color." *The Brickfield* exemplifies the probity and intelligence of Fry's endeavor, with its reluctance not to lose touch with tradition—a prudence that is generally to be observed even in the more radical responses to the challenge of modernism in Fry's own work and that of his artistic peers in Britain of the time. In that sense, this little watercolor is an instructive intellectual document as well as an appealing object of art in its own right.

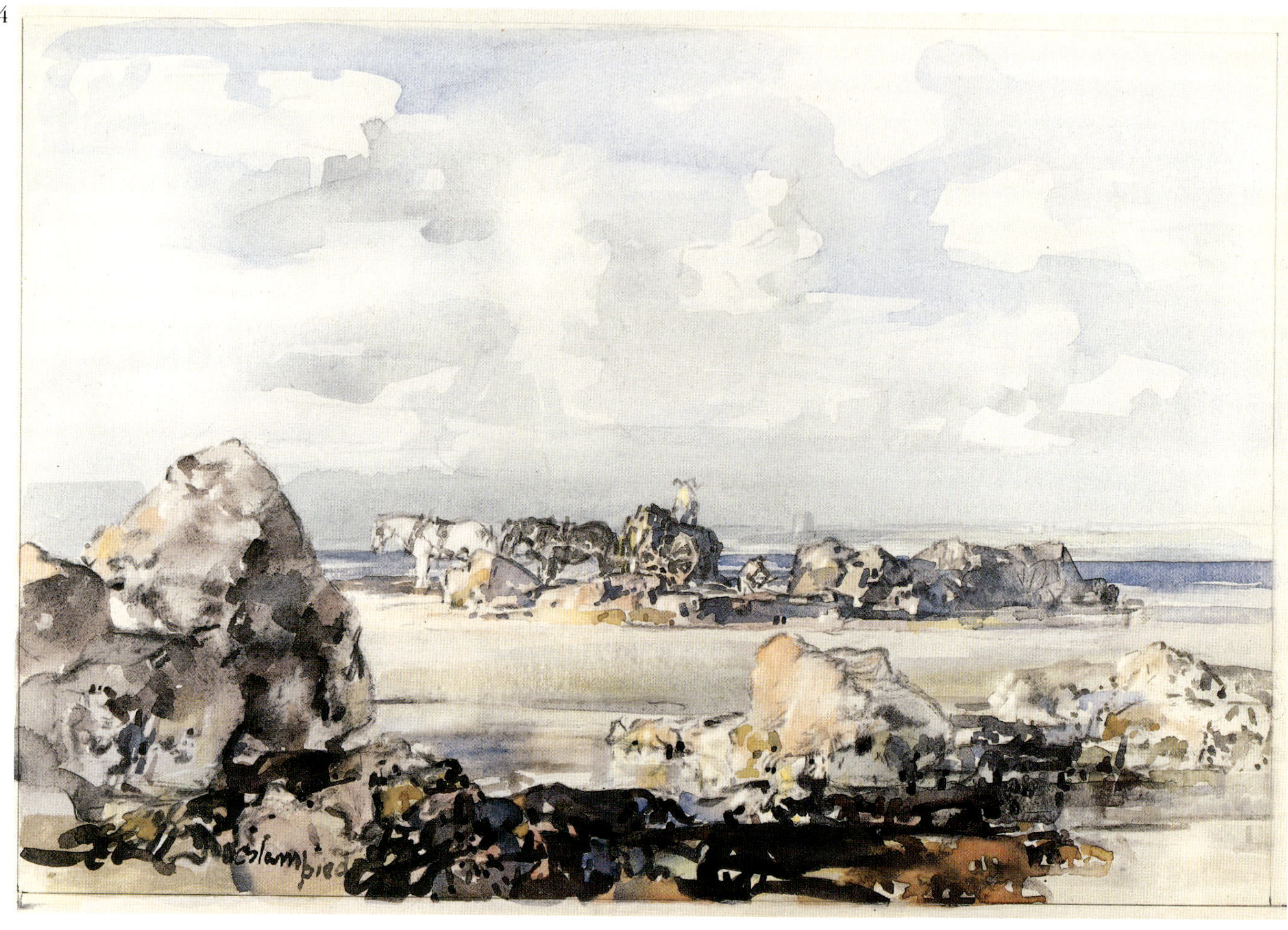

EDMUND BLAMPIED (1886–1966)

44. *Low Tide, Jersey,*
    Watercolor, 13 x 18½ in. (33 x 47 cm)
    Museum Purchase
    1956.94

Edmund Blampied represents the no less honorable tradition of a more single-minded involvement in his craft, wherein he earned a wide following for his skillful performances, both as a painter and as a graphic artist. Blampied's much admired and copious production as an etcher and lithographer is discussed below (see No. 67). A product of the rural environment of the island of Jersey, Blampied experienced a rudimentary exposure to art in classes at St. Helier's, before departing to London in 1903 for further study at the Lambeth Art School. His facility in the employment of the graphic techniques to which he eventually turned is attractively reiterated in the practiced freedom of his performance in watercolor and oil painting. Indeed, it

was as a painter that he first showed his mettle. Later, in 1912, he turned to the study of etching (see No. 67), and still later, in 1920, he took up lithography.

Blampied's watercolor paintings in particular depend upon the effects of spontaneity of execution which had by his heyday become popular as natural to the medium. *Low Tide, Jersey* typifies his production as a watercolorist. A virtual anthology of his technical approach, it is marked by the practiced conventions he predictably observed. They favored the extensive use of transparent washes, freely combined with preliminary notations in line, and an effective use of the untouched paper surfaces. His technical facility was well suited to the range of subject matter in which he specialized, as he turned with conviction to depicting the farmlands and coasts of his native Jersey and to scenes drawn from the life of the islanders, observed with sympathetic good nature. His conviction at rendering the look of the workhorses of the island as well as the action of human laborers at their work has won special praise from his admirers.

3. Printmaking

As in painting, a native British school was slow to emerge, in large part because the wants of the more sophisticated class of patrons were customarily satisfied by artists from the Continent. Indeed, as in painting, it was not until William Hogarth (1697–1764; No. 45) that the art of printmaking took on true momentum in England. First apprenticed to a silversmith, Hogarth had learned the rudiments of the engraver's craft as a youth before studying drawing at the St. Martin's Lane Academy. In 1720 he set up his own shop as an engraver. As was the case with many earlier artists, Hogarth's commercial fortunes as a painter and printmaker came to be intimately linked. The replication of the painted subjects he soon began to produce not only afforded necessary income, but also served to advertise his skills and assure his reputation. Like such great predecessors as Albrecht Dürer and Peter Paul Rubens, who profited from their involvement with the production of prints, Hogarth was understandably protective of his personal rights in those matters and scrupulous about the high standards of any work that bore his name. In this as in other respects Hogarth is justifiably respected as the founder of a thriving school of native artists. Those who emerged as dominant figures in the years to come varied greatly in personal bent, but it seems fair to point out that many of them shared Hogarth's own fascination for narrative, much of it directed toward didactic purposes, often with a moral edge.

Hogarth's concern for legal protection against what had become common practices of commercial infringement was justified by the experience of seeing his own subjects cheapened by callous imitations, prior to Parliamentary passage of the Engraver's Copyright Act of 1735. In the improved climate of artistic entrepreneurship that followed reform, other artists were encouraged to have graphic editions of their painted subjects undertaken. Portraits were especially popular, and the worthy first president of the Royal Academy, Sir Joshua Reynolds (1723–1792), especially benefited from both the popularity of portraiture, in which he excelled, and the renown promised by graphic replications of his subjects.

Developments in the craft of mezzotint engraving reached high levels of sophistication in the late eighteenth century. Specialists could render a range of tone and subtleties of transition admirably suited to the painterly effects cultivated by Reynolds and other popular painters of the era, such as Gainsborough and Romney. In due course, the facile transcriptive properties of mezzotint gained it an international popularity. Because of the high standards maintained in London that mode of reproductive engraving came to be known abroad as the "English manner." Many notable practitioners, including James Watson (1739–1790; No. 46), were employed to create convincing reproductions of paintings. (Ironically, Watson and some of his fellow masters of the English manner had immigrated to England from Ireland, because of the more active commercial climate of London.)

In response to popular demand amongst a bourgeois clientele with growing material aspirations, reproductive prints were sometimes done at a large scale, to be framed and hung as adornments on the walls of domestic interiors. Though not an absolutely novel practice—prints had apparently been so used in Europe virtually from the beginning of printmaking—the fashion for this form of pictorial display assumed new proportion in the late eighteenth century, especially in England. Many editions of prints were also published for the alternative purpose of being kept in albums or portfolios, and many plates were made as book illustrations. For that reason they have become desirable items of collection in their own right.

The invention of a totally new printmaking process of "chemical printing," which came to be known as

lithography, provided new possibilities for the thriving
market of reproductive prints. Invented by a Bavarian
playwright named Alois Senefelder, that appealingly
facile technique soon attracted attention abroad, and
by the early years of the nineteenth century, both
artists of rank and dilettantes explored its promise.
Although Senefelder's novel procedures were only developed in 1798, they were already known in England
by 1801. As elsewhere, however, especially in France,
it was not until the end of the second decade that
renditions in lithography took on sophisticated form.
From then onward, the technique was subjected to
many ingenious adaptations.

The eminent Victorian painter Sir Edwin Landseer (1802–1873; No. 16) himself applied his considerable skills as a draftsman to the occasional rendition
of one of those animal subjects that so endeared him
to his contemporaries. More often, however, Landseer
employed specialists to supply his eager public with
convincing replications of his paintings, as may be
seen in another of his subjects here on view (No. 50).
The development of photogravure processes in the
decades after mid-century so seriously undercut the
market for the more time-consuming techniques of
hand-crafted reproductive printmaking that interest
in the making of mezzotint or lithographic transcriptions rapidly declined.

Although the main thrust of these developments
in British printmaking centered on the provision of
fine replicas of unique works originally done in other,
more costly mediums, a few artists such as William
Blake (1757–1827; No. 47) and John Martin (1789–
1854; No. 51) chose to explore the possibilities of
printmaking for its independent possibilities of expression. In the process they produced works of outstanding
merit. Among the available techniques, lithography
in particular was attractive to some artists of that
inclination because of its comparative ease of han-

dling. Those who were not initiated in the demanding discipline of engraving were especially drawn to
try their hand at lithography, with its less formidable
technical requirements. This was especially the case
on the Continent, where such notable converts as
Francisco Goya (1746–1828), Théodore Géricault
(1791–1824), or Eugène Delacroix (1798–1863), may
be singled out for their precocious attraction to lithography.

In Britain that medium enjoyed no comparable
vogue as an original medium. Many artists had, of
course, been trained to some extent as printmakers in
their youth, as had been the case with Hogarth. Other
members of the British School, such as the painter
John Sell Cotman (1738–1842; No. 49), eventually
turned to graphic means—usually some form of etching—to render what were in effect drawings of a sort,
depicting the kinds of subject familiar in their painted
works. In that respect, printmaking served them as an
ancillary skill more than as an end in itself. Cotman's
fellow landscapist from Norwich, John Crome (1768–
1821) or their colleague Thomas Girtin (1775–1802),
showed a real flair for adapting soft-ground etching to
their own purposes. Although they cannot be regarded as real innovators in the purer sense of printmaking—they struck upon no original applications
of the basic techniques they inherited from current
practice—they did produce a number of admirable
images within the traditional mold, which earned
them an honorable place in the history of printmaking.

Among those who would by contrast apply themselves to the print processes as the mainstay of their
artistic enterprise, by all odds the most conspicuous
and original was William Blake. Indeed so inventive
was Blake in some of his technical applications that
his colored prints in the so-called mixed mediums
remain somewhat baffling in material character, but
stunning in their expressive impact. On the other

hand, Blake was not immune to the vast practical potential of printmaking for giving palpable form to his "visions," and at times he employed the more traditional forms of engraving. These he had learned thoroughly during his youthful apprenticeship to James Basire (1730–1802), who had set him to work drawing Gothic monuments in Westminster Abbey and other churches. Blake's love of line, inculcated in those formative experiences, is to be admired in the illustration from his *Book of Job* (No. 47). A late work, published in 1825, the volume of plates from Blake's *Book of Job* stands as one of his culminating achievements. Unfortunately, Blake's lifelong devotion to the task of giving graphic form to his visions was not requited by commercial success or prosperity, save in a small coterie friendly to his aspirations.

More traditional views of subject matter—particularly landscape representations—had broader popular appeal and a wider currency in the world of prints. Joseph Mallord William Turner (1775–1851; No. 48) had envisaged his *Liber Studiorum* (1807–19) as a rival to Claude Lorraine's *Liber Veritatis*, with its safeguard record of Lorraine's compositions. Although the project was never completed as Turner originally envisaged it, the plates of the *Liber Studiorum* comprise a landmark essay in the history of landscape composition, even as Turner had wished it to be. The plate included in the review of British printmaking is a first state, entirely by the master's own hand. In many instances, plates from the series were elaborated in mezzotint (or occasionally, in aquatint) by assistants working under Turner's supervision.

As the nineteenth century progressed, however, many artists took an increasing interest in etching as an expressive medium in its own right. That trend was initiated mainly in France amongst the Romantic masters, especially Delacroix, and shortly thereafter within the Barbizon School which flourished after the mid-century. It soon had repercussions amongst their British counterparts, some of whom had, in fact, benefited from study of printmaking in France. Without regard for reproductive applications the stature of etching as an artistic medium was thus asserted, in recollection of the traditions maintained by Rembrandt and other masters of etching, to whom fresh attention was directed. In Britain that movement, which began in the 1850s, was above all indebted to the influence of James A. MacNeil Whistler (1834–1903; No. 56), but many other distinguished graphic artists, including Whistler's brother-in-law, Sir Seymour Haden (1818–1910; No. 55) contributed to what came to be known as the "etching revival."

The towering figure in that phase of the etching revival in Britain was the cosmopolitan, American-born Whistler, whose career as an artist was fundamentally rooted in the French experience of his formative years in Paris (1855–59). There he had enjoyed close associations with the avant-garde of the time. The example of Gustave Courbet (1819–1877) inspired his early efforts, and the stimulus of his associations with such younger figures as Edgar Degas (1834–1917) and Henri Fantin-Latour (1836–1904) contributed much to his realization of his own, highly original ends. Supremely individualistic in his art as well as his behavior and theoretical utterances, Whistler found in the graphic mediums, particularly in etching, drypoint, and engraving, vehicles admirably suited to his poetic vision, in which an elegant understatement prevails. His penchant for subtleties of line and tone or for the suggestive moment of virtually unencumbered space was alert to the importance of the act of printing itself. Indeed his attentiveness to the surface tones in some of his later plates has invited description of them as virtually monotypes in their uniqueness of execution. The singular range of Whistler's technical variety as well as his seemingly effortless skill of manipulation and deftness of design earned him a lasting reputation as one of the preeminent printmakers of the modern era.

A number of contemporaries shared his fascination with the expressive capacities of the printer's art, emancipated from the service to reproduction. Their wish to associate the creative side of their work with the arts of drawing and painting was intended to declare their independence from the primary reproductive traditions of printmaking, for not all of those who claimed the special status of "painter-etchers" were also practicing painters. Such was the case, in fact, with one of the most conspicuous of that company: Whistler's own brother-in-law, the first president of the Society of Painter-Etchers, Sir Francis Seymour Haden (1818–1910). A physician by profession, Haden was nonetheless a man of parts and far from a mere amateur as an artist. He was a distinguished connoisseur and collector, as well as one of the finest landscape etchers of his century. And in part due to the immigration to England of the notable French artist-teacher Alphonse Legros (1837–1911), the involvement of British artists in the practice of printmaking gained momentum during the late Victorian era. It was at the invitation of Whistler, whom he first met in Paris in 1859 that Legros decided to immigrate to London, where he came fully into his own. Well known for his connoisseurship as well as his practical command of the print processes, Legros served as an authoritative spokesman for the cause of printmaking. One of his pupils was William Strang (1859–1921; No. 59), who rose to distinction as one of the finest printmakers of his generation, in whose works the inclinations to brooding, symbolic overtones in subject matter are to some extent reflective of his teacher's own literary predispositions. Whistler's own artistic mantle fell to some degree upon the sturdy shoulders of another naturalized Briton, Sir Walter Sickert (1860–1942; No. 60), who became known for his theatrical subjects and interiors, in which his impressionistic sense of light and inventiveness of composition gained him a sustained reputation, both as a graphic artist and as a painter.

Frank Brangwyn (1867–1956; No. 62) no less staunchly held his own in the development of large-scale plates notable for their maker's exploration of bold, novel effects in design and technique. By contrast, Gerald Brockhurst (1890–1979; No. 68) worked in small format and at a virtually miniature scale of execution in the portraits which gained him an international reputation.

Virtuosity of technique thus assumed overt importance as a vehicle of personal expression, and the legacy of modern printmaking was vastly enriched. For Britain, one of the most notable gains in that regard was the emergence of a company of Scottish artists who devoted themselves to exploring the artistic promise of the graphic mediums. Their representation in the present selection of prints enhances its value as a review. David Young Cameron (1865–1945; No. 61) portrayed the special beauty of the highland North, with glimpses of the lives of its people in their daily activities; Muirhead Bone (1876–1930; No. 64) turned mainly to exquisitely detailed renditions of architecture; James McBey (1883–1959; No. 66) spiritedly captured the special visual character of the many parts of the world to which he traveled in his search for fresh experiences. Through the efforts of these artists and their many dedicated colleagues from other parts of the realm, the legacy of printmaking in Britain was extended into our own century.

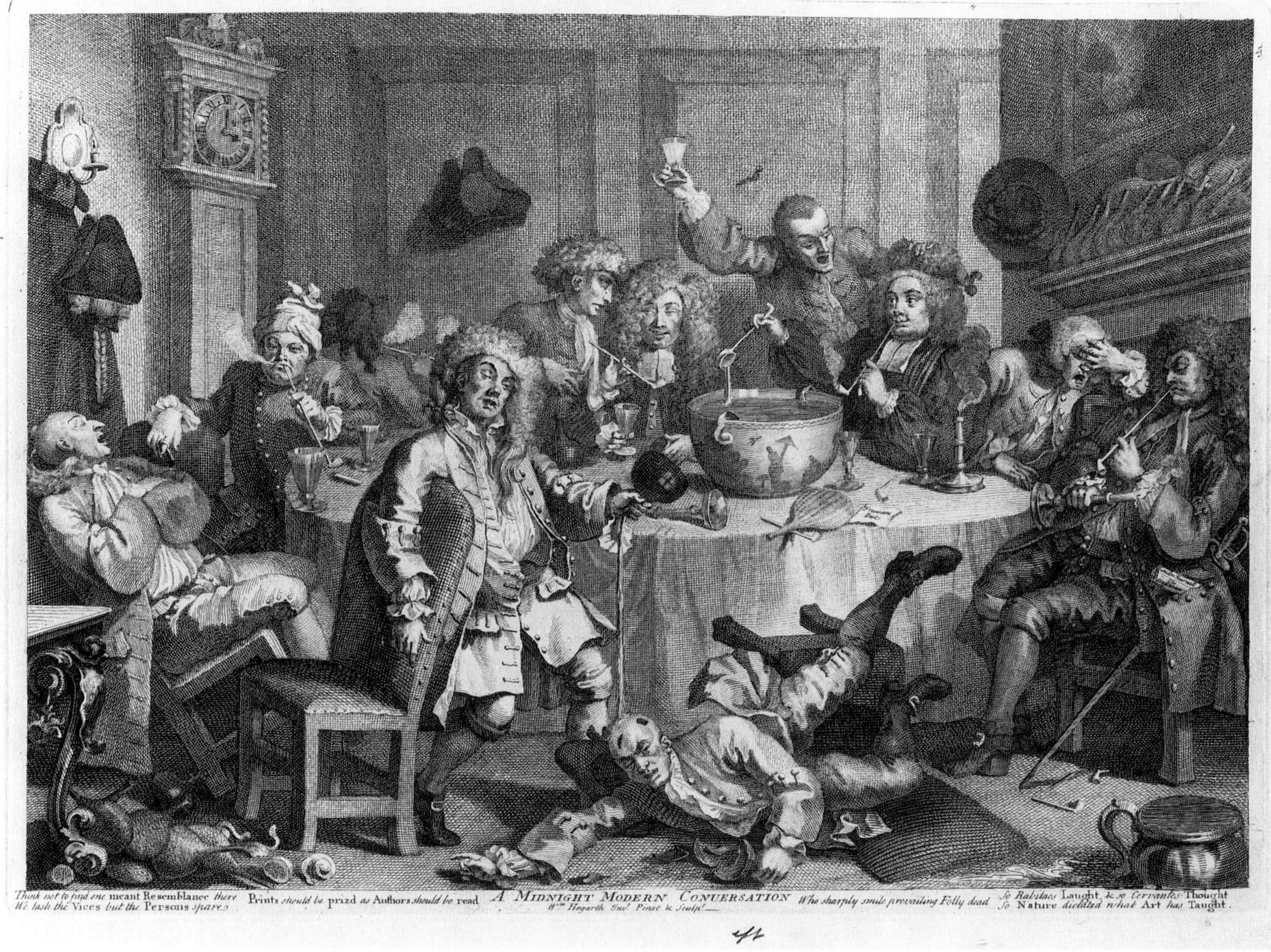

WILLIAM HOGARTH (1697–1764)

45. *A Midnight Modern Conversation*, 1732–33
   Engraving, 2nd State of 3, 16 x 20¼ in. (40.6 x 51.4 cm)
   Museum Purchase, the William K. Allison, '20
   Memorial Fund
   1982.33

Hogarth had learned the fundamentals of engraving while still a youth apprenticed to an engraver of arms on silver, Ellis Gamble (active 1712–18). In 1720, Hogarth established his own shop for making engravings on copper, but it appears that he already entertained higher, artistic ambitions. He took drawing lessons at an academy in St. Martin's Lane run by John Vanderbank (1689–1727) and later arranged for private tutoring with Sir James Thornhill (1676–1734) whose decorative paintings in the dome of St. Paul's Cathedral Hogarth admired. He also admired Thornhill's daughter, with whom he eloped in 1729. A reconciliation with Thornhill was eventually managed, however,

and when Thornhill died, Hogarth inherited his father-in-law's school, which he made into an important institution of its kind.

Ambitions for success as a painter in oils led Hogarth first to specialize in painting portraits and conversation pieces. But he soon became bored with those forms of art, preferring instead to compose the series of canvases that were, in effect, the "morality plays," for which he is justifiably best known. Completed first as oil paintings, these theatrically conceived commentaries on the misadventures of naive victims of cynical exploitation or on human follies in general, were then reproduced as engravings which made Hogarth famous. Aside from three elaborate sets of those scenes—*Harlot's Progress*, *Rake's Progress*, and *Marriage à la Mode*—Hogarth published other, paired or single plates after his paintings of the kind, such as *Beer Street*, *Gin Lane*, and *Calais Gate*. *A Midnight Modern Conversation* is one of Hogarth's earliest ventures into that vein.

As the title of the print clearly indicates, Hogarth's bawdy satire on self-indulgence weds the Netherlandish traditions of group portraiture with what came to be known as "low-life" genre. The antics of the lower social classes are depicted, often with coarse humor, as in the paintings of Adriaen van Ostade (1610–1685) or Adriaen Brouwer (1605–1638). Hogarth's gifts for narrative invention along those lines won him a ready following amongst those attuned to the satirical edge of such contemporary writers as Henry Fielding and Jonathan Swift. The "conversation piece" to which allusion is made in the title was a related fusion of group portraiture with the more polite form of "high-life" genre, wherein the ways of polite society are amiably presented. Unfortunately for Hogarth's commercial interests this subject in particular was subjected to widespread pilferage by callous copyists. Among other indignities, it was appropriated as a novelty for ornamenting commercial products such as snuffboxes. Accordingly, Hogarth took measures to protect his proprietary interests in his own inventions and was instrumental in Parliament's passage in 1735 of the Engraver's Copyright Act, a statute that has henceforth been known as "Hogarth's Act."

As an early example of its type within Hogarth's production, *A Midnight Modern Conversation* lacks some of the finesse of drawing and execution that would later pertain. Nor does it exhibit the rococo flair for elegant line that the master would soon cultivate, as in his series, *Marriage à la Mode*. On the other hand, it is a telling demonstration of Hogarth's powers of narrative invention; the picture was his stage upon which his cast of characters present a kind of dumb show. While his inscription disclaims reference to particular persons, resemblances to individuals of his acquaintance have been inferred. And the pungency of his comic observation would assume even bolder tone in his broadsides aimed at societal reform, such as *Beer Street* and *Gin Lane* or *Industry and Idleness* (1747), where the imagery is unsparing.

The penchant for broad humor exhibited by Hogarth was echoed in the work of Thomas Rowlandson (1756–1827), James Gillray (1757–1815), and others, who took advantage of the freedom of expression that pertained in their land to create a preeminent school of satirical representation. In this as in many other respects, Hogarth took the lead in establishing a strong school of native-born British artists. It is above all the reputation of his prints that first created, then sustained that enviable reputation.

Jᴀᴍᴇs Wᴀᴛsᴏɴ (1739–1790)

46. *Sir Jeffery Amherst*, 1766
    Engraving, after Sir Joshua Reynolds, 13 x 18 in.
    (33 x 45.7 cm)
    Gift of Dr. William J. Turner and Miss Isabel J. Turner
    PR 1939.90

The great age of mezzotint engraving in England during the second half of the eighteenth century was dominated by several skilled craftsmen who immigrated to London from Dublin during the latter decades of the eighteenth century. Aside from Watson, their number included James McArdell (b. ca. 1729), Richard Houston (ca. 1721–1775), Edward Fisher (1730–ca. 1785), and John Dixon (ca. 1730–after 1800). A growing market for reproductive prints after the old masters as well as the reigning English portraitists of the era, particularly Sir Joshua Reynolds, encouraged a high level of production in that vein. One of the ablest members of that Irish group was the prolific James Watson, who showed his wares at Spring Gardens in 1775. Watson soon became closely associated with the fashion for portrait subjects after Reynolds, Gainsborough, and other fashionable portraitists of the era. One of Watson's notable achievements as a printmaker is his engraving of Sir Joshua Reynolds' famous portrait of Dr. Samuel Johnson (1772) in which Watson's breadth of handling has won the special admiration of connoisseurs.

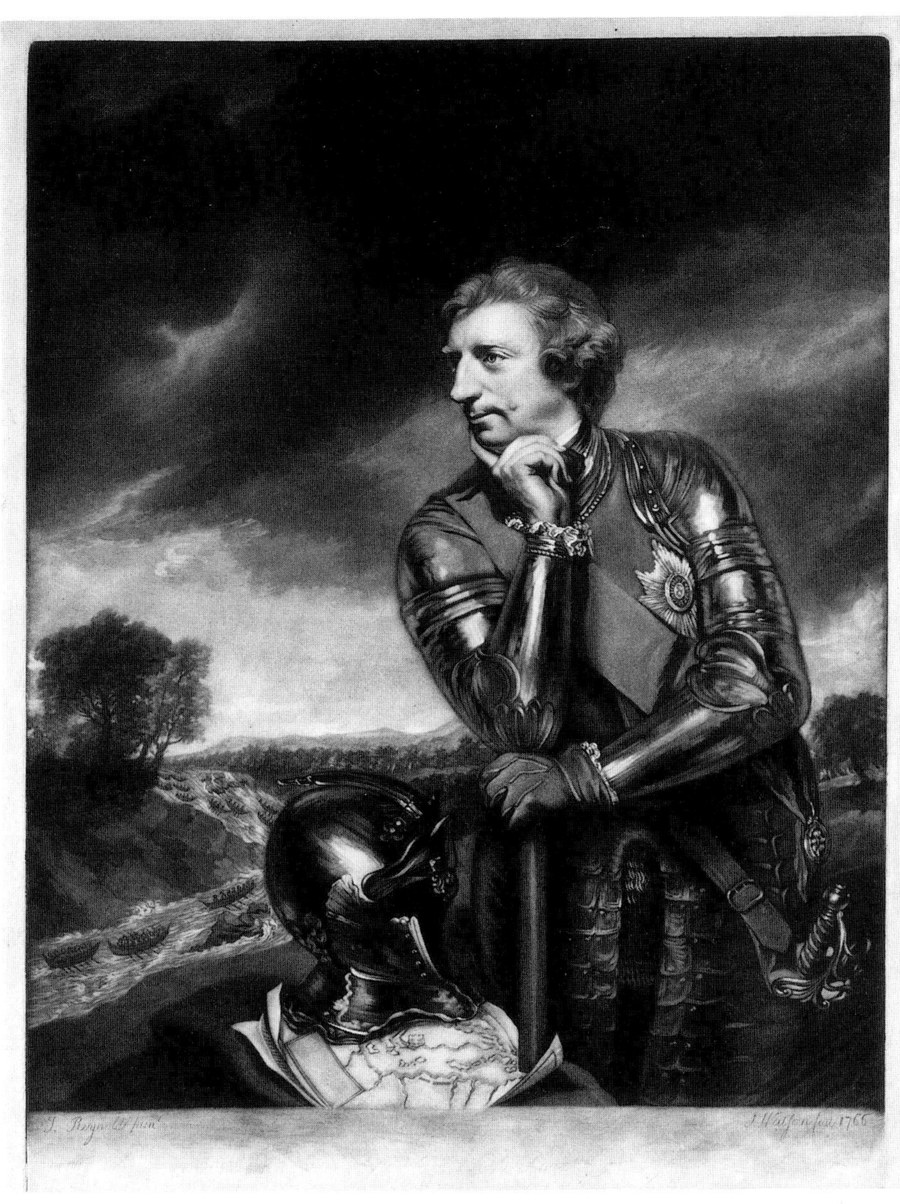

Watson's version of *Portrait of Sir Jeffery Amherst* after
Reynolds' painting (No. 6) exemplifies the qualities of
largeness and simplicity of handling which are associated
with his reputation as an outstanding members of those
Irish practitioners of mezzotint reproduction. Although
his plates have been criticized as lacking the force of those
produced by his compatriot Fisher, Watson's mastery at
rendering tonal gradations with finesse has been rightfully
praised. In this case it is of especial interest in this regard
to observe Watson's capacity to translate the qualities of
Reynolds' painted surfaces into the more restricted terms
of the printed sheet, with an artistic eloquence all its
own. Needless to say, Reynolds keenly appreciated the
importance to his reputation by the dissemination of these
translations of his subjects, so he was careful to employ
the finest workmen, such as Watson, to ensure optimum
results. In this concern for the protection of his professional reputation, Reynolds adhered to the traditions of
excellence maintained by such eminent predecessors as
Rubens and Hogarth, who were similarly mindful that
transcriptions of their works be as faithful as possible to
the original model.

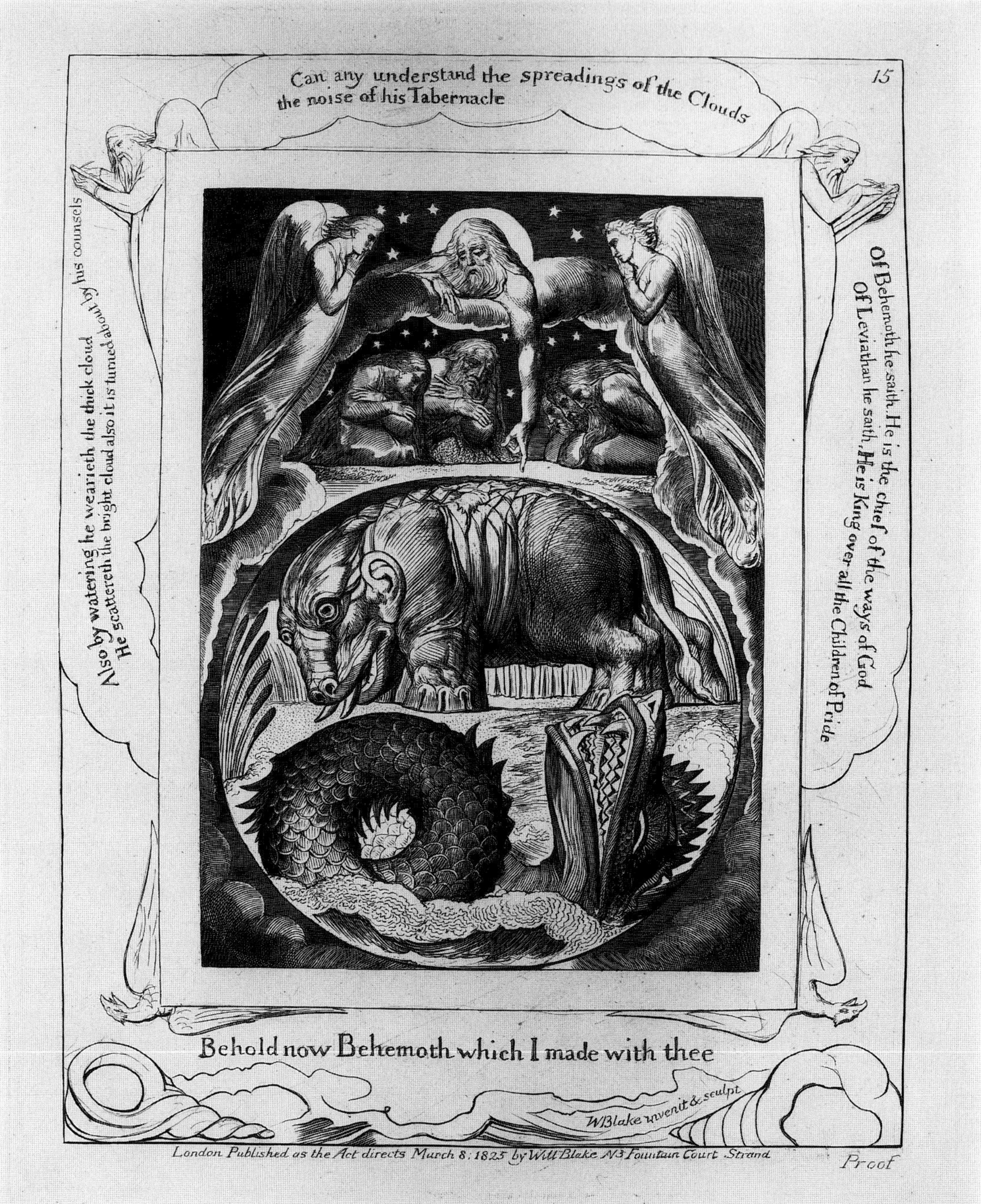

WILLIAM BLAKE (1757–1827)

47. *Illustration of the Book of Job: Behold Now Behemoth
    Which I Have Made With Thee*, 1825
    Engraving, 8¼ x 6⅝ in. (21 x 16.8 cm)
    Museum Purchase
    1966.6

Blake's early artistic inclinations were encouraged by his
father, who sent him to drawing classes with Henry Pars
(1742–1782) and later, in 1867, apprenticed him to the

engraver, James Basire (1730–1802). During the seven-
year term of Blake's work for Basire, his tasks included
drawing from medieval sculptures in Westminster Abbey
and other London churches. Those youthful experiences
with Gothic art left lasting marks upon Blake's art. Brief
study at the Royal Academy in 1878 was less congenial, it
seems, and while he occasionally exhibited at the academy
for some years (1780–1808), he never became formally
associated with that organization, even though he remained on good terms with Henry Fuseli (1741–1825) and
James Barry (1741–1806), who taught there.

By 1784, he set up a printing shop, and later in that decade, began to publish his characteristically original writings, all illustrated and printed by himself. Those "illuminated" books were designed in the spirit of decorated medieval manuscripts, in which the texts and the ornamental embellishments are conceived as intimately related to each other as parts of a greater whole. They include, among other masterpieces, *Songs of Innocence* (1789) and *America: a Prophecy* (1793). As intellectual contradictions, they represent a richly individualistic amalgam of current thinking in philosophy, religion, and radical politics. Artistically, they are no less original, though equally indebted to multiple sources of visual inspiration, ranging from the Gothic, through Michelangelo, to the contemporaneous efforts of Fuseli, Barry, and John Flaxman (1755–1826). Those tomes, impressive in format, were printed in small editions in a complicated technique, special to Blake. It apparently involved a kind of relief etching with final colorations hand-applied in watercolor, to make each a unique product. In the latter 1790s, Blake turned increasingly to illustrating the texts of other writers, most conspicuously Dante and Milton. In spite of commercial hardships and lack of appreciation or support except from a few, Blake doggedly pursued his own course of realizing his "visions," as he regarded them, whether undertaken in printed form, in drawing or watercolor, or in the tempera painting that he explored in the 1810s.

Blake's set of twenty-two plates illustrating the *Book of Job* is sometimes regarded as the culminating evidence of his accomplishment in that vein. The set was commissioned by Blake's fervent admirer, John Linnell, himself a painter of quality, whom Blake had met around 1818. Although the plates were executed at the very end of the artist's life, his interest in the story of Job had surfaced earlier, as prior representations of the subject done in other mediums attest. As with Blake's own, mythic figure of Albion in *Jerusalem*, Job represented for him the hero granted redemption after falling from grace. In this regard as in other respects, such as the vivid materialization of the demonic *Behemoth* or the threatening energies of *Job's Evil Dream*, Blake presents a personal commentary upon the synoptic flow of the Biblical account of Job's destiny. The relationships with the page design of medieval manuscript illuminations observed in the earlier books appear again, but those conventions are realized in the more traditional technique of line engraving on copper plates, not in his idiosyncratic "mixed medium" of former years. Blake's consummate skill in the employment of that demanding process is strikingly embodied in *Behold Now the Behemoth Which I Made With Thee*.

JOSEPH MALLORD WILLIAM TURNER (1775–1851)

48. *Near Blair Athol, Scotland*
   Etching, from *Liber Studiorum*, 1st state,
   7 x 10¼ in. (17.8 x 26 cm)
   Gift of Edward C. Crossett, '05
   1951.2080

Joseph Mallord William Turner played a singular role in the establishment of landscape painting as a major aspect of the art of his time. Turner's genius was recognized early. His watercolors had been exhibited regularly at the Royal Academy since 1775, when the artist was a mere lad of fifteen. In 1799 he was elected an associate member of the academy, and in 1802 he was honored by a full membership. As had been the case with earlier artists, Turner soon recognized the importance of distributing reproductive prints of his paintings as a means of furthering his reputation. He recruited the finest available craftsmen for this purpose and supervised their efforts closely, to assure fidelity to his intentions. Sometimes Turner took a personal hand in the process by completing the initial line etching of the composition, with the understanding that tonal elaborations could be added later by specialists in mezzotint or, occasionally, aquatint. Needless to say, the earlier states done entirely by the master are now especially prized, although many of the toned impressions are also of admirable quality as master prints.

Turner's keen sense of personal rivalry with his seventeenth-century French predecessor, Claude Lorrain (1600–1682) led to his decision, around 1807, to compile a book of landscape representations, or *Liber Studiorum*, in emulation of Claude's *Liber Veritatis*. Turner was by that point already well advanced in his career, so his hubris in inviting comparisons with the "Divine Claude" is easier to understand. Indeed, Turner's lifelong obsession with Claude's art and its reputation guided him to provide in his last will and testament that the mass of his works accumulated in his studio be left to the nation on the strict condition that one of his paintings hang side-by-side with one by Claude in the National Gallery of Art, London. That promise has been respected. The group of drawings comprising Claude's famous *Liber Veritatis* were made, quite literally, to *verify* that the compositions contained in his record book were authentic. Reproduction of that important corpus, then

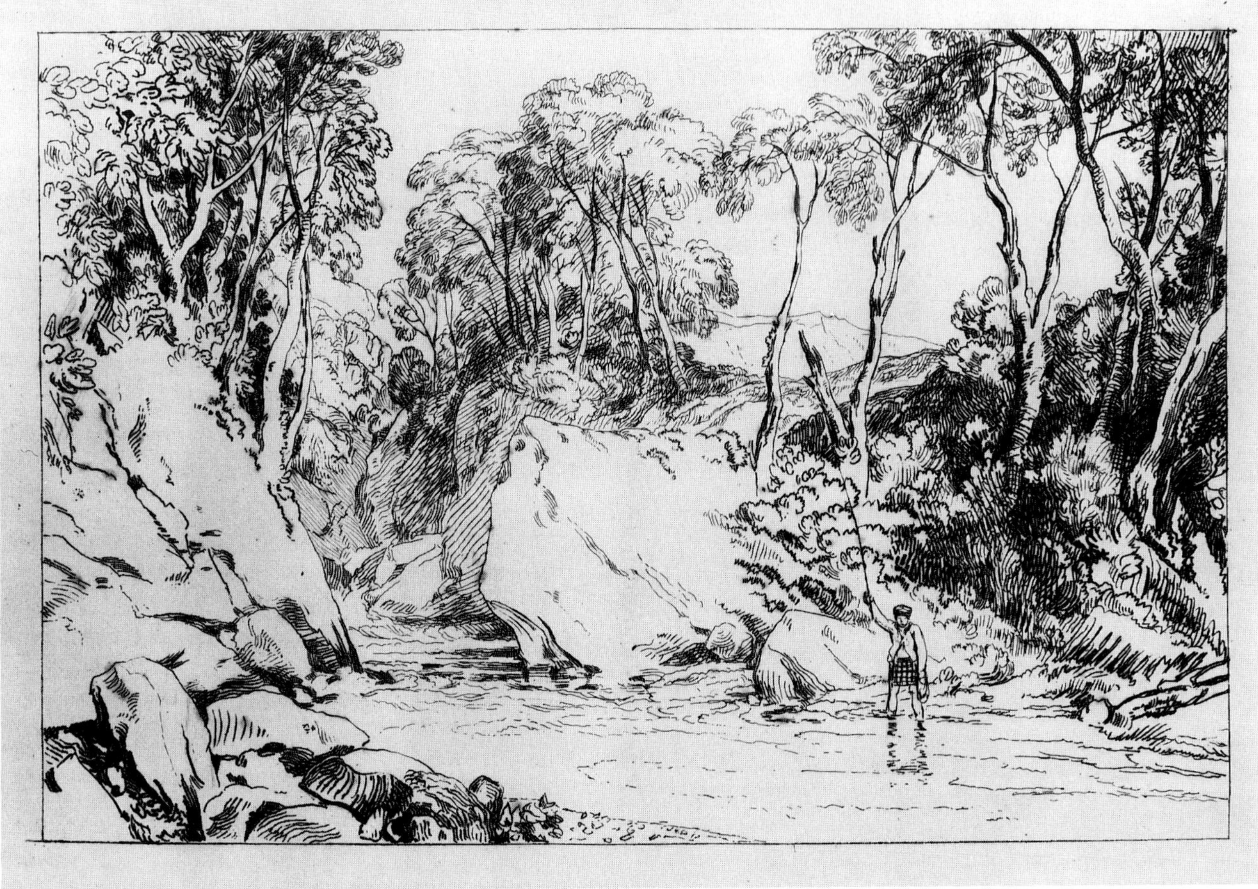

conserved in the collection of the Duke of Devonshire, had been undertaken with admirable results by the well-known English engraver, Richard Earlom (1743–1822). Employing a combination of mezzotint and etching processes, Earlom had completed a set of two hundred plates which were published in 1777 by the London entrepreneur, John Boydell. They are a notable achievement in the history of reproductive engraving in England.

Turner's *Liber Studiorum* was conceived not as a record of completed works, but rather as a kind of essay in the possibilities of landscape composition. It included suggestions for works not yet undertaken. Extant works were revised to avoid literal repetition. Of some one hundred subjects originally contemplated, only seventy-one plates were eventually published as the *Liber Studiorum*. Most of them were begun by Turner but completed by others. Only about ten of the published series were completed by Turner himself. Some of the plates that were undertaken as part of the project did not feature in the set as it was issued, and some of the drawings made at the time were not translated into prints until afterward. It should be also noted that some of Turner's plates and drawings were much later in the century etched by his ardent admirers Sir Seymour Haden (1818–1910) and Sir Frank Short (1857–1945).

Near Blair Athol, Scotland is a first-state impression from the *Liber Studiorum*, in which the freshness and strength of Turner's special vision of landscape are to be appreciated. The composition, with its sweeping, baroque reach into vast distances, has the unity and power associated with Turner at his best. It also demonstrates the fact that for all of Turner's preoccupation with the art of Claude, he was responsive to other, somewhat contrary sources of traditional inspiration. Not least of all he owed much to the informally disposed or "rustic" modes of composition that had evolved in seventeenth-century Netherlandish landscapes. Less closed in form than the "classic" modes cultivated by Claude, the looser, more irregular character of forms to be seen in that approach to landscape had a picturesque appeal, not only to Turner but also to his compatriot and great rival in historical importance, John Constable (1776–1837).

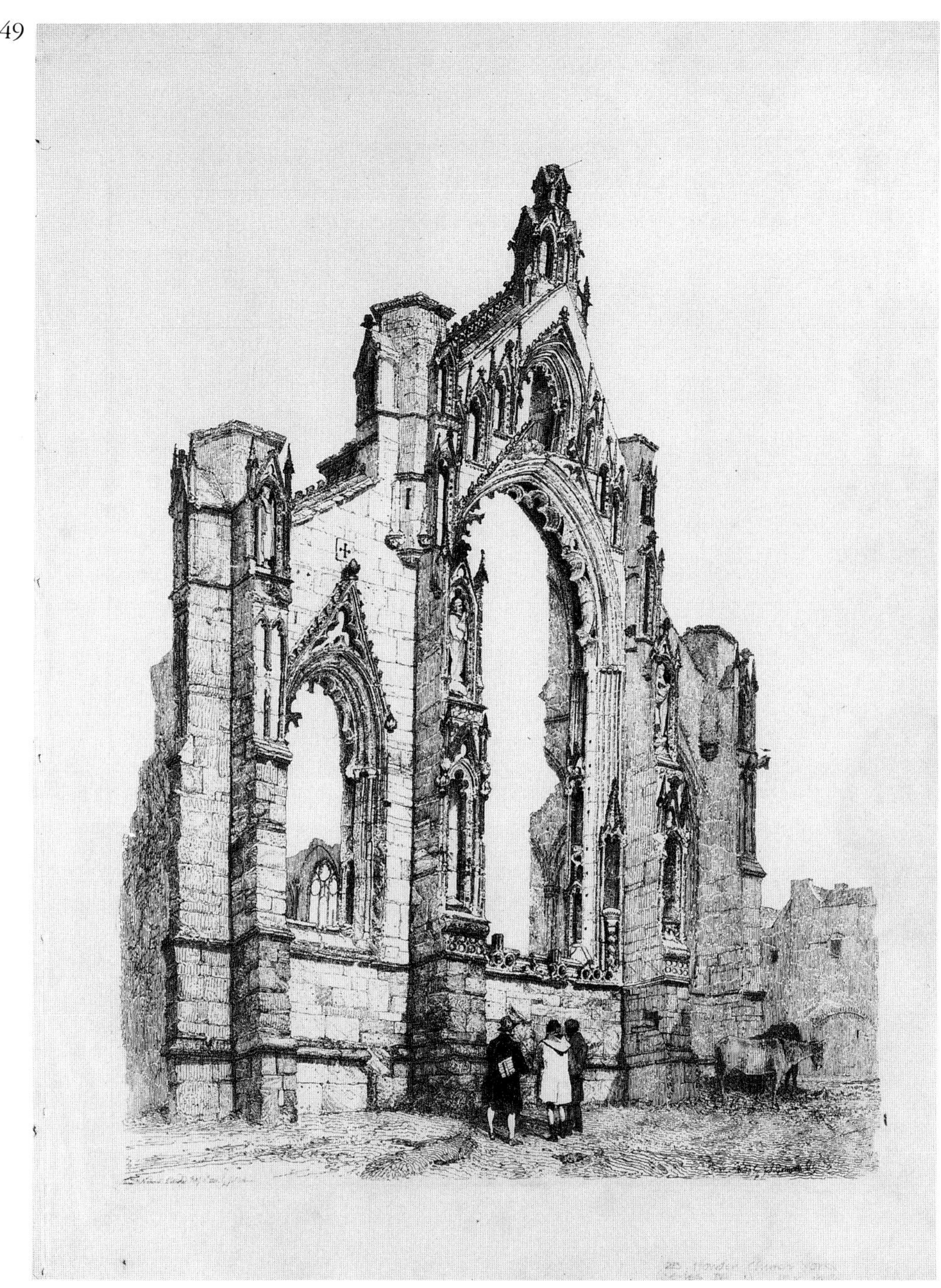

JOHN SELL COTMAN (1782–1842)

49. *Howden Church, York*
  Softground etching, 15 x 20⅞ in. (38.1 x 27.6 cm)
  Museum Purchase
  1979.60

Although Cotman is best known as a painter, particularly a specialist in watercolor, his performance as an etcher is also distinguished and bears out his reputation as one of the great British landscapists of the nineteenth century.

Briefly active in London, where he went in 1798, he benefited from employment by the great collector, Dr. Thomas Monroe, in 1799. Through Monroe he became acquainted with Thomas Girtin (1775–1802), another of the many young artists aided by the doctor. His interest in sketching landscape took him to Wales in 1800 and subsequently, to Yorkshire in 1803, 1804, and 1805. Discouraged with his professional prospects in London, however, he returned to his native city of Norwich, East Anglia, in 1806. There he worked closely with John Crome (1768–1821), known as

"Old Crome," in forwarding the cause of local artists. They formed an artistic association, known as The Norwich Society, later to become the Norwich School, which was dominated by Crome. Somewhat shaded by that esteemed colleague, in 1812 Cotman moved to Yarmouth, but he returned to Norwich after Crome's death in 1823. There he took up teaching, and after 1834, taught at King's College, London.

Auxiliary though it may have been, Cotman's serious attention to printmaking was sustained over a long period of years. Around 1809/10 Cotman was attracted to etching as a vehicle for expressing his interest in the tonalities of light, as well as a means of making known his ideas, whether to collectors or to his fellow members of the society. He turned to softground etching around 1820, but only a few trial proofs of these plates were pulled before a combined edition of Cotman's plates was issued by Bohn in 1838. Between 1812 and 1822, Cotman traveled extensively in Normandy, where he compiled a noteworthy album of plates, the *Architectural Antiquities of Normandy*, which were published in 1822, accompanied by a text written by J. M. W. Turner. Cotman's name is above all associated, however, with the representation of his native countryside, especially with scenes showing architectural monuments of Norfolk, Suffolk, and York. *Howden Church, York* is representative of his renditions of the kind, in which an eye for characteristic detail is sensitively registered within a prevailing atmosphere of soft light.

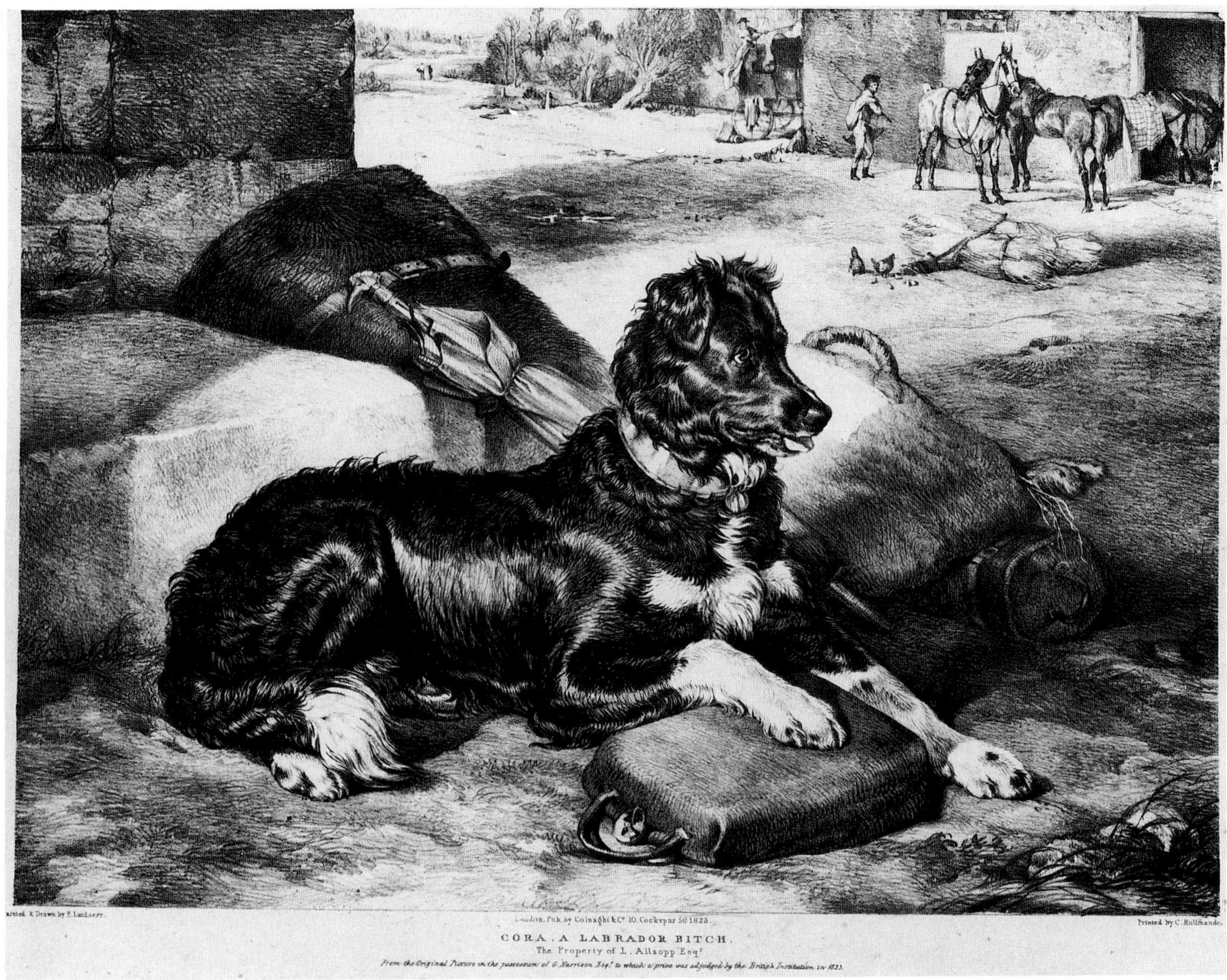

CHARLES JOSEPH HULLMANDEL (1789–1850)

50. *Cora, A Labrador Bitch*, 1823
Lithograph, after Sir Edwin Henry Landseer,
14 x 17¼ in. (35.6 x 43.8 cm)
Museum Purchase
PR xx 80

A pioneer in the practice of lithographic printing in Britain, Charles Hullmandel was born in London of German parents. After a period of training with an otherwise obscure printer named Farraday, in 1819 Hullmandel set up his own press in London. He promptly proceeded to develop the lithographic techniques that would increasingly serve the commercial appetite for faithful, graphic replications of works created by artists working in other pictorial mediums. Among the many who benefited from his skills was Edwin Landseer.

Executed in 1823, at what was yet a fairly early stage of technical development in the lithographic processes, Landseer's canine image, *Cora, A Labrador Bitch*, retains the inherently draftsmanly properties which mark the early stages of the employment of the lithographic crayon. At this juncture, Hullmandel had not yet developed the technical means to simulate the painterly effects he would eventually command in his works of a decade later. He came to extend the resources of the lithographic process to include the use of washes closer to the material character of the paintings he was called upon to reproduce. Still, the admirable drawing Landseer here rendered under Hullmandel's direct supervision for printing in his shop is a superb embodiment of early lithographic production. At the same time it serves as a sample of Landseer's own, natural virtuosity as a draftsman which had marked him from the beginning of his career as one of the most celebrated artists of the Victorian era.

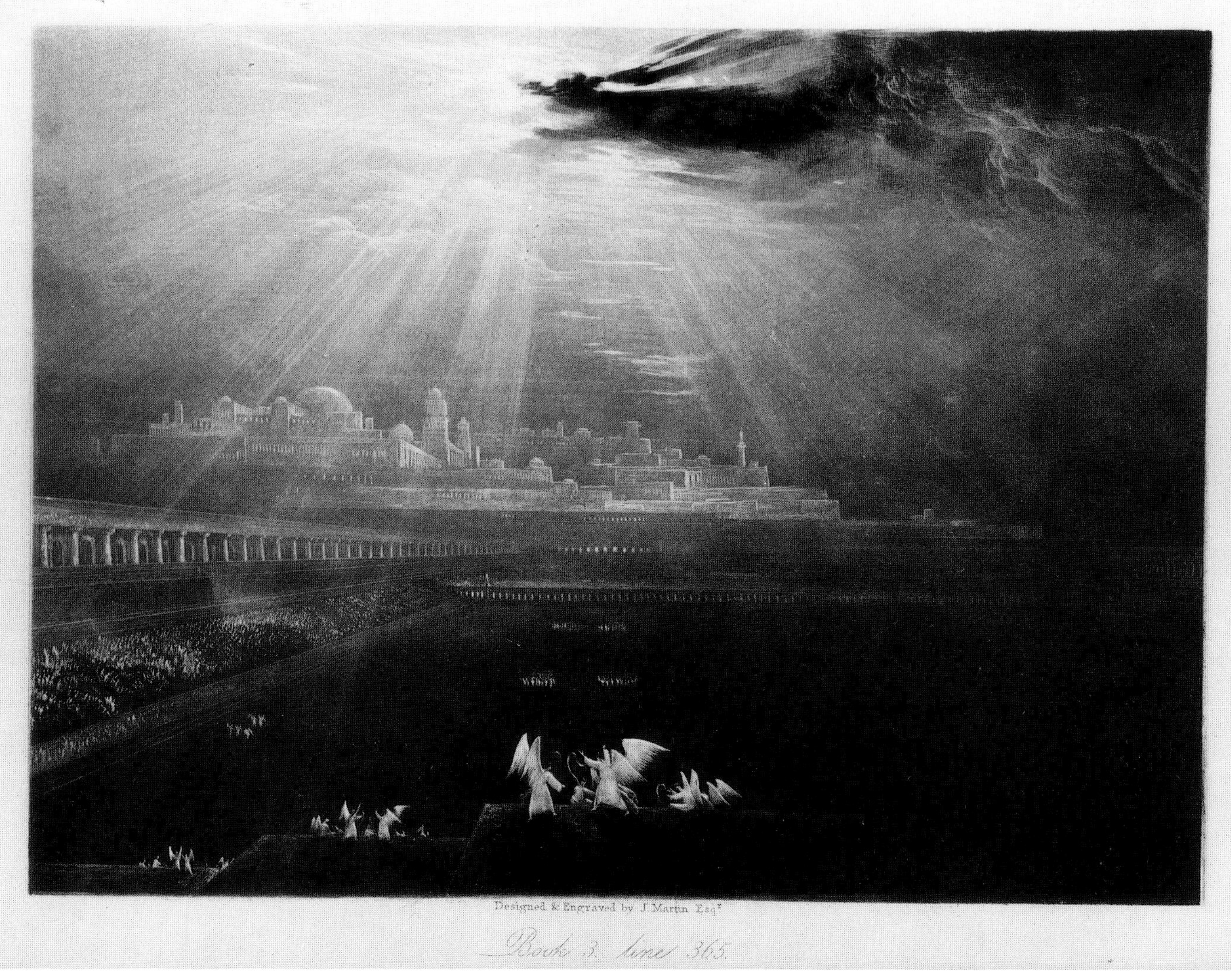

JOHN MARTIN (1789–1854)

51. *Heaven, Rivers of Bliss*
Engraving, from *Paradise Lost*, 6¼ x 8¼ in.
(35.6 x 43.8 cm)
Museum Purchase
1978.26

Following a youthful apprenticeship to a Newcastle coach painter, John Martin benefited from the tutelage of an Italian painter, Bonifacio Musso, who had settled in Newcastle. Of particular value to Martin was the opportunity to study a large collection of prints by Salvator Rosa, Claude Lorraine, and other earlier masters which his mentor had brought with him. In 1806 he gravitated to London, where he found employment painting enamel decorations for a glass manufacturer. That commercial experience had lasting influence on his art, in which a somewhat stylized precision of execution is to be noted. First exhibiting as an independent painter at the Royal Academy in 1811, his Romantic involvement with sublimely visionary themes inspired favorable comparisons of his art with that of Turner.

As a printmaker, Martin stands as an entirely original figure in the history of British art, for he was one to realize the creative promise of the traditionally reproductive technique of mezzotint engraving. His two series of illustrations of Milton's *Paradise Lost* are justly regarded as masterpieces in the employment of mezzotint as an independent means of expression and the culminating embodiment of their maker's arresting talent as a printmaker. Commissioned in 1823 by a little-known publisher, Septimus Prowett, Martin's illustrations for *Paradise Lost* took the form of two editions. They differed slightly in format and certain component details, but each was marked by the same richness of contrast, ranging from velvety black to almost incandescent creamy whites. *Heaven, Rivers of Bliss* is one of the twenty-four subjects Prowett issued in 1827, now known as the "small" plates. The larger prints had first appeared "in parts" in 1825 and were issued as a full series of twenty-four illustrations in 1826/7. In either format, these small masterpieces by Mad Martin (as he was sometimes called) remarkably encapsulate his capacity for exalted vision, regardless of the physical size at which his fantasies were projected. In their minuteness of detail, one is reminded of Martin's youthful employment as an enamelist for the decoration of china and glass. At the same time, his compositions reveal a grandeur of conception and a taste for the sublime that link Martin with the artists of visionary inclination in the United States, most notably, Thomas Cole, whom Martin directly influenced.

DAVID LUCAS (1802–1881) AND JOHN CONSTABLE (1776–1837)

52. *The Lock—Large Plate*, 1834
   Mezzotint in black ink, 22¾ x 19½ in. (57.8 x 49.5 cm)
   Museum Purchase
   1987.7

David Lucas was "discovered" by the well-known mezzotint engraver, Samuel William Reynolds (1773–1835), who was also the master of Samuel Cousins (1804–1887). While Lucas would unfortunately enjoy nothing like the professional success of Cousins—indeed, he came to a sadly destitute end—in his earlier years he produced some of the greatest masterpieces in the history of mezzotint engraving. Reynolds had done well in recognizing the youth's talent, and in the seven years of his apprenticeship to Reynolds, Lucas had learned his craft impeccably. He was thus admirably suited to serve in turn the purposes of John Constable, whose intention was to publish at his own expense an edition of prints after his landscape paintings that would bring his accomplishments to the attention of a wider public—much as Turner had set out to do with his *Liber Studiorum*.

The collaboration between Constable and Lucas resulted in a set of twenty-two subjects published in 1833 as *Various Subjects of Landscape—Characteristic of English Landscape Scenery*. Working directly from sketches by Constable, Lucas developed first proofs which were retouched by Constable and reworked to the point where they faithfully represented Constable's own sense of each scene. They comprise a major document in the history of printing in mezzotint, not only for the uniquely close collaboration in the production of that initial series, but even more so for the outstanding artistic quality of the resultant plates. The capacities of mezzotint to render the atmospheric interaction of light and shade, creating an impression of natural verity is also to be admired in six plates comprising an appendix to the original set, prepared under the same collaborative circumstances. Work on the appendix was begun in 1833, but the set was not published until 1838.

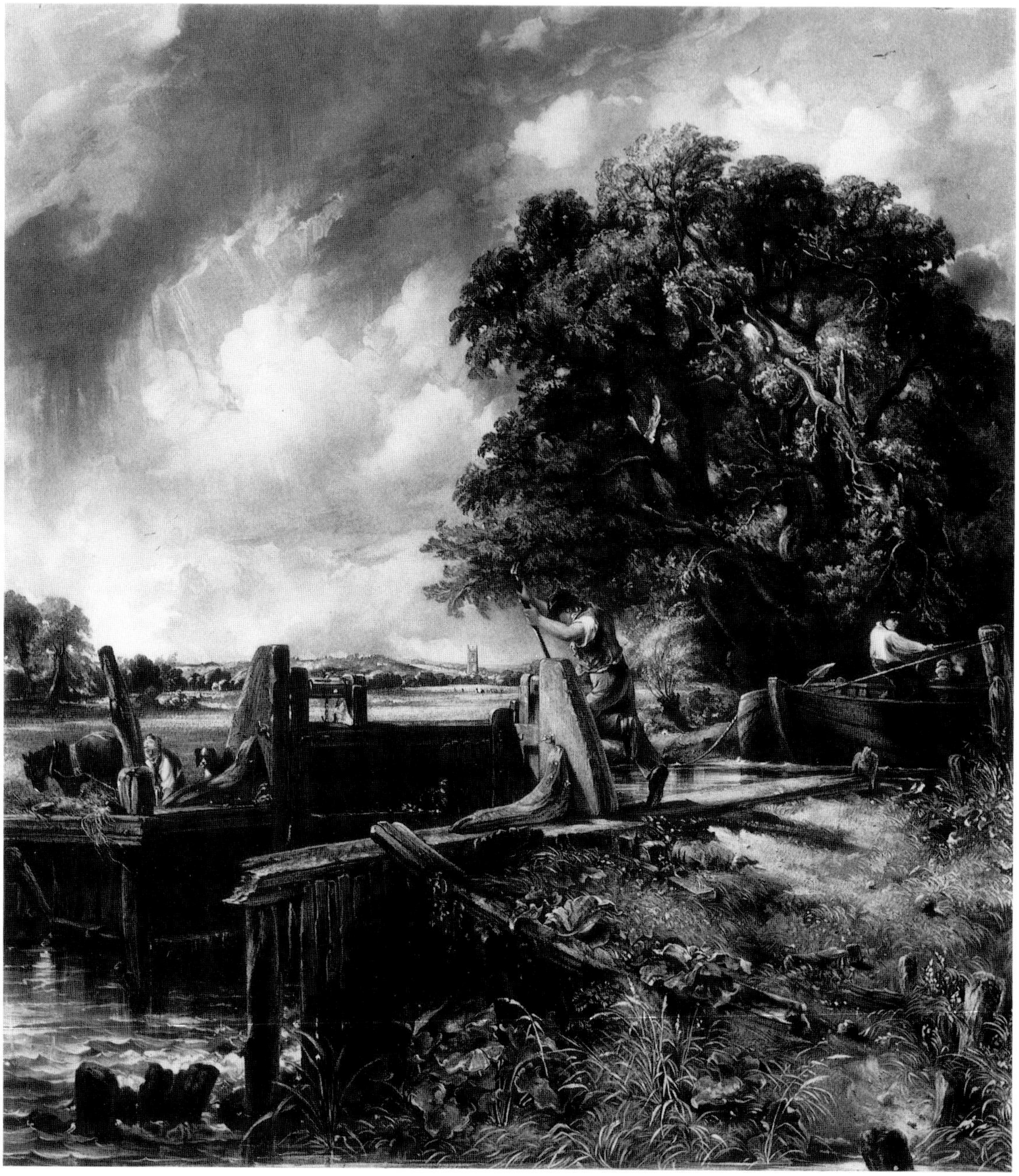

Fortunately it has been possible to acquire both editions of these splendid prints for the collection of the Mead Art Museum.

In spite of the fact that the initial products of that artistically auspicious collaboration were accorded but scant commercial success, Lucas undertook to reproduce other compositions by Constable, among them a series of five large plates, the first of which is *The Lock—Large Plate*. A very early and brilliant impression of the first plate, issued in 1834, it testifies to the virtuosity of Lucas in capturing the tonal essence—and even the textural dynamics—of Constable's canvases. Although the painter did not personally retouch proofs of the later plates, his correspondence indicates that the project benefited from his supervision. With its richness of tone and grandeur of scale, *The Lock* stands as a true masterpiece of British printmaking. It beautifully satisfies Constable's original intention for his prints as stated in the introduction to his 1833 edition: "... to display the phenomena of the Chiaroscuro of Nature, to mark some of its endless beauties, to point out its vast influence upon [the art of] landscape [painting], and to show its use and power as a medium of expression."

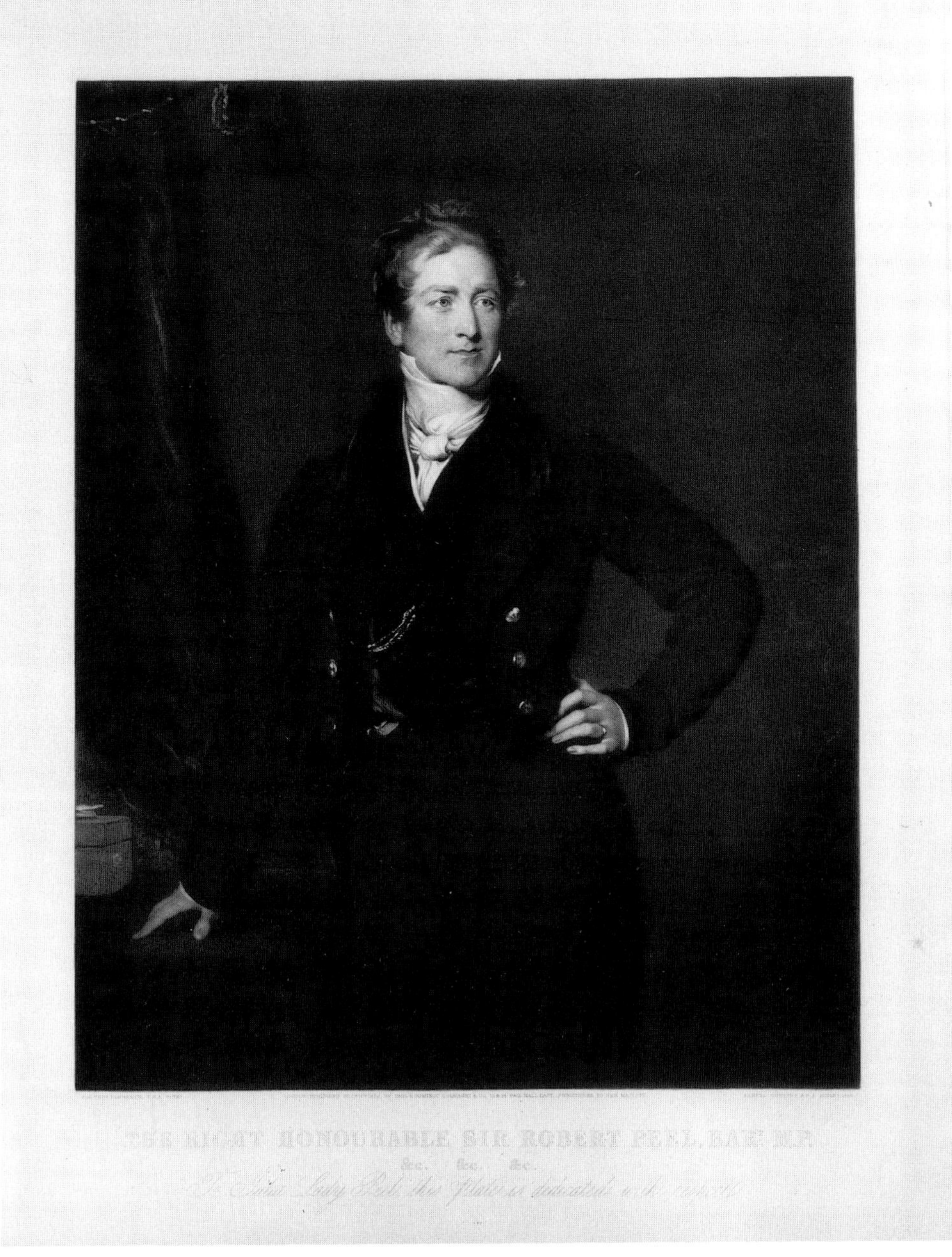

SAMUEL COUSINS (1804–1887)

53. *Portrait of Sir Robert Peel*
Mezzotint engraving, after Sir Thomas Lawrence, 21½ x
15¾ in. (54.6 x 40 cm)
Gift of the Children of Dwight W., '95, and Elizabeth
Morrow
1955.486

The use of mezzotint as a means of transcribing painted portrait images was transformed by nineteenth-century engravers, who desired reliable means of replicating large editions of prints. Originally trained in mezzotint by the prolific Samuel William Reynolds (1773–1835), Cousins assisted his master in the production of many of his series of some 357 plates after paintings by Sir Joshua Reynolds. (Cousins later claimed to have been the sole author of eighty-four of that number.) In his independent production, Cousins devised a new way of satisfying commercial demands for increasingly large editions. He took the lead in using more durable, steel plates in place of the softer copper ones hitherto employed. The changes in technique necessitated by that material development had significant aesthetic results upon the products of that process. To avoid the difficulties of "scraping" the resistant surface of steel, mezzotint engravers began to employ a "mixed style" involving the use of stipple engraving and forms of the etching treatment sometimes augmented by the additional employment of rocking-tools and roulette implements.

Cousins gained great admiration for his virtuosity in the employment of those complex technical means. He was the first specialist in engraving to be honored by election in 1855 to full membership in the ranks of the Royal Academy, where printmaking had been traditionally regarded as a craft, valuable as a reproductive form, but not to be equated with the "higher" arts of painting and drawing. Unfortunately for Cousins' posthumous reputation, the invention of photographic process soon outmoded the mezzotint, and changes of taste rendered the look of his images unpleasantly harsh and mechanical in the eyes of later critics. Fortunately, it is no longer fashionable to accept any such disparagement of Cousins' powers.

His *Portrait of Sir Robert Peel*, engraved after a portrait in oils by Sir Thomas Lawrence, shows the great British statesman in the years of his ascendancy to political leadership. The nation was then caught in the social and economic tensions of rapid transition from an agricultural state to that of the foremost mercantile and industrial power of the nineteenth century. Peel was a handsome and popular figure throughout a career that saw him twice serving as prime minister, and his image was widely circulated among his admirers.

CHARLES GEORGE LEWIS (1808–1880)

54. *Lion*, 1856
   Engraving, after Sir Edwin Henry Landseer,
   8¼ x 10¾ in. (34.3 x 43.2 cm)
   Donor unknown
   PR xx 90

His own redoubtable talents aside, Sir Edwin Landseer was the beneficiary of a number of capable graphic artists who helped extend and perpetuate his fame as a leading artist of his day. Among them his friend and childhood neighbor Charles George Lewis did yeoman service as an engraver of some sixty plates after paintings by Landseer, as well as transcriptions of popular animal subjects by Landseer's world-renowned, French counterpart, Rosa Bonheur

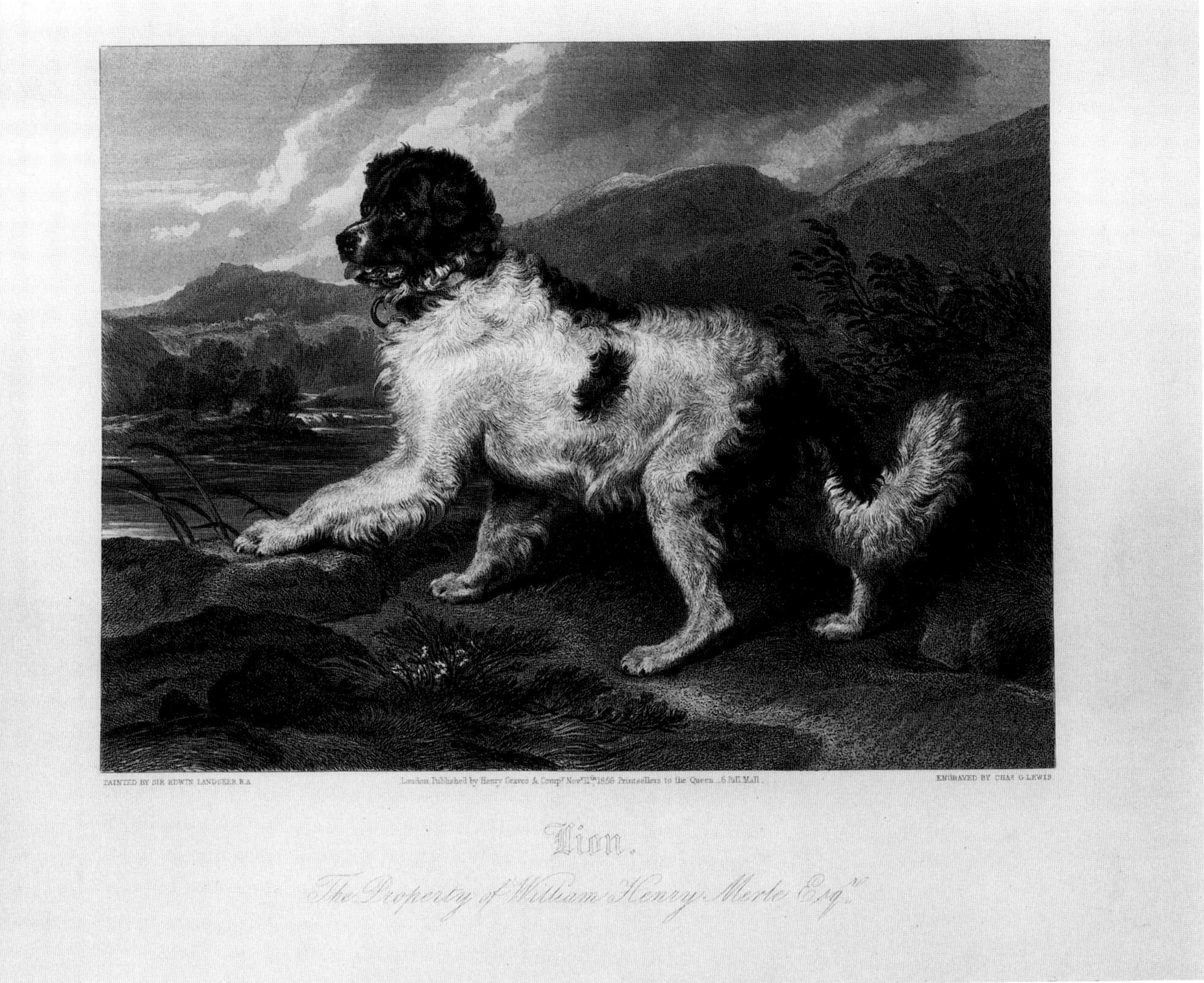

(1822–1899). The son and pupil of the accomplished engraver Frederick Christian Lewis (1779–1856), Charles George Lewis was raised in a family tradition of devotion to fine craftsmanship. Among other distinguished associations, the father had been briefly one of Turner's collaborators in his project of compiling the *Liber Studiorum*, having completed the first plate of the series in aquatint. Also reputed as a specialist in mezzotint and other processes, he was well prepared to pass on a range of skills to his capable son Charles who served other famous and original artists.

Quite understandably permission to issue fine reproductions after such artists as Landseer and Bonheur were much sought after by publishers whose interests were, of course, more commercial than aesthetic. In the interest of printing the larger, more profitable editions his employers desired, Charles Lewis adopted the traditional medium of engraving, which could more closely approximate the tonal effects of painting than could lithography, yet avoided the quick wear of the soft copper plates traditionally used for mezzotints. With a practical turn of mind, Lewis was alert to modern advances in engraving techniques, such as the use of a ruling machine to avoid much of the laborious hand work hitherto required. By laying in general areas of tone in that mechanical way, he could conserve his attention to particularized detail for where it counted most, especially for the spirited, texturally convincing rendering of *Lion*. Ingenious though artisans like Lewis were in the inventive exercise of traditional printing techniques, they could not forestall forever the intrusion of photography as a nemesis which would bring to an end the time-honored role of the handmade print as the means of producing reproductive images.

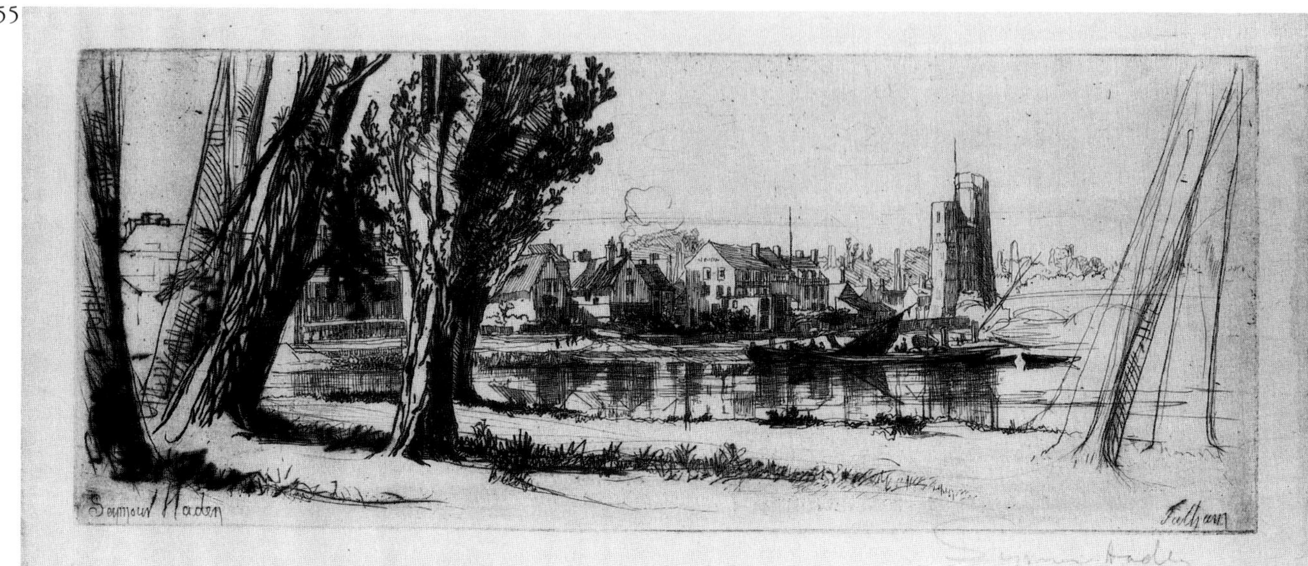

SIR FRANCIS SEYMOUR HADEN (1818–1910)

55. *Fulham*
   Etching, 4½ x 11 in. (13.3 x 28.6 cm)
   Gift of Katherine Rounds for the
   Arthur C. Rounds Collection
   PR 1929.12

At the time when reproductive techniques of engraving had been brought to such sophistication as appears in the work of Charles George Lewis and his fellow practitioners, there ensued a widespread reaction to those standards of mechanical artifice. Other artists pursued the expressive freedom of technique associated with the grand traditions of etching as practiced by Rembrandt and other earlier masters of that art. Earlier signs of a thirst for a more spontaneous release had been strongly evident in the graphic efforts of the French Romantics, especially Eugène Delacroix. And in England, a groundwork for sentiments of the kind had been laid by such artists as Turner and Cotman. But it was above all in France where the revival of interest in etching as an art of original expression took place. The younger generation of artists known as the Barbizon School found in etching a medium ideally suited to their interests in realism as it could be studied in the rural surroundings in which they lived and worked. Charles Emile Jacque (1813–1894) and Jean François Millet (1814–1875) were preeminent pioneers in that movement, which soon took on international proportions.

In England, Sir Francis Seymour Haden played a leading role in the etching revival and served as the first president of the Society of Painter-Etchers, which he founded in London in 1880. Eventually honored with royal patronage, the Society of Painter-Etchers was established to promote the cause of etching as a creative activity fully on a par with the sister arts of painting and drawing. It was intended to dispel long entrenched notions that the practice of printmaking was somehow an inferior pursuit, to be classed more with craft than with art. Even though some members—most notably Haden himself—did not profess to be painters, they nevertheless adopted a title that would announce the lofty aspirations of their society.

A distinguished member of the medical profession, Haden had studied at the Sorbonne and thus was exposed to French influences in the arts, as well as the sciences. It is likely that the prints of Charles Jacque inspired Haden's first venture into printmaking, after a trip to Italy (1843–44), and it was the French critic, Philippe Burty who first took notice of those admittedly slight, but promising efforts. Encouraged in his artistic interest by his brother-in-law Whistler, Haden later pursued a serious career as an etcher. He had married Whistler's half-sister in 1859, shortly after publication of *French Set*, a work Whistler dedicated to Haden. Haden had at the time taken a renewed interest in etching and was encouraged in that enterprise by close association with Whistler. Unfortunately, that bond was severed in 1867.

Haden's representations of landscape are accounted by connoisseurs as especially remarkable examples of the use of drypoint with etching. In their directness and clarity of atmospheric vision, these etchings seem to reflect a remarkable direct lineage from the etched landscapes of the greatest master of the medium, Rembrandt, whom Haden admired above all others. *Fulham* is a fine example of his gifts. In it, his sensitivity to nuances of light and shadow, and his ability to capture their essence in line, are admirably present. The freshness of the handling reflects Haden's fondness for transcribing his image onto the plate with the subject directly in view, as may well have been the case in this instance. At the same time it should be noted that Haden sometimes reworked his plates to enrich the tones and sometimes to achieve more dramatic effects. In this side of his art one is reminded of his deep appreciation of Rembrandt, whose works were so often remarkably revised in accordance with artistic second thoughts.

56

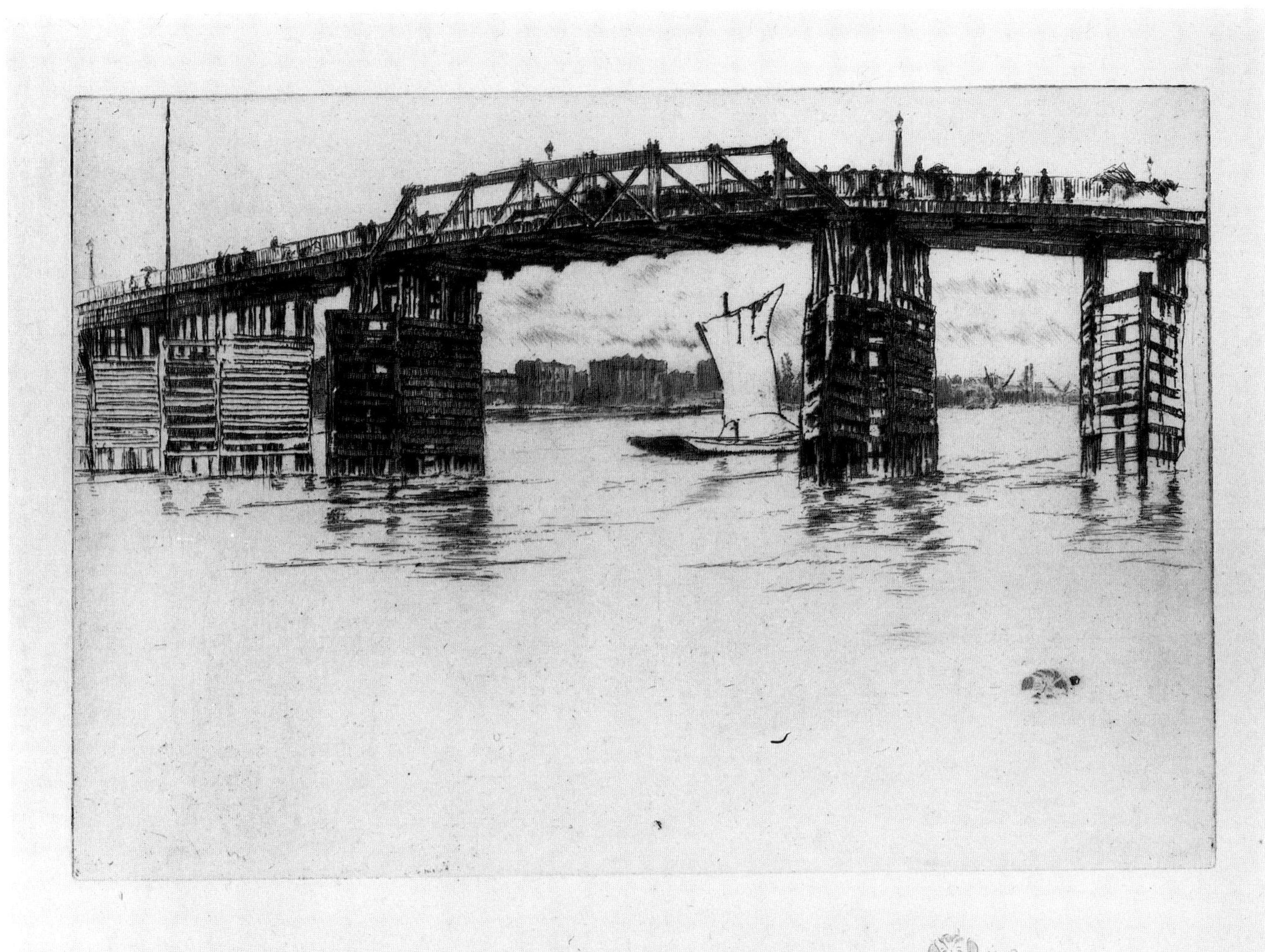

JAMES ABBOTT MCNEILL WHISTLER (1834–1903)

56. *Old Battersea Bridge*, 1878–79
   Etching, 8 x 11¾ in. (20.3 x 29.9 cm)
   Bequest of Charles W. Cole
   1978.19

Although Seymour Haden was older than Whistler and had been the first of the two to try his hand at etching, it was Whistler who proved to be the greatest etcher of modern times and an inspiring figure in the etching revival. Whistler's contribution to the history of etching is too complex to summarize here—leaving aside as well his significance in the practice of other artistic mediums or in the development of aesthetic theory and criticism. Cosmopolitan in background, the American-born Whistler is perhaps more readily identified with the British or Parisian scene than with the United States. It should be said, however, that his contribution to art in his native land was, to say the least, also richly significant.

His artistic training began in 1845 at the Imperial Academy of Fine Arts, Saint Petersburg, where his father was employed as a railroad designer. Following the death of his father, the family moved to London, then in 1849, back to the United States, where he was briefly enrolled at West Point. More important for his art was a year's service with the U.S. Coast and Geodetic Survey, where he learned the rudiments of etching. From there he went directly to the Bohemian life of Paris and a brief period of study with Charles Gleyre (1808–1874). His artistic development benefited from his personal acquaintance with such important avant-garde masters as Gustave Courbet (1819–1877), Edouard Manet (1832–1883), Edgar Degas (1834–1917), and Henri Fantin-Latour (1836–1904). In 1859, he left Paris to take up residence in London, perhaps out of pique at the rejection of his first important painting, *At the Piano*, from the salon of that year. He had also just completed his suite of *Twelve Etchings from Nature* (also known as *The French Set*) recalling a walking tour of northern France, Luxembourg, and the Rhineland. Printed in Paris but actually published after the artist's move to London, *The French Set* served as a significant catalyst in the intitiation of the etching revival in Britain.

Old Battersea Bridge shows one of Whistler's favorite landmarks, drawn as part of a second series of studies he made along the Thames River around 1878. It is, therefore, a product of his mature, middle period, when his plates were of the highest technical quality and further distinguished by an avant-garde flair for compositional design. Whistler delicately marked expanses of the plate with open linear patterns, suggesting the effects of diaphanous mist that he would cultivate later in his Venice and Amsterdam periods yet to come.

Bankrupted by his notorious libel suit against Ruskin and his expenditures upon his White House in 1879, Whistler was commissioned by the Fine Art Society to undertake a set of twelve etchings of Venice. He stayed in that locale for fourteen months, rather than the mere three months originally contemplated, and returned to London with nearly fifty plates. A dozen of his favorites were issued in 1880 as a set. They marked a new phase of his remarkable career as one of the greatest printmakers of all time. Fortunately, Whistler generally fared well with his efforts as printmaker, so that his production was not only large and varied, but also illustrates his general artistic development over the course of many years.

Sir Hubert von Herkomer (1849–1914)

57. *An Arab's Head*, 1895
    "Herkomergravure," 7 x 9 in. (17.8 x 22.9 cm)
    Museum Purchase
    1980.79

The Bavarian-born Hubert von Herkomer, came to England while still a youth in the company of his father, a wood engraver who set up shop in Southampton around 1862. By 1870, the son gravitated to London, where he was to win attention first as a painter of genre and history subjects, then as a portraitist. Especially in that latter guise he won acclaim in France as well as England, where he became a member of the Royal Academy in 1879 and, the following year, a professor at Oxford. His technical flair extended into his performance as watercolorist and printmaker.

Herkomer is known for his invention of an ingenious process, "Herkomergravure." *An Arab's Head* illustrates the facile effects made possible by that process. It involved making an electrotype or metallic mold from a plate painted like that of a monotype and dusted with black lead or some

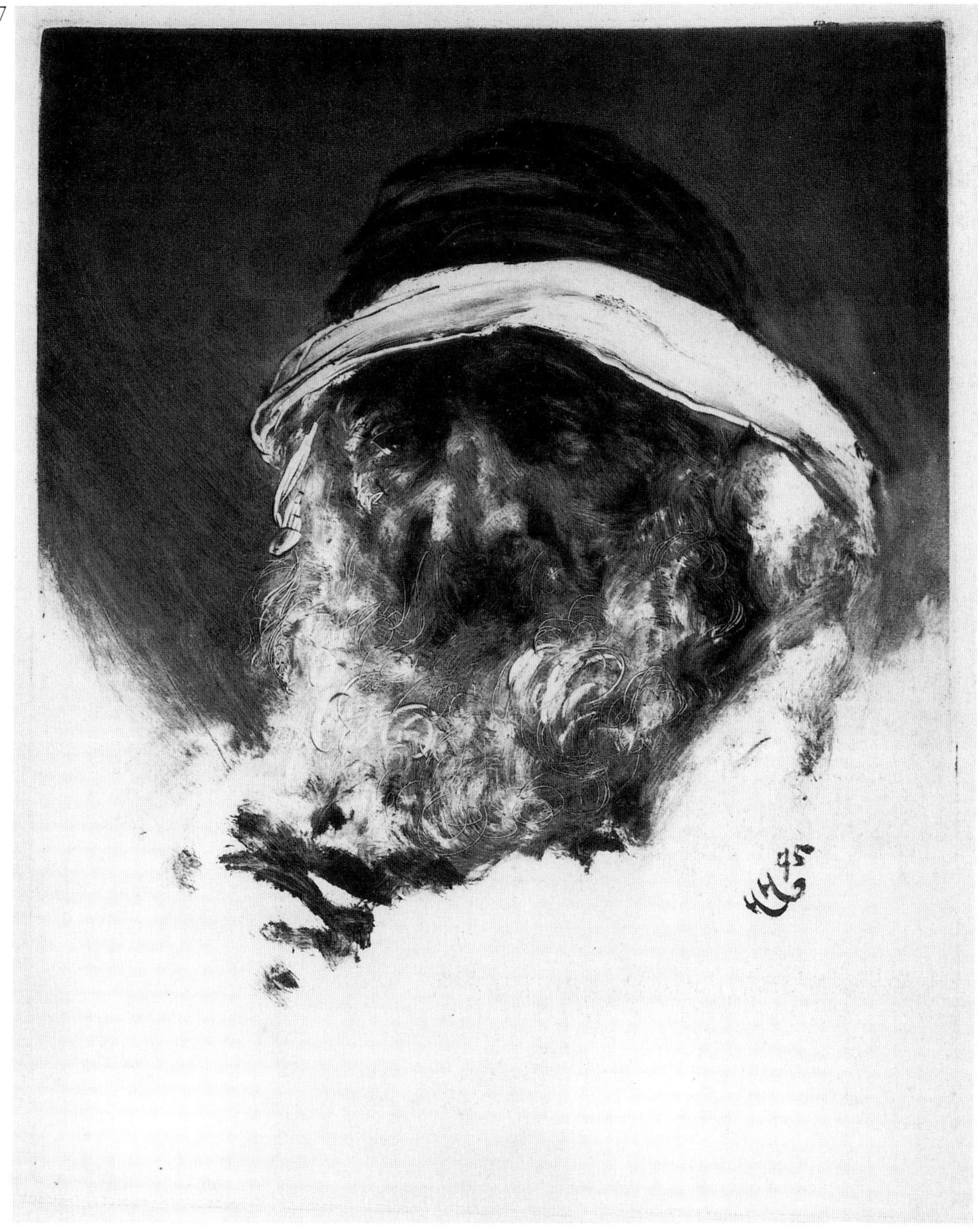

other substance of the kind. By adding the further step of depositing a copper surface on the monotype, he was able to make multiple images resembling those obtainable in a monotype. Herkomer was proud of his process and patented it, but it was never widely adopted by other artists and remains unique within his own oeuvre. It nevertheless is a curious example of the Victorian fascination with ingenuities which those of more puristic inclination are apt to regard as idiosyncratic or even perverse excursions from the mainstream of artistic developments.

Herkomer's subject is very much in the mainstream, for the tradition of representing exotic people and places had persisted throughout the nineteenth century. Romantic fascination for the Orient had especially fixed upon Islam. And in Britain the massive involvement with the affairs of the empire had quickened popular interest in far-off lands. Images such as *An Arab's Head* were therefore much in line with the European urbanite's lively sense of living at the crossroads of the known world and, indeed, at the apex of world history as well.

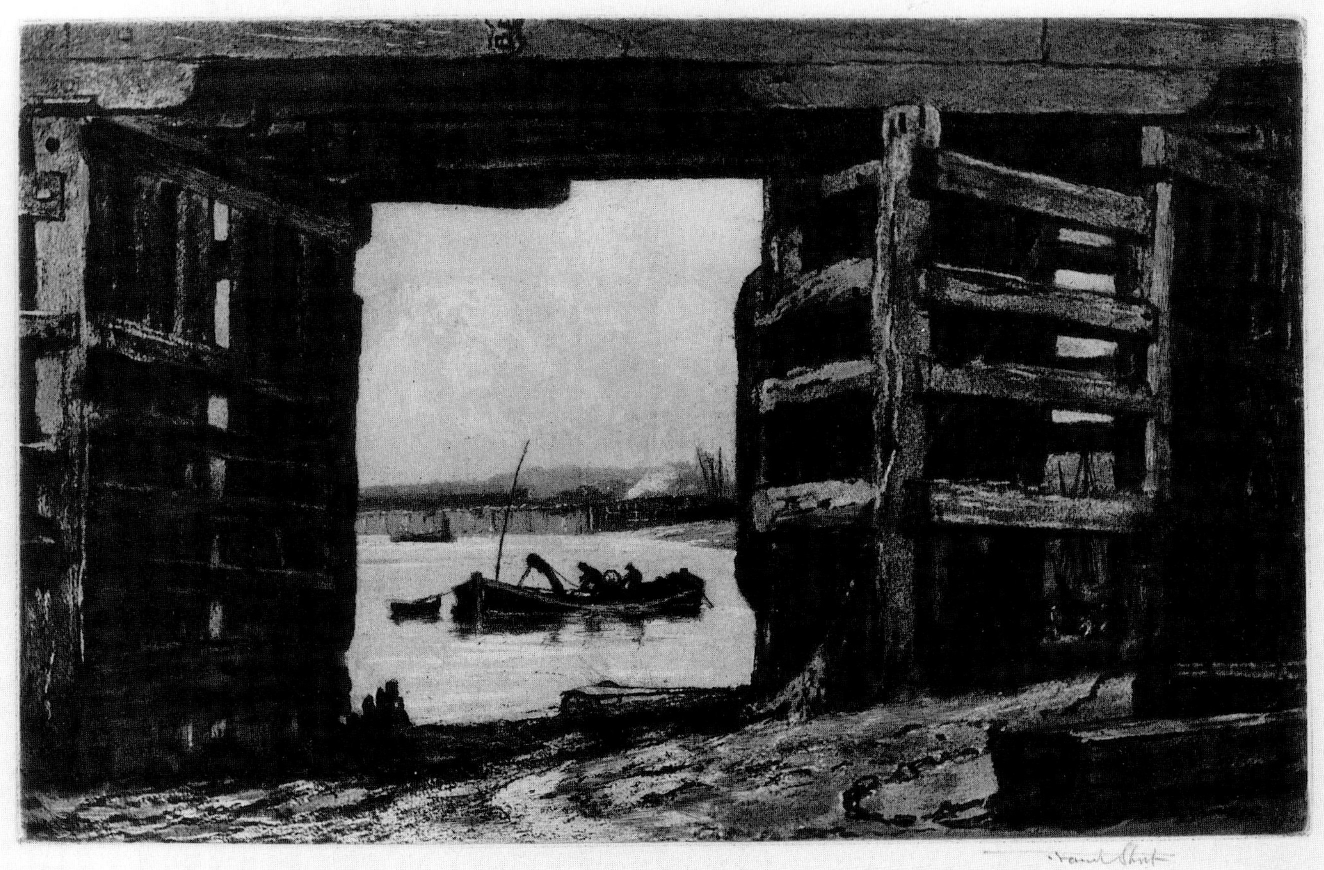

SIR FRANK SHORT (1857–1945)

58. *Span of Old Battersea Bridge,* 1899
   Aquatint, 7½ x 11½ in. (19.1 x 29.2 cm)
   Gift of Edward C. Crossett, '05
   1951.1989

A noted teacher at the Royal College of Art, South Kensington (1891–1924), Frank Short exerted a pervasive influence upon younger printmakers for many years. He was admired for his deep appreciation of the traditions of his chosen medium as well as for a brilliant technical mastery exhibited in some 206 plates produced in his long career. Upon the death of Seymour Haden in 1910, Short had succeeded to the presidency of the prestigious Society of Painter-Etchers, a post he held until 1939. Short also followed that distinguished predecessor in other ways. Affinities between the art of the two men are to be seen, for example, in Short's equal fascination for light as suggested by free networks of line disposed within otherwise unembellished expanses of the plates of his etchings. Understatements of the sort, with their invitation to bold, free, linear invention had been introduced into British etching

in Haden's work of the 1860s. Among his contemporaries, however, Short admired Whistler above all as the chief exponent of the etching revival. Remarkably, Short was able to maintain a cordial relationship with that "great man" with whom so many had personal difficulties. And with both Whistler and Haden, he looked back to Rembrandt as the foremost master in the history of etching and drypoint.

Span of Old Battersea Bridge reveals the complexities of Short's responses to these and other influences. A fine impression of the only state of a small edition, it clearly relates to Whistler in representing one of the artist's favorite landmarks along the Thames. On the other hand it differs significantly in style from Whistler in Short's more insistent compositional massing of forms and in its strength of contour and tone. And Short's adoption of mezzotint in this and other instances harks back to his long nurtured love of Turner's art and, in that respect, owes no debt to Whistler.

As a young man Short had harbored the ambition of completing the *Liber Studiorum* with plates "after" Turner. In the process of approaching that never realized project, he came to appreciate the special appeal of the long-neglected medium of mezzotint, following the general decline of interest in reproductive engraving at mid-century. As in his approach to etching and drypoint, Short employed mezzotint and sometimes aquatint, with a savor for the creative effects invited by the special nature of that technique and the pictorial effects its use invited. Influential both as a teacher at South Kensington and a diplomat in artistic circles, Short is justly regarded as a leading spirit in the British School of etching for the long span of his active life.

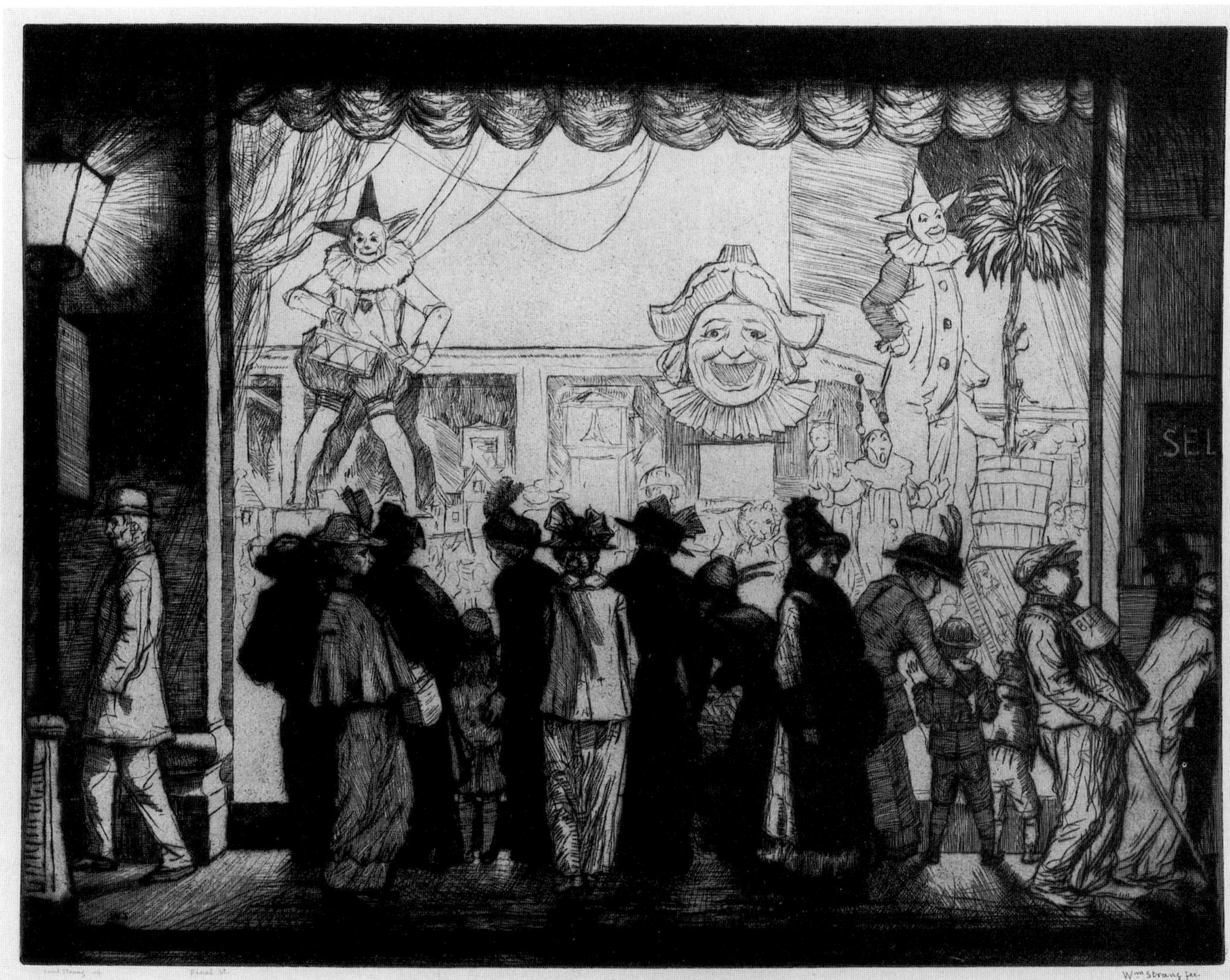

WILLIAM STRANG (1859–1921)

59. *Selfridge's Toy Window*
Drypoint and etching, 17¾ x 14 in. (45.1 x 35.6 cm)
Museum Purchase
1979.70

William Strang was the beneficiary of thorough training under the guidance of Alphonse Legros (1837–1899), who was his teacher at the Royal College of Arts, South Kensington. At Whistler's suggestion, that eminent French master had emigrated from Paris in 1866. As a teacher at the Royal College of Art and later, as Slade Professor at University College, Legros exercised an enormous influence both on the practice of printmaking and on the opinions of connoisseurs of his day. His personal bent for depicting macabre subjects full of a death-ridden symbolism based on sixteenth-century Germanic antecedents had peculiar meaning for Strang, who often adopted themes of the sort for his own work. At the same time, schooled as he was by Legros in the traditional processes, Strang was not averse to indulging his spirit of fancy in exploring ingenious technical inventions, as well. Technical purists, such as

Joseph Pennell (himself a fine exponent of etching), greeted Strang's fondness for experiment as well as his thematic emphasis with mixed feelings. And technical considerations aside, Strang's independent series of plates, such as those devoted to war or *The Dance of Death*, show overtly literary pretensions consistent with the rather heavy symbolic involvements of the Pre-Raphaelites or of eclectic historicists such as George Frederick Watts (1817–1904). That Strang's work as an illustrator is consistent with those interests may be seen in his interpretations of Milton's *Paradise Lost*, Bunyan's *Pilgrim's Progress*, and Cervantes' *Don Quixote*.

A prolific worker, Strang produced some 751 catalogued plates in the course of his career. His facility made him perhaps too susceptible to outside influence even in his mature years, when echoes of Rembrandt, Daumier, and Jean-Louis Forain have variously been detected by experts. Still, there are enormous strengths as well as contradictions in Strang's performance. This may be seen in *Selfridge's Toy Window*, with its somewhat bizarre and threatening juxtapositions of reality and fancy. Overcast with an aura of droll, but grim humor, it shows the store manikins looking out from the warmth of their display window, seemingly more alive than the holiday shoppers exiled to the dark, wintry chill outside, along London's Oxford Street. This subject is unusual in its treatment of a contemporary subject, yet it vividly shows the artist's redoubtable skills in his chosen mediums.

WALTER RICHARD SICKERT (1860–1942)

60. *Noctes Ambrosianae*, 1906
   Etching, 7 x 8⅝ in. (17.8 x 21.9 cm)
   Museum Purchase
   1984.61

Whistler's most important disciple of the next generation, Walter Sickert, was also an immigrant to Great Britain. Born in Munich, he had come at age eight with his family to England and is staunchly regarded as an outstanding representative of the British School. In 1881 he entered the Slade School of Art, but in 1882 he joined Whistler with whom he served for a time, both as pupil and assistant. In that latter capacity, he accompanied Whistler's famous painting of his mother when it was sent to Paris for exhibition in 1883. There, thanks to introductions from Whistler, he met Degas and was received by Manet in his studio. On his honeymoon in Dieppe in 1883 Sickert reestablished his acquaintance with Degas. He visited Dieppe regularly from 1885 and lived there from 1899 to 1905, when he returned to London.

Thanks to his association with Whistler, he became seriously involved with the graphic processes as well as with printmaking and painting as mutually reinforcing and virtually interchangeable means of self-expression, Sickert conformed in the most literal sense to the notion of the painter-etcher that had been earlier advanced by Whistler, Haden, and other masters. At the same time, he subscribed to the notion, initially French, of prints as objects for display on the wall, like paintings, not as something akin to books, to be stored for the most part in portfolios. Repercussions of that shift of emphasis are evident today, as some modern prints are conceived on a monumental —one is tempted to say, gigantic—scale.

In his fascination for scenes of the music hall and theater, around 1885/90, or for domestic interiors fraught with psychological overtones in the relationships of the personages portrayed, Sickert is understandably associated with French counterparts, particularly with Degas. Still, his characterizations lack the steely edge of Degas or the laconic silence of Vuillard. *Noctes Ambrosianae* is a characteristic expression of his love of the theatrical scene and, most of all, the common people who found pleasure there. Boldly bitten to create a rugged strength of line, and broadly organized in its compositional design, it embodies Sickert's approach to the print as visually large in scale, even when comparatively small in size, as this plate actually is. Sickert's glimpses into the world of popular entertainment have a character all their own. This is to be seen particularly in the architecture of the compositional design, which is more forthright than Degas', with little or none of his elusiveness of structure. In handling, too, the treatment is more decisive—even brusque—in contrast to

the tantalizingly tentative quality encountered in Degas' raking glances at actuality. At any rate, by this time Sickert had come to share more in the ideals of Impressionism than of Whistler's world.

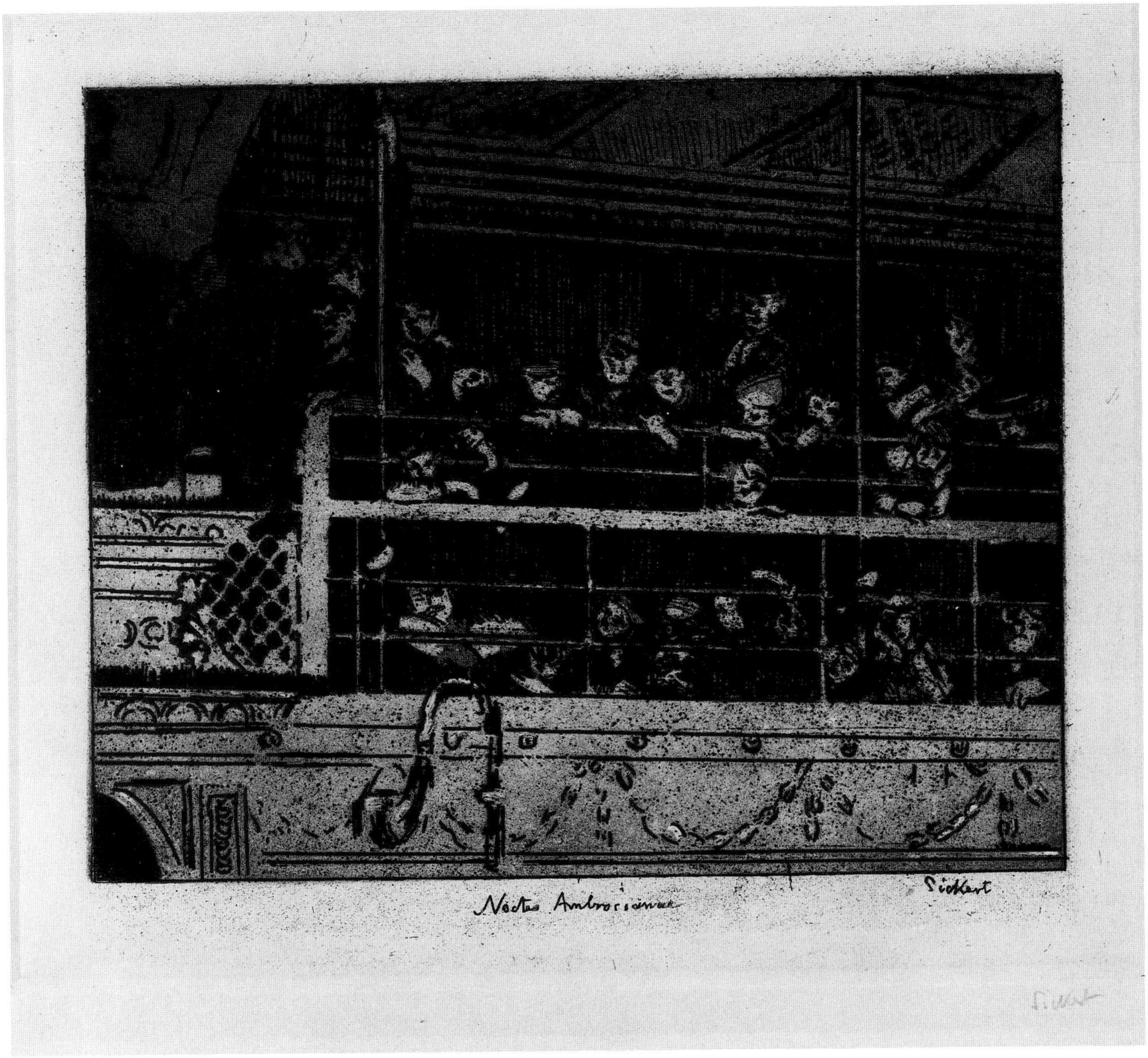

In 1897 Sickert broke with Whistler following the latter's lawsuit about transfer lithography. Later, Sickert became interested in issues aroused by Roger Fry's landmark exhibition, *Manet and Post-Impressionism*, presented in November 1910. The following year, Sickert took the lead in forming the Camden Town Group, an early manifestation of the avant-garde in Britain, which presented four group exhibitions between June 1911 and early 1913. Ex-

cept for John and Lucien Pissarro (sons of the famous Impressionist), the members were mainly linked by a common fascination for the seamier aspects of urban life—all rendered with an eye for striking tone and color. Spencer Gore (1878–1914), whom Sickert had met in Dieppe in 1904, served as president during the brief existence of the controversial group—a kind of British equivalent of the Ashcan School in the United States. Only Sickert, the dominant figure, and the Pissarros were deeply involved with printmaking. Sickert maintained this interest for many years, but on the redefined terms of the new artistic principles which began to infiltrate the British scene.

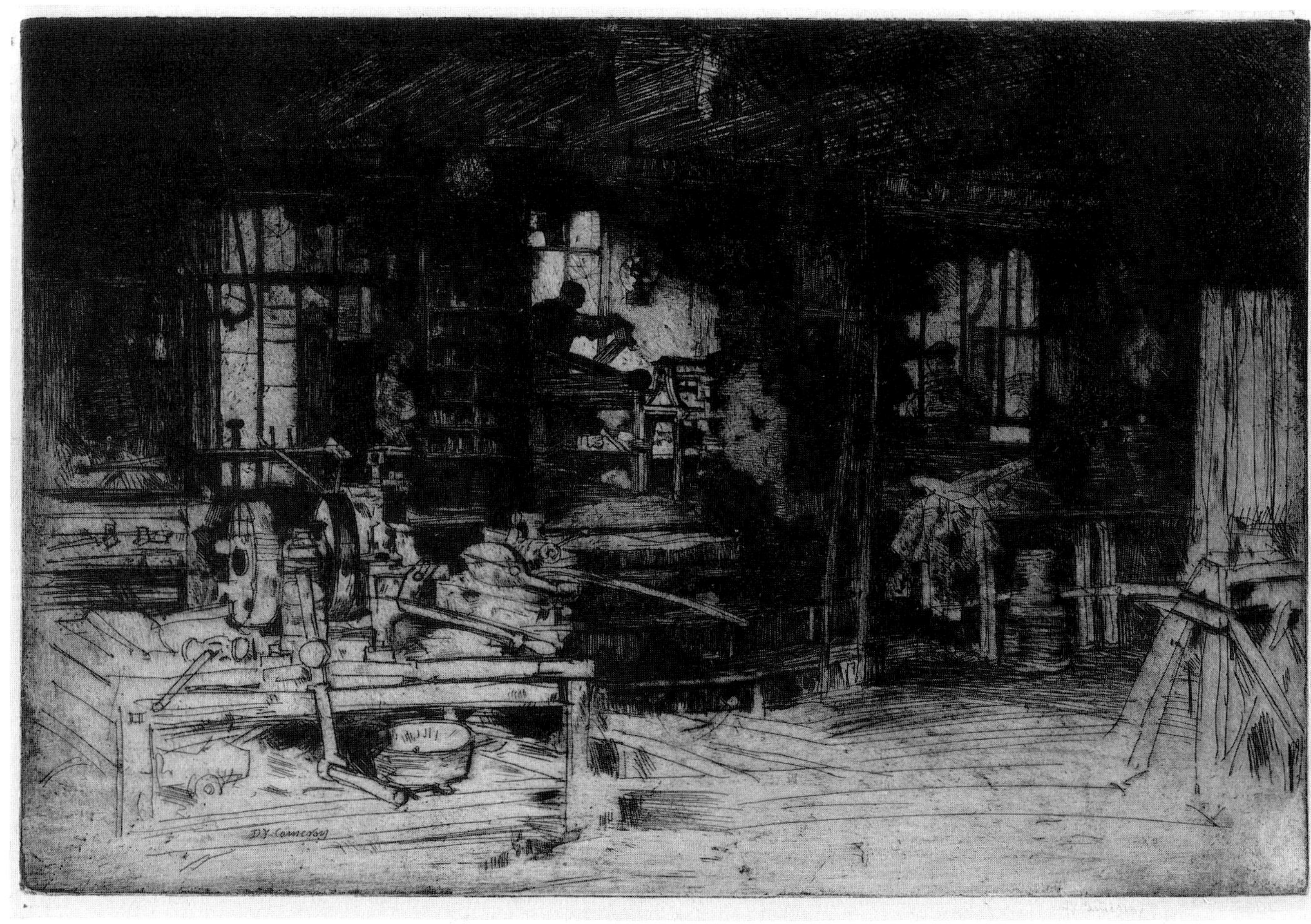

DAVID YOUNG CAMERON (1865–1945)

61. *The Workshop, Stirling*, 1905
   Etching and drypoint, 2nd state of 4, 8½ x 12 in.
   (21.6 x 30.5 cm)
   Gift of Edward C. Crossett, '05
   1951.771

The third son of a Glasgow minister of the Scottish church, David Young Cameron was the first of several of remarkable talents to emerge in Scotland toward the end of the century. Cameron received his introductory professional training in the progressive atmosphere of the Glasgow School of Art. The artistic ethos of the era around 1880/95 into which Cameron matriculated was set by a group of younger artists known as the "Glasgow Boys," who were bonded more by personal friendship and freedom of spirit than by any shared ideals of specific technique or subject matter. The leading member of the group in its early days was William York Macgregor (1855–1923), who had studied under Legros at London's Slade School of Art. Follow-

ing comparatively brief formal beginnings at the Glasgow School, Cameron transferred at age twenty to the Edinburgh School of Art. He profited greatly in his early years from the encouragement of one George Stevenson, who was a friend of Haden's and himself an amateur etcher. At Stevenson's urging, Cameron took up etching in 1887 and embarked on a professional career which soon saw his works represented at the international exhibitions which had by then come much into fashion. Like other printmakers who were to gain recognition as members of a thriving Scottish School, Cameron was greatly indebted to the artistic examples of Whistler and Seymour Haden in their insistence upon the artistic dignity of printmaking, in line with the ethic of the painter-etcher. Whistler in particular had strong associations with Scotland. The city of Glasgow enjoyed an especially vigorous and liberal cultural climate at the time. Most important of all, it was at Glasgow that for the first time a work by Whistler was acquired by a public gallery, when in 1891 Whistler's *Arrangement in Grey and Black, No. 2: Thomas Carlyle* (1872–73) was purchased.

Cameron followed the example of Whistler and others of his calling in traveling extensively in search of suitable subjects. Cameron's sojourns in picturesque surroundings on the Continent began in the mid-1890s. He undertook the depictions of architectural landmarks of Italy and France which set the direction of his future production. Among those ventures, the *Paris Set* of 1904 is especially admired as a kind of tribute to the art of Cameron's great French predecessor, Charles Meryon (1821–1868). Cameron sought to emulate Meryon's command of detail within a prevailing sense of atmosphere. At the same time, however, there is more than a little deference to Haden, as well, in Cameron's discerning inclusion of comparatively unworked passages in his composition to convey the sensation of outdoor light. Cameron's views of Italy, including those of Venice,

bear comparison with the finest products of his predecessors in the etching revival movement.

Cameron was not constrained solely to the representation of landscape and architectural exteriors, however, despite his great gift at capturing the interplay of sunlight and outdoor shadow. Among the interior studies he undertook fairly early in his career, one of the most impressive is *The Workshop, Stirling*, in which his command of shadowed complexity of spatial extension is authoritatively registered. It is easy to see in this superbly realized plate how Cameron's etchings came to be regarded as a measure of excellence by print connoisseurs of his day. Despite violent shifts of aesthetic judgment since the apogee of Cameron's popularity, his posthumous reputation continues to enjoy the respect of knowledgeable collectors of our own day.

SIR FRANK BRANGWYN (1867–1956)

62. *Venetian Canal*
   Drypoint, 6 x 8 in. (20.3 x 15.2 cm)
   Museum Purchase
   PR 1930.1

Born in Bruges of Welsh parents but raised in England, Frank Brangwyn shared the enthusiasm of many of his fellow British artists for periods of travel and work abroad. He also perpetuated the established mid-nineteenth-century tendency to consider serious engagement with the print medium a proper extension of his total artistic commitment. Apprenticed to William Morris (1834–1896) at the age of fifteen, he learned about textile design. His period

of tutelage with Morris lasted from about 1882 to 1884. After the sale of his first independent picture in 1885, Brangwyn spent a time at sea, voyaging to Africa and Asia. Themes of the ocean and an affection for oriental art would later feature in his development as a painter. Brangwyn won international favor for his architectural decorations, one of which was painted in 1932 for Rockefeller Center, New York City.

True to his schooling in the versatility of artistic accomplishment preached by Morris, Brangwyn was equally at home as a designer for pottery and stained glass and a book illustrator. He thus conformed to his great teacher's insistence upon the equal value of the traditionally more lowly handicrafts with other aspects of creative design.

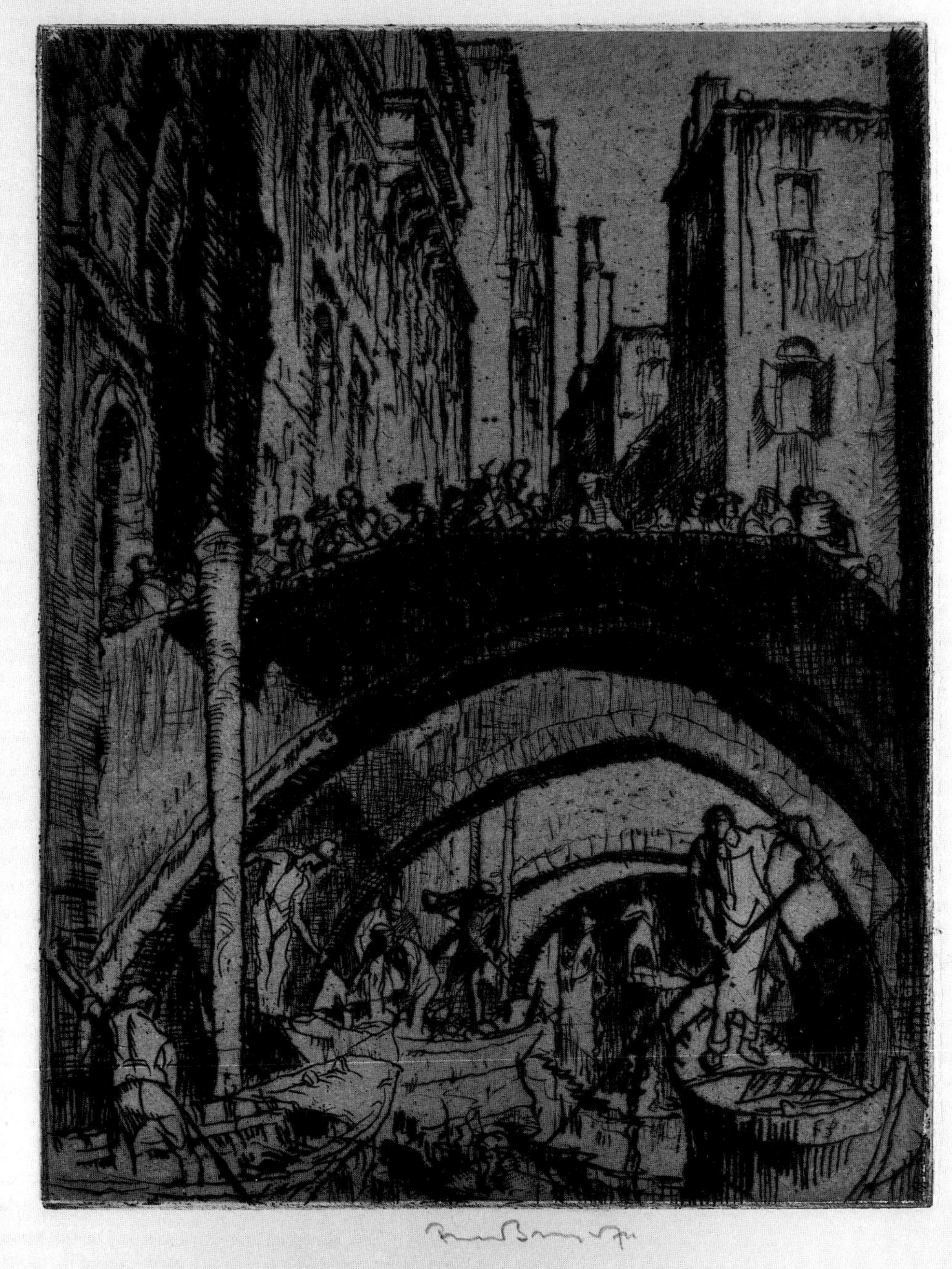

Morris' dictum was central to the Arts and Crafts Movement that emerged in the light of his efforts to gain recognition for the natural independence of function and decorative appeal.

For Brangwyn, etchings offered a welcome respite from the demands of work on his larger commissions. His breadth of handling and forcefulness of approach to design as a printmaker relate directly to the qualities that were admired in his monumental efforts. Similarly, the thickness of his etched line and the heavy inking of his plates share in the bold spirit of his performance as a painter. Brangwyn's *Venetian Canal* recalls Whistler in subject, but it should be noted that it openly contradicts Whistler's well-publicized disapproval of large plates. To other eyes, however, Brangwyn's "transgressions"—if such they may be called—are nevertheless admirably in harmony with the character of his own work in other mediums. Brangwyn reconciled the demands of decorative design with those of convincing representation, an accomplishment to be appreciated.

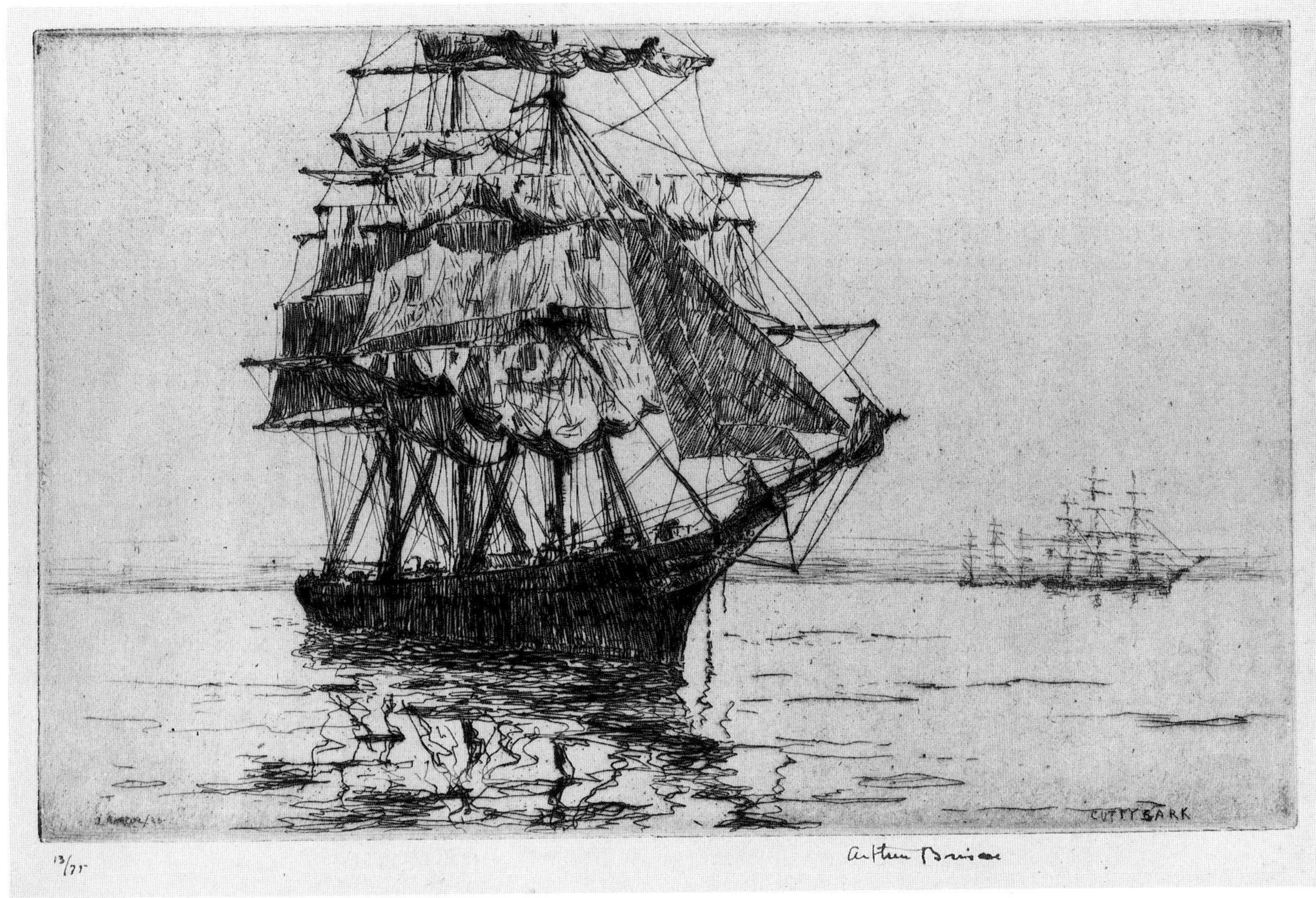

ARTHUR JOHN TREVOR BRISCOE (1873–1943)

63. *Cutty Sark*, 1924
   Etching, 7 x 10¾ in. (17.8 x 27.8 cm)
   Gift of Edward C. Crossett, '05
   1950.85

Esteemed by connoisseurs for technical finesse as an etcher, Arthur Briscoe gained great popularity for the marine subjects that he treated almost exclusively. After his studies at the Slade School, London, Briscoe had sought further training in Paris, but the student life of the French capital did not suit him. Returning to England, he bought a boat and throughout his life pursued the life of what has been called a "freelance" sailor.

For a long time Briscoe specialized in watercolor painting, at which he showed great proficiency, but in the 1920s he turned to etching. His etchings, some 189 in number, were all executed within the span of roughly a decade. In them, Briscoe's special understanding of the sea and ships, gained through his intimate acquaintance with shipboard activities, takes shape with seemingly effortless conviction. His rendition of the great clipper ship, *Cutty Sark*, embodies those qualities which made his plates al-most a mandatory part of any sophisticated print collection formed in the heyday of his reputation. Briscoe's preference for working quickly marks the character of his images with their look of spontaneity. A rare gift for rendering movement equipped Briscoe to portray stunningly the drama of man's contest with the natural forces of the sea. For his many admirers in an island nation fascinated by the sea and drawn to its majesty and might, his message was a telling one.

After a flush of popular success with his prints, Briscoe suffered reverses of fortune around 1930 with the collapse of the fashion for print collecting at the onset of the Great Depression. Subsequent developments in artistic preference for a time further dampened enthusiasm of the cognoscenti for the contribution of those working out of so descriptive a conviction—although in Britain they suffered least of all, it may be said. Whatever the case, more recent turns of fashion and a moderating of prejudices in some circles against descriptive art have argued for the much deserved rehabilitation of artists of Briscoe's persuasion, with his unapologetic enthusiasm for setting forth a straightforward record of the places, people, things, and events he knew and liked best.

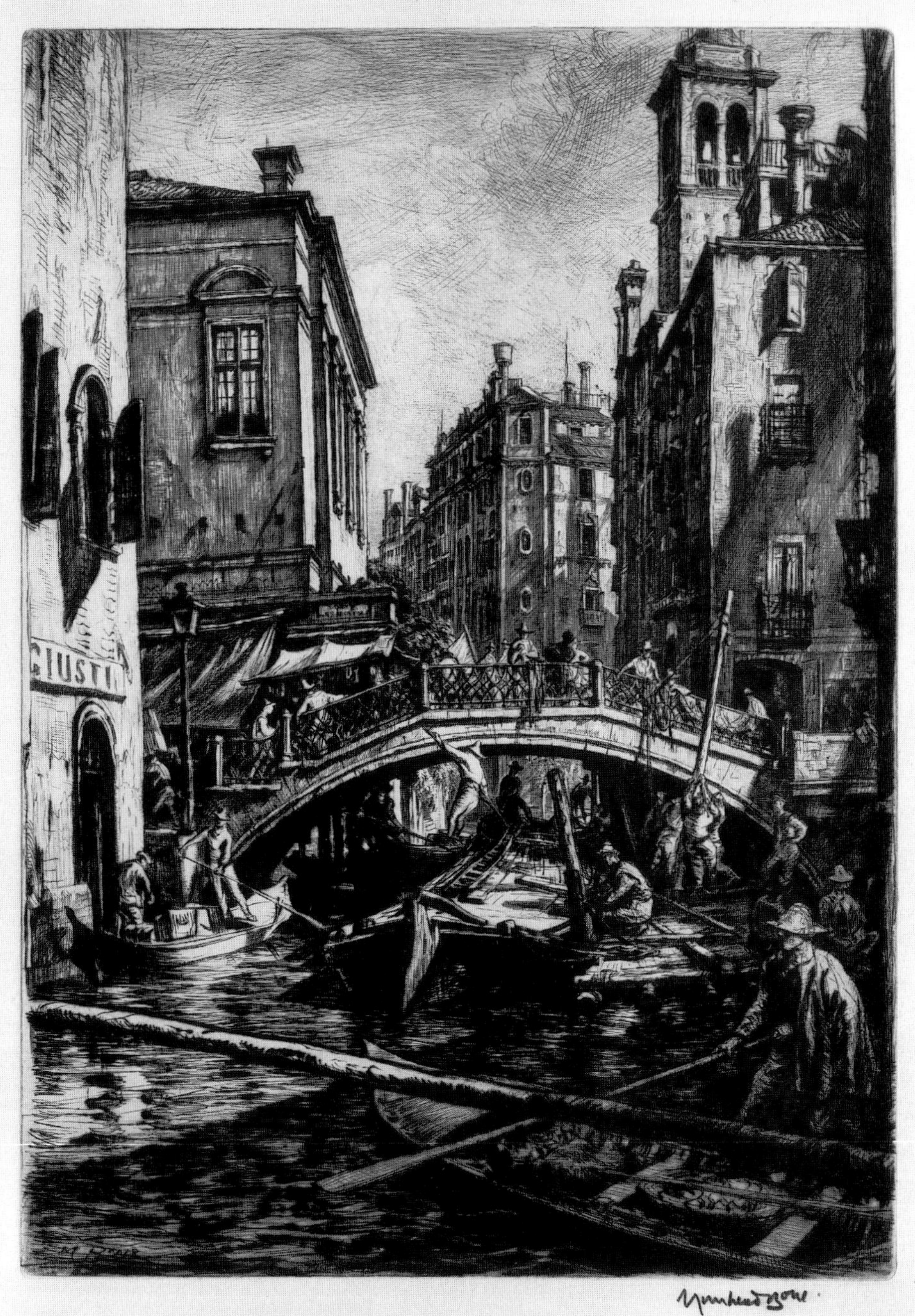

SIR MUIRHEAD BONE (1876–1953)

64. *Canal and Bridge of S. S. Apostoli, Venice*
Drypoint, 9 x 12¾ in. (22.9 x 32.4 cm)
Gift of Edward C. Crossett, '05
1951.588

Another of the Scottish masters of printmaking, Muirhead Bone received his initial training at the Glasgow School of Art. His first efforts in etching and drypoint, *Etchings of Glasgow*, were issued in 1899. Although he had little for-

mal training in the graphic media, he evolved a remarkable technical command and is now regarded as one of the leading masters of drypoint. Bone's early employment as a draftsman with an architectural firm doubtless contributed to the exercise of his acute eye for architectural detail. Coupled with his responsiveness to patterns of shadow and light, that feeling for keen observation gives special life to the architectural vistas that often attracted him. Widely traveled in Europe from 1909 onward, Bone customarily made drawings and watercolors along the way—habits and skills that served him well in the periods he served

as official artist of the military services during the two
world wars.

More appealing in some ways, however, are the products of his independent travels abroad, particularly his explorations in Spain, which culminated in 1936, with the publication of his lavish, two-volume edition, *Old Spain.* With an accompanying text by David Young Cameron's wife Gertrude that edition was illustrated by drawings and watercolors by Bone.

Canal and Bridge of S. S. Apostoli, Venice recalls one of Bone's productive visits to Italy, which commenced as early as 1910. This subject demonstrates his virtuosity in the use of drypoint to achieve effects of broadly massed tone enlivened by clearly wrought but never finicky detail. To some extent Bone's achievement of those effects reflects his attentiveness to the process. He was fastidious in wiping the plate in the course of the print run—a concern for the niceties of execution that recall his individualistic involvement with the pulling of each impression. He also frequently reworked his plates to retain a freshness of the burr, which is so vulnerable to wear in soft copper plates that have been overprinted. For that reason some of his editions, though small, exist in many states.

AUGUSTUS EDWIN JOHN (1878–1961)

65. *Portrait of William Butler Yeats*, 1907
    Drypoint with etching, 6¾ x 4⅞ in. (17.2 x 12.4 cm)
    Museum Purchase
    1987.19

The Welsh-born Augustus John commanded the attention of the London art world throughout a long and controversial career. John's precocity had already drawn him notice while he was still a student at London's Slade School of Art. There he completed the regular curriculum under the tutelage of Sir William Orphen (1878–1931), among others, and Henry Tonks (1862–1937) who was an ardent admirer of Degas and enjoyed a great reputation as an inspiring teacher. It was Tonks in particular who recognized and encouraged young John's gifts as a draftsman. In 1898 John was awarded the Slade Prize. On a visit to Paris in 1899, the year of his first solo exhibition, he was first struck by the art of Puvis de Chavannes (1824–1898), and for a time the influence of Puvis' emphasis on decoratively patterned form left its mark on John's own efforts.

After a brief stint as a teacher at Liverpool University (1901–2), John detoured onto less orthodox paths in joining a troupe of gypsies and learning their language and ways. Finding inspiration among outcasts from "polite" society, he loved to portray the life of the vagabond in scenes of gypsy encampments or of beggars or itinerant musicians. Indeed, it seemed for a time that it was Augustus John in whom the ideal ingredients of modern artistic individualism were to be identified. Future developments proved that supposition premature, as far more fundamental forms of radicalism were released by the advent of Post-Impressionism and the cult of what the English writer Clive Bell dubbed "significant form." Even so, John's personal exhibitionism appealed to many who were disposed to accept literary notions of the free spirit as tantamount to creativity, so that literary portrayals of The Artist were in some degree often apt to resemble Augustus John. It is worth noting that at the 1913 Armory Show in New York City, John's individual representation by thirty-eight works was second in size only to the collection of some forty pieces by Odilon Redon (1842–1916). Years later, in 1938, the testy John scandalized his contemporaries by resigning his seat in the Royal Academy to which he had been elected in 1928—only to accept reelection in 1946.

John's etchings date mostly from the 1910s and 1920s. From the 1920s onward, portrait painting became his major

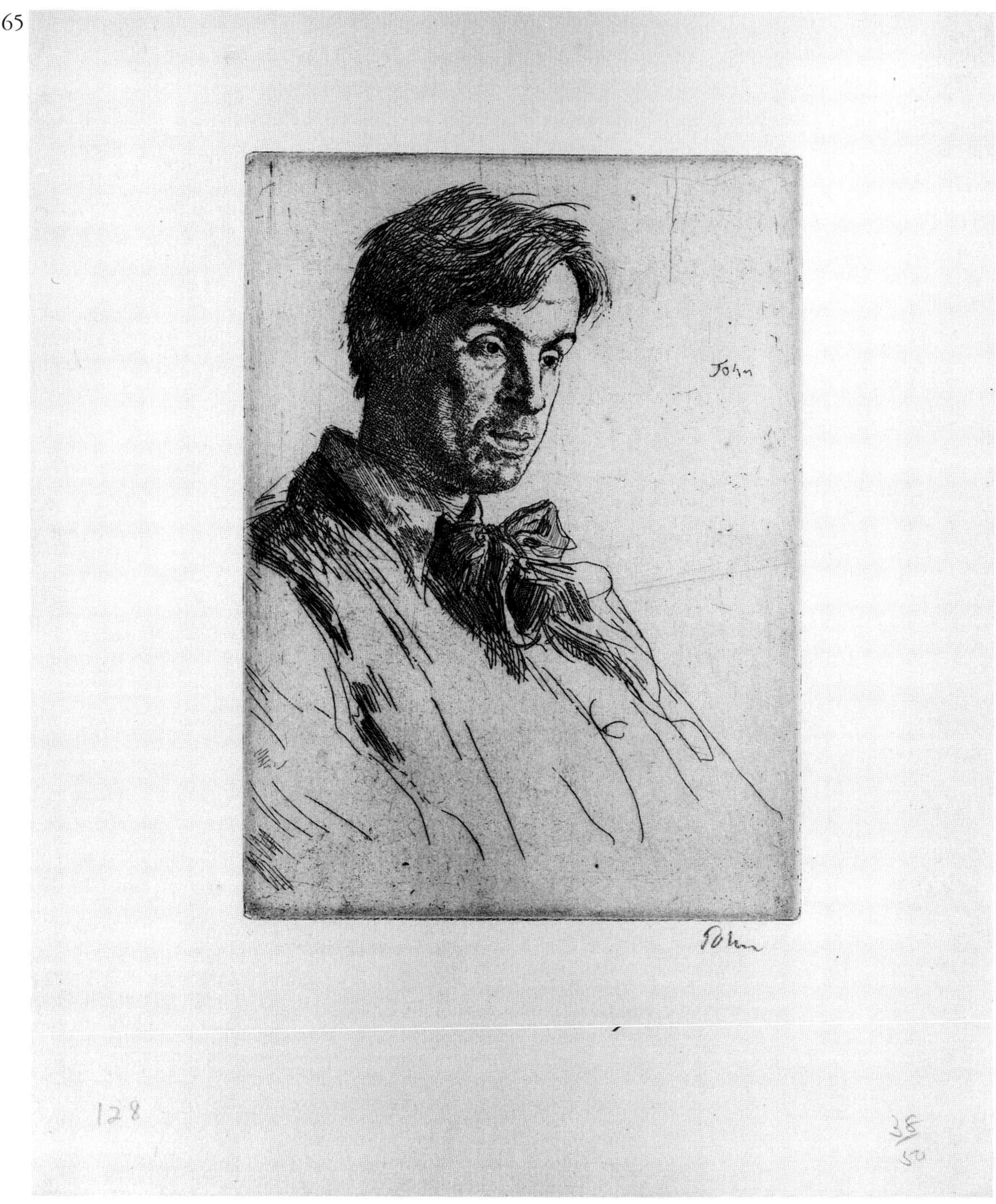

vehicle of self-expression. He had turned to portraiture shortly after his student days, however, and his interest in that genre is prominent in his etched subjects. All of them fairly small in size, these ventures into the graphic processes prominently include trenchant portrayals of other sitters as well as portraits of himself. Among them, John's *Portrait of William Butler Yeats* is generally accepted as the epitome of his accomplishment as an etcher. One of only fifty impressions pulled from the plate, it shows the great Irish poet and dramatist just as his involvement with the new Abbey Theatre in Dublin reached a climactic pitch of intensity. John eloquently captures the writer's rare combination of sensitivity and strength with a complementary manipulation of his line and tone. These qualities of expressiveness and the directness of execution it encapsulates are shared by his more complex scenes showing his favorite vagabond types. In them he reiterates his admiration for the vitality and freedom enjoyed by the gypsies, tinkers, and strolling musicians, whose activities caught his eye.

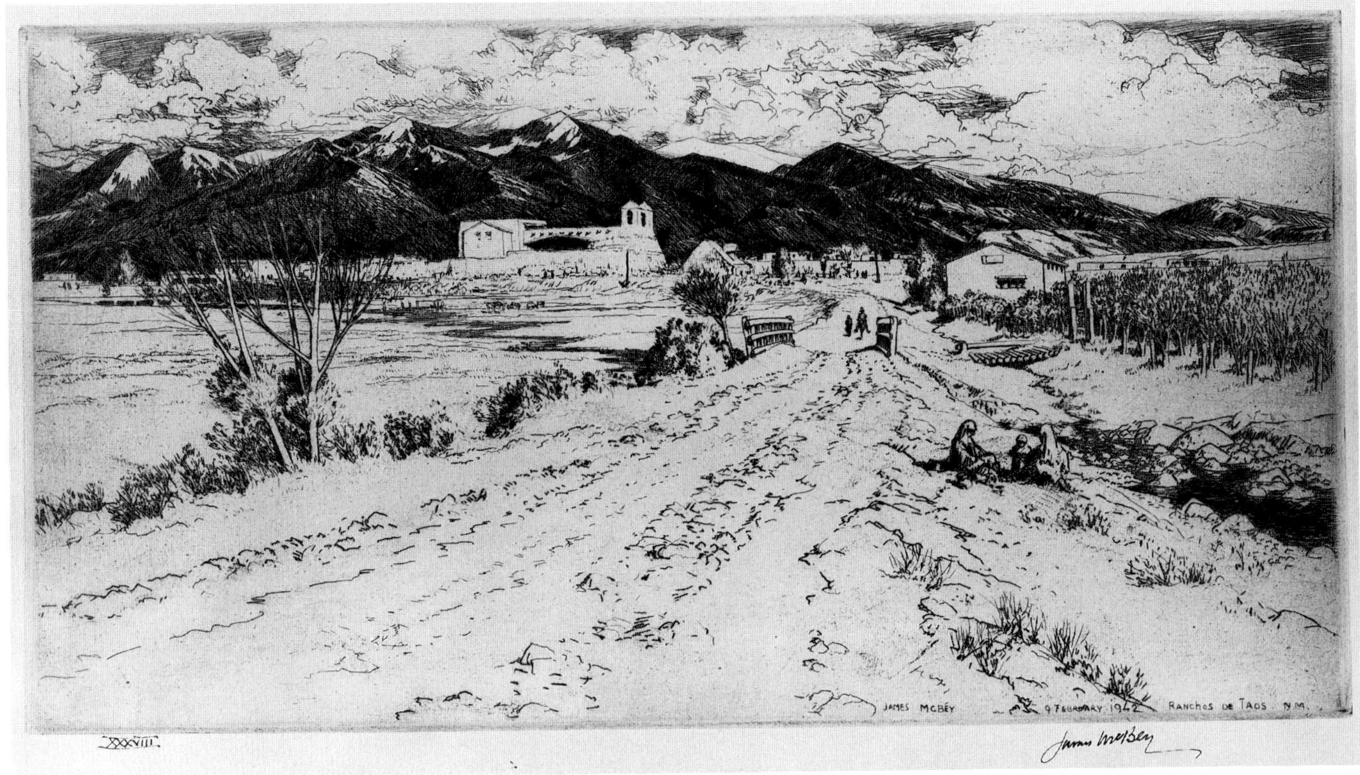

JAMES McBEY (1883–1959)

66. *Ranchos de Taos, New Mexico*, 1942
    Etching, 7 x 13¾ in. (17.8 x 32.4 cm)
    Gift of Edward C. Crossett, '05
    1951.1759

Essentially self-taught, James McBey profited from little formal training before embarking on his professional career as a watercolorist and etcher. He was drawn to an interest in etching while yet a youth of seventeen, in part at least by reading a translated edition of a treatise on etching written by the well-known French printmaker, Maxime Lalanne (1827–1886).

Disposed as he was from the first to meticulousness in matters of craft, McBey was closely attentive to the practical processes of printing and regularly sought out special papers to enhance the quality of his proofs. Beginning with the native Scottish scene as a focus of his descriptive talents, he proceeded to expand his repertory thanks to the experiences of travel on the Continent, beginning with a trip to Holland in 1910 and to Spain in 1911. During the years just prior to World War I he expanded his horizons further with travel in Morocco during 1912. He was thus prepared for the exotic, Islamic environment that he would again encounter during his service as a military illustrator for the British Expeditionary Forces in World War I. After

service in France in 1916, the following year he began a lengthy assignment in Palestine. While in the Holy Land, McBey assembled the impressions, notes, and studies that would serve him in the later publication of three *Palestine Sets*, which appeared after the war—in 1919, 1920, and 1921, respectively. Typical of his working method throughout his career, he preferred to execute his plates in the studio. He was well served in this approach with his outstanding gifts of memory.

McBey's first visit to Venice in September 1924 had an even more crucial effect upon his artistic development, however, as it had for so many of his predecessors. There, he succumbed to the provocative spell of that city so rich in artistic tradition. His eye was quickened as never before to nuances of light and atmosphere, studded with accentuations of picturesque detail. Once developed as part of his working vocabulary, those traits of apt perception were translatable into other visual terms. McBey used it in his treatments of other subject matter in the course of subsequent travels, whether in the canals of Amsterdam as well as those of Venice, or in the marine prospects he also came to favor.

Ranchos de Taos, New Mexico is a souvenir of McBey's travel in the United States during the 1940s. A comparatively late work, it was inspired by the aspect of desert country of the American Southwest. There, McBey must have recalled prior experiences in North Africa and Palestine. At the same time any viewer of this fine plate who may be directly acquainted with the special look of that region will surely be struck by the accuracy with which McBey has captured the qualities of space, scale, and even the traits of light and atmosphere particular to that part of the world. At this point in his career, the heyday of the craze for collecting of etchings had seriously waned because of the financial conditions following the Wall Street crash of 1929. That he had nevertheless maintained his skills is readily apparent in his view of a new part of the world that he had just come to experience.

67

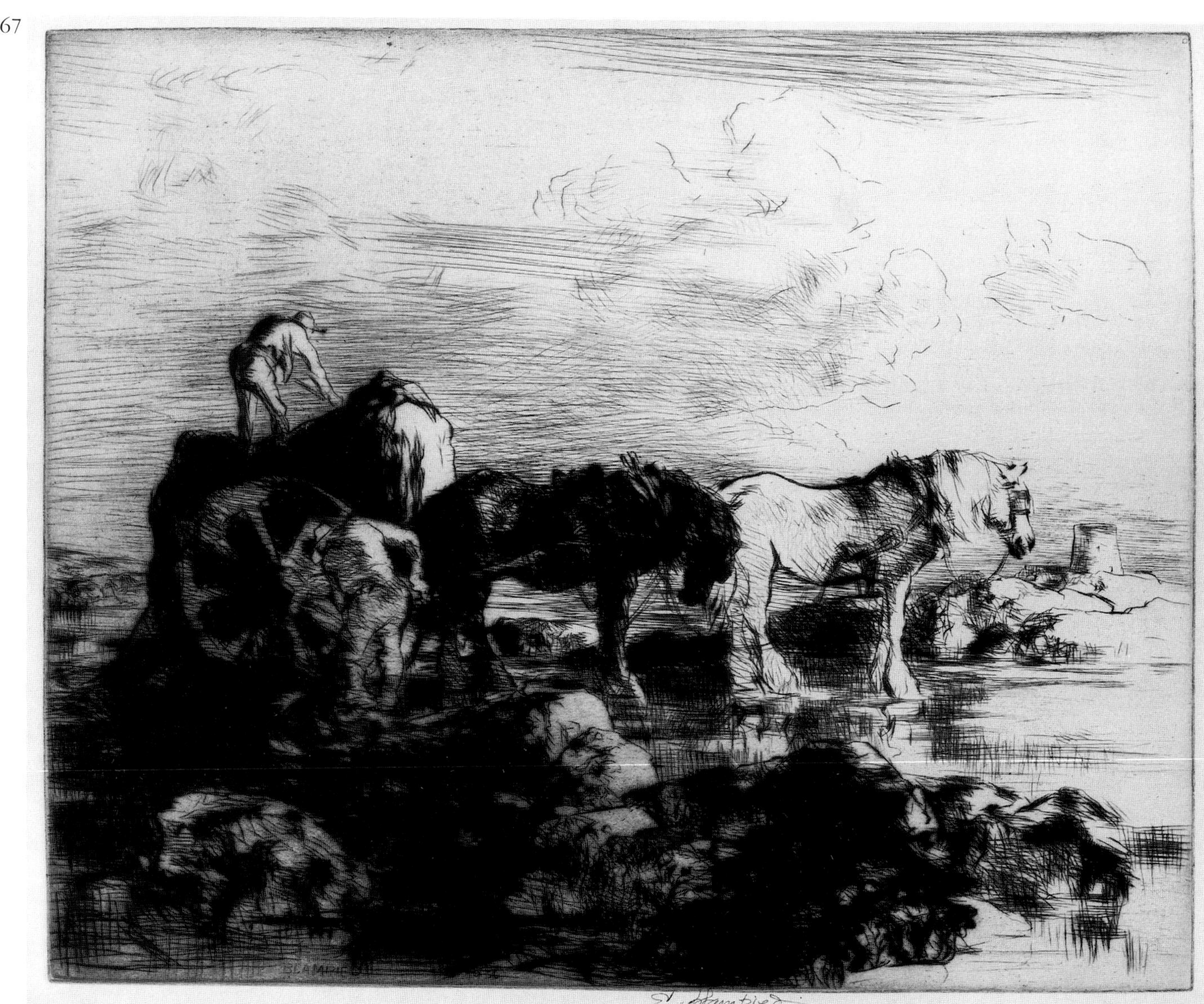

EDMUND BLAMPIED (1886–1966)

67. *Seaweed Harvest, Jersey*, 1936
    Drypoint, 12 x 14¼ in. (30.5 x 36.2 cm)
    Museum Purchase
    PR 1937.2

The son of a poor peasant family in the island of Jersey, Edmund Blampied was raised in humble rural circumstances in St. Martin's parish. At fifteen years of age, he attended art classes at St. Helier's conducted by a Miss Klintz. Two years later Blampied left for London, where he enrolled in the Lambeth Art School. It was not until 1912, however, that he took up the study of etching, with a teacher named Walter Seymour at the L. L. C. School, Bolt Court. He soon developed an amiable skill in the use of that medium and an especial facility with drypoint.

Much later, in 1920, he turned to the use of lithography. Master of many mediums, Blampied gained perhaps his most sustaining artistic fulfillment as an etcher.

Whether in drypoint or lithography, Blampied sustained qualities of exceptional verve and spontaneity that won him an enthusiastic following for his characterizations of Channel Island life. His great popularity rested in large part on his responsiveness to the life of the folk on his native island of Jersey, amongst whom he had been raised. Whether working at close range or at greater distance, as here in *Seaweed Harvest, Jersey*, he had a flair for catching the essentials of place, gesture, or facial expression, bespeaking a warm understanding of his subject. Often his characterizations of the Channel Islanders among whom he dwelt are humorous but affectionate in tone, without descending into caricature.

In his concentration upon life in the small island villages, on the farms, and along the shores, he accumulated a warmly humane documentation of a culture that is neither English nor French nor, precisely, in-between the two. Something of Blampied's aptitude for capturing the essentials of a situation is to be enjoyed in the brio with which the action of his workman is caught in *Seaweed Harvest*, even to the suggestion of his personal quirks of gesture and the hang of his workclothes. Blampied's knowing response to the look of the sturdy workhorses of the island farms has also been singled out for special praise by admirers of his art.

Gerald Leslie Brockhurst (1890–1979)

68. *The Black Silk Dress*, 1927
    Etching, 6¼ x 8¾ in. (22.2 x 15.9 cm)
    Gift of Edward C. Crossett, '05
    1951.646

Gerald Leslie Brockhurst harks back to the roots of a native preoccupation with portraiture. A native of Birmingham, at age twelve he was enrolled in the Birmingham School of Art and later attended classes at the Royal Academy. A gold medal and scholarship for his academy performance took him to Paris and Milan for further study. His skills both in etching and in painting, however, seem to have evolved independently, with no direct reference to his training. In eschewing the broadly Baroque heritage of tonal realism that had come to prevail in the wake of the etching revival, he reverted to pictorial terms in which the hard-edged precision of detail dear to many of Victorian predecessors was revived. Interestingly, while still a young student at Birmingham he won praise as a "Young Botticelli." Lingering traditions of Pre-Raphaelite attention to detail had remained especially strong there. By Brockhurst's day that stance of maintaining closed contours and carefully defined modeling of the interior forms, constituted in effect an individualistic aloofness from either the established modes of the painter-etcher, with the looser, more atmospheric qualities of pictorial form, or the avant-garde novelties of arbitrary drawing and composition then gaining prominence in some cosmopolitan circles. Brockhurst's

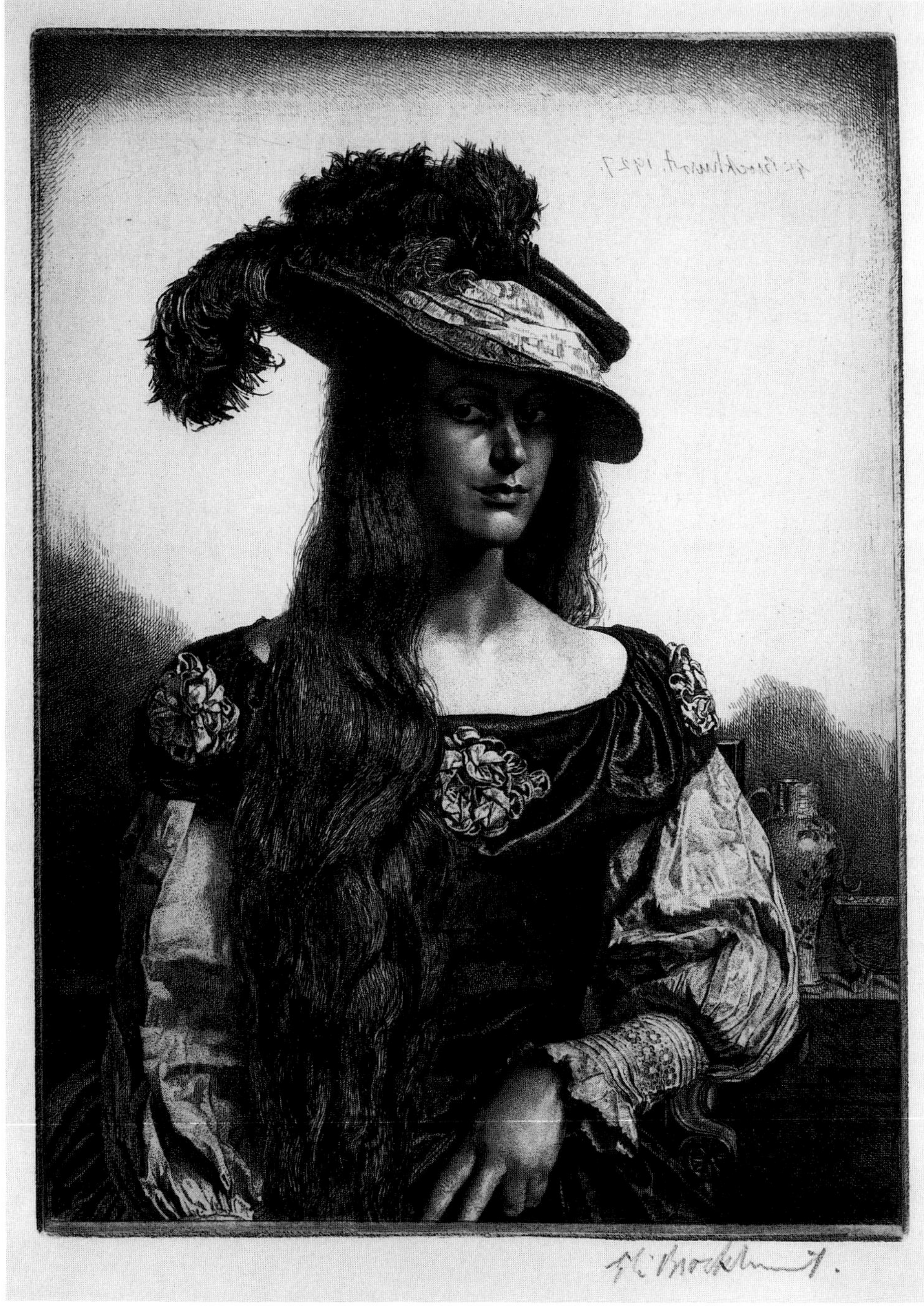

frequent device of posing his models close to the viewer and within confined pictorial setting strongly suggests Renaissance usage. The impact of his closely defined, almost metallic surfaces once seemed almost anachronist in the context of the more "painterly" looseness of execution that commonly prevailed among his contemporaries. Now, his insistent definition of form is in some ways analogous to the sharp-focused realism that has since come into vogue in many quarters.

The Black Silk Dress is often regarded as the epitome of Brockhurst's attainment as a graphic artist, with its richness of tone and conviction of textural differentiation. These effects are achieved with an admirable delicacy of touch yet strength of plastic realization. Not least of all, Brockhurst regularly exhibited the portraitist's eye to distinctiveness of facial feature and bodily bearing, which he characteristically observed with elegant reserve. He nevertheless arouses the viewer's curiosity about the personal nature of his sitter. And yet there is a note of temporal distance maintained in the historical rather than contemporary cut of the costumes in which he customarily clad his sitters.

4. Decorative Arts

A representative selection of works of decorative art from the Amherst College Collection has been included here to complement the pictorial examples which comprise the main substance of the exhibition. The Mead Art Museum houses numerous objects of decorative art which are either too fragile or too bulky to travel. Obviously, too, the magnificently paneled Jacobean interior ensemble of the stately room from Rotherwas Manor, our most significant holding in the decorative arts category, is permanently installed in the Museum and must accordingly be enjoyed *in situ*. These few examples, therefore, must suffice to give the flavor of the collection.

Furniture

The earliest examples of English furniture to be shown in the present exhibition date from the Restoration period, following the return of Charles II from exile on the Continent. While there, King Charles had taken a fancy to the High Baroque fashions currently in vogue. In matters of taste, the court of Louis XIV exerted an almost inescapable influence on the other courts of Europe. The popularization of the sumptuous modes supported at Versailles was quickened after 1785, when the Edict of Nantes was revoked. Many of the fine Huguenot artisans of all kinds of specialty took refuge in the Netherlands and England. Still at the peak of their commercial and cultural prosperity, the Netherlandish patrons and their craftsmen had already exerted a strong independent influence in England. Old cultural ties were, if anything, strengthened by residence of the Stuart Court in Holland during the Cromwellian interregnum. For example, English furniture makers of the Restoration era widely ly adopted the use of walnut, following the lead of

their Netherlandish counterparts. By contrast, under James I and Charles I there had been no radical departures from the preferences expressed in the Tudor period, when the sturdy, heavier forms of English Renaissance design continued to be articulated and oak was the primary choice of material.

These trends may be seen in a side chair (No. 69) that dates from the reign of Charles II (1660–85). It shows the high-backed design of the period with spiral turnings and carved cresting. The extensive use of caning on the seat and back also reflects sources in Dutch usage. British craftsmen were not merely imitative, however. Characteristically, their continued preferences for an elegant decorativeness that had long been implanted in their land, inspired them to treat the basic schemes set in foreign prototypes with an elegance of proportion and detail that are distinctive to British cabinetmaking.

With the approach of the eighteenth century, further changes of taste rendered the High Baroque styles of the Restoration old-fashioned. This period of transition to the more comfortable—one is tempted to say, the more "modern"—forms that were generally preferred by eighteenth-century patrons is conveniently classified with reference to the reigns of William and Mary (1689–1702) and Queen Anne (1702–14). The ascent to the thrones of England, Scotland, and Ireland by William, who was at once a descendant of King Charles I and a member of the House of Orange, only strengthened old cultural bonds between the two realms. Appropriately enough, the term *Anglo-Dutch* is commonly applied as a classification of furniture of that period. As in other matters, however, the influence of France is discernible throughout. For example, Prince William III of Orange, the future king, had early come to admire the Paris-born architect, Daniel Marot (1663–1752). As a Huguenot, Marot had abandoned his promising

113

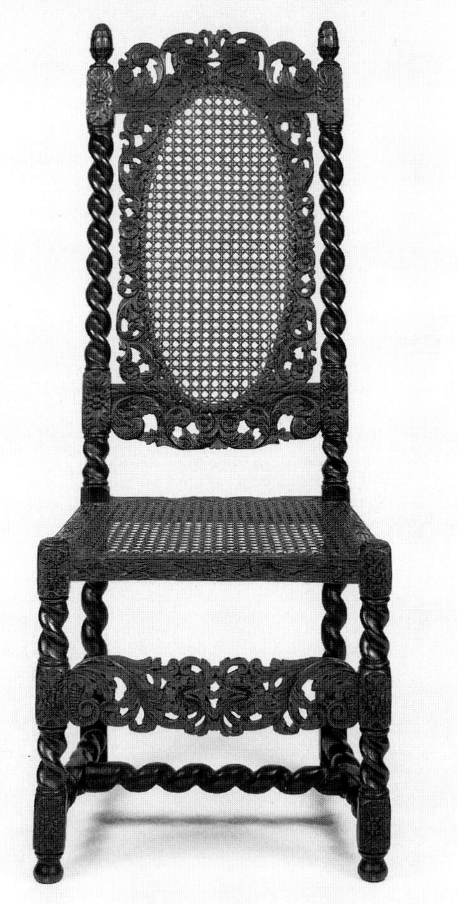

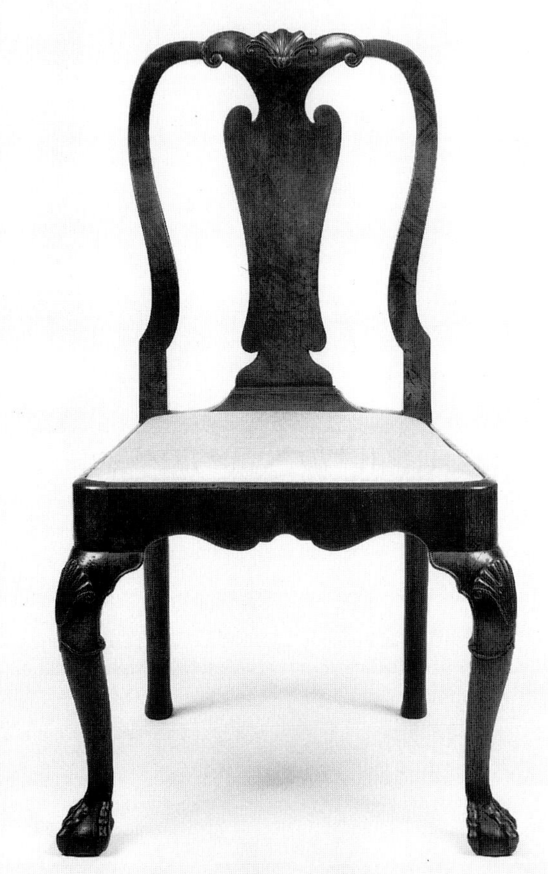

71

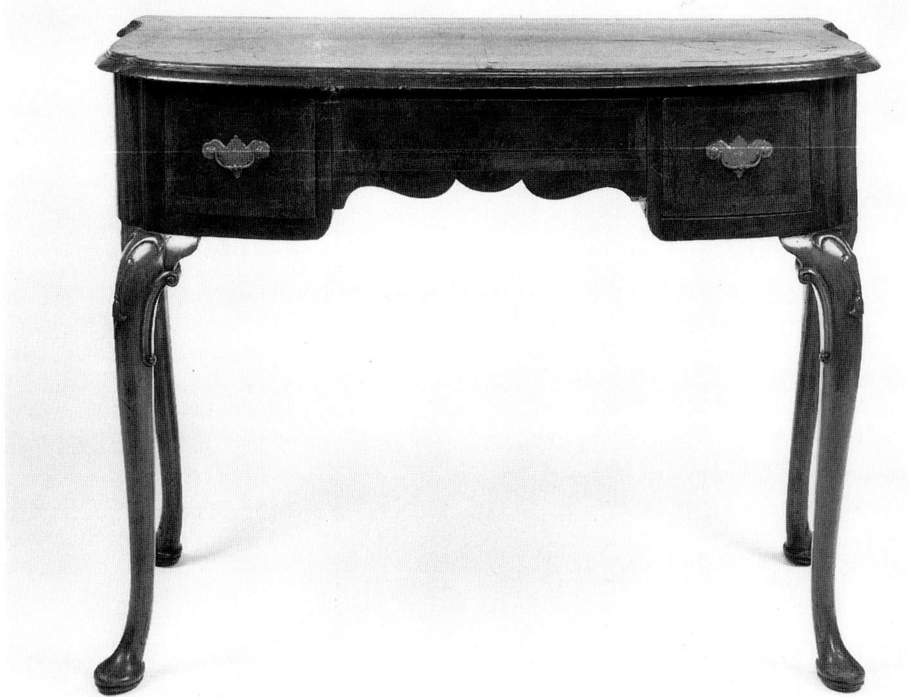

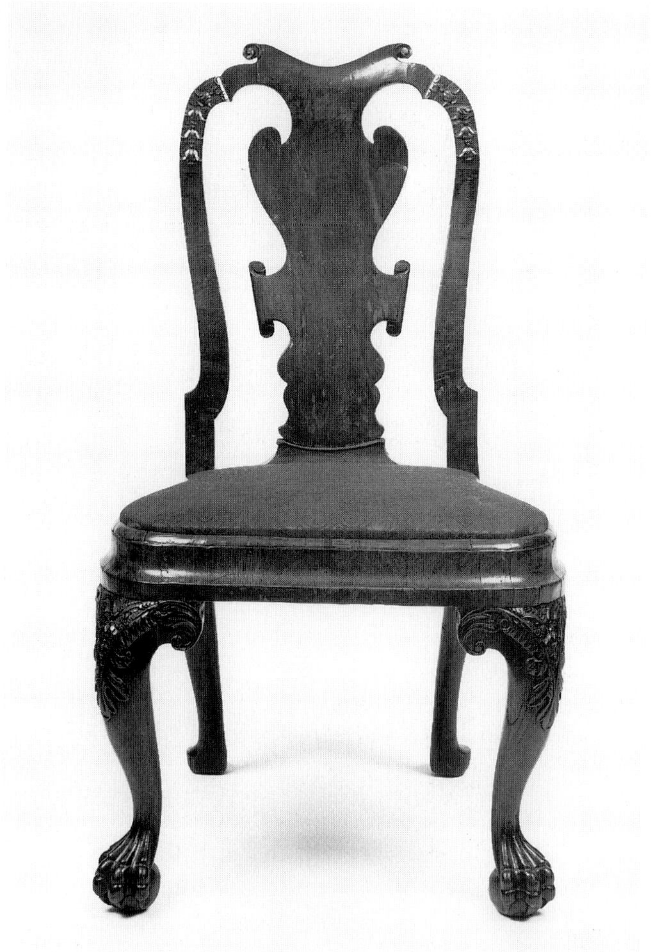

professional beginnings in France to seek political assylum in Holland, where he gained prominence as a designer for the decorative arts as well as in architecture. His success was largely due to his publications, the first of which appeared in 1702, the year Queen Anne succeeded to the British throne. Thanks to these publications, and to contemporary documentation on the work of other artisans, from this time onward the history of furnishings is known in greater detail than was formerly possible.

Examples of "Queen Anne" fashion in the present exhibition include a chair and side table typifying the quite striking change in furniture of the Restoration period. The chair (No. 70) is made of walnut with an upholstered seat. It illustrates the basically broader, more comfortable dispositions of shape that announce the beginnings of eighteenth-century modes. The splat-back structure, designed equally for comfort and sturdiness, is visually softened by elegant curvatures of basic shape. Those surfaces are tastefully formed and further ornamented with carved detail. Traits of the sort are to be appreciated as well in the serpentine, or cabriole, treatment of the legs, indicative of derivations from French models. Almost a hallmark of pieces created at this period, the leg design is occasionally said to have been inspired by Chinese prototypes, patterned after animal anatomy. Transformations of the sort, however, have occurred in utilitarian objects since antiquity in many parts of the world. Whatever the case, the motif of the cabriole leg prominent in Queen Anne seating furniture, tables (No. 71), or cabinets, ordinarily turns on a pad foot or goat's foot support.

With the death of Queen Anne in 1714, the royal succession passed to the Hanoverian line. During this so-called Georgian period, after the four kings George, there developed a fascination with the classical precepts espoused by Italian architect Andrea Palladio (1518–1580). His *Four Books of Architecture* first

appeared in English translation in 1715, and his views on architecture were taken equally to apply to the arts of furnishing—with happy results. Colin Campbell's book, *Vitruvius Brittanicus*, also published in 1715 and also dedicated to the new king, George I (1714– 47), served to reinforce the primacy of architectural design and a respect for classical principles. By the time of George II's reign, (1727–60), those ideals were fully assimilated.

A pair of side chairs (No. 72, one shown) from the same era relates to that emergence of characteristically early Georgian treatment, as contrasted with the Queen Anne style. As time went on, however, the comparative restraints of Palladianism gave way, in turn, to the brilliant fancies of the Rococo, as they were converted into a distinctively insular vernacular style by such gifted designers as Thomas Chippendale (1718–1779). Chippendale's book, *Gentleman and Cabinet-maker's Director* (1754), was a profusely illus-

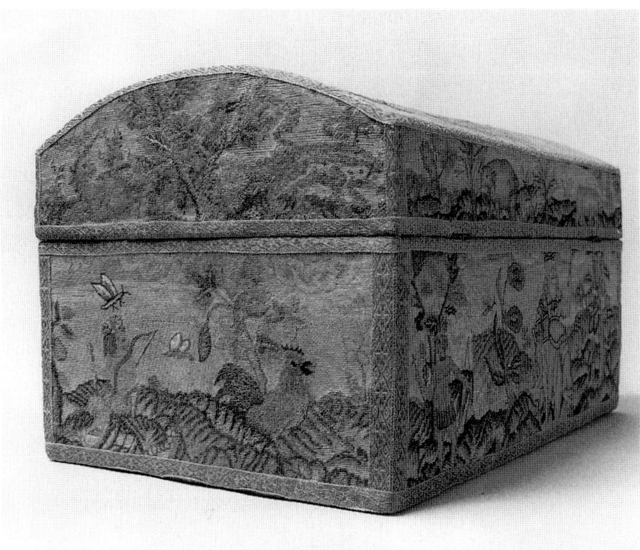

73

trated source of inspiration even for those who lacked access to the study of original products from his London shop in St. Martin's Lane.

The eighteenth century produced other inventive designers who were responsive to the ever-quickening shifts of taste and conditions of patronage that marked the era. Among them, Robert Adam (1728–1792) was a towering figure. Unfortunately, our reserves at the Mead Art Museum do not yet contain examples of those later periods to compare with earlier selections. Nor do our holdings from the Victorian era argue for any special attention, save in a few isolated instances. The objects just described nevertheless seemed to constitute a small grouping in itself.

One final item of special interest and appeal has also been included among the household goods: a needlepoint box (No. 73) with a domed cover and compartmented interior, lined with green velvet. While the object is indisputably old, its precise historical derivation remains uncertain. Its exterior covering of finely executed needlepoint, with an engaging representation of figures in a landscape, unquestionably reflects the rich legacy of textile art produced in Britain over the course of many years. Inasmuch as this object is the most impressive of our holdings of the kind, it has been included as an example of another form of decorative application by the artisans of Britain.

SILVER

The sampling of silver included in *The Grand Tradition* mainly illustrates the significant developments and shifts of taste characteristic of the Queen Anne (1704–1727) and mid-Georgian (1728–70) periods. The later examples relate to some aspects of Adam style (1771–1800), but they hardly suffice in themselves either to illustrate that high point of English mastery of the silversmith's art or to suggest the range of the Regency that followed. They do represent certain types of precious utensil which are not otherwise shown, so it seems useful to include them.

The two earliest pieces are both coffee pots (Nos. 74 and 75) with the tapered sides that identify them as so-called lighthouse coffee pots. They share basic design chracteristics of their genre: a curved pouring spout that came into use just before 1700 and a wooden handle permitting safe use. Lids intended to keep the liquid warm were hinged as an added measure of safety in pouring. Coffee had been introduced to England from Abyssinia, during the Commonwealth (1649–60). Hence, that beverage made its appearance earlier than tea, which only came to be imported later in the century. Although coffee was initially regarded as a drug and accordingly distrusted, it soon became so popular that many serving pieces such as these were produced.

The same direct but elegant accommodation of formal and functional dictates is to be observed in a tea kettle (No. 76) also of Queen Anne design. The English process for making tea differed from the Chinese method, for while the Chinese poured the heated water into the cup or bowl onto the leaves from a pot, in England the beverage was "infused" or brewed in the pot. The first metal teapots were based on the type of ceramic vessels employed in China. It was soon found, however, that the hot metal damaged table surfaces and, therefore, it was not only safer, but

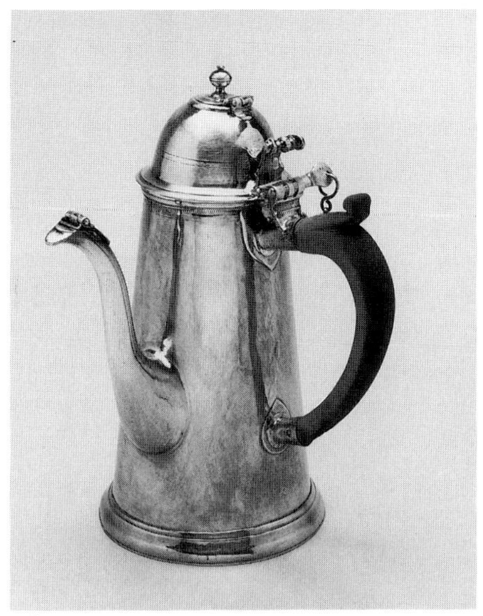
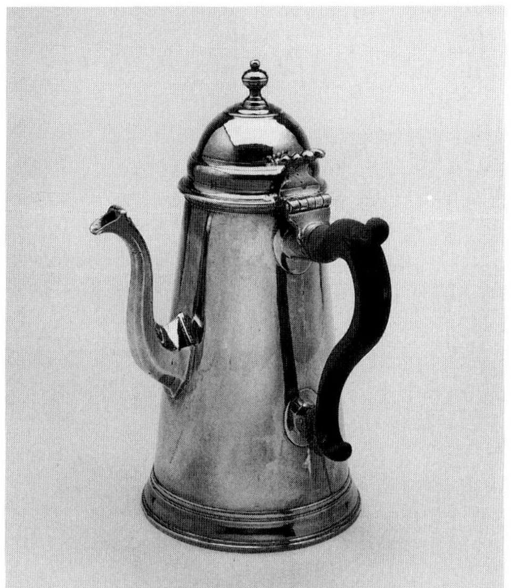
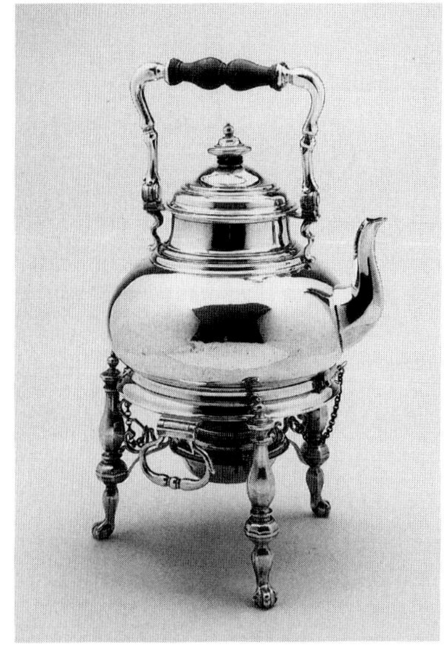

74 75 76

more convenient, to heat the kettle only when fresh tea was desired. That economy of effort was made possible by the provision of specially designed kettle stands with built-in spirit lamps as sources of heat. This ingenious outgrowth of the simple teapot became popular in the Queen Anne period. At first, the basic design of tea kettles was pear shaped or polygonal. Later, a globular design was adopted, as in the piece in the Amherst collection. The polygonal form remains evident, however, in the shape of the pouring spout. Eventually, the globular body shape was displaced in fashion by an inverted-pear shape. Sometimes a teapot was made to match the kettle, but the notion of a "tea set" with pieces of a coordinated design is more modern.

A tankard (No. 77) dating from roughly a year later than the tea kettle shows the extension of Queen Anne taste into the years immediately following its height. Basically a simply formed drinking vessel, this tankard exhibits straight, slightly inward sloping sides broadly resembling the design of the coffee pots already discussed. It also has the domed and hinged top which was especially favored from about 1710 to 1735, but which finally passed entirely out of use around 1765. In general form, the tankard was a traditional form of large drinking vessel designed to contain strong drink, not least of all, malt beverages. Of northern European origin, it usually was made with a hinged cover and thumb piece. The decorative mold-ings, normal to the design are reminiscent of the earlier traditions of fabricating drinking vessels of the sort from combinations of other materials, with only the rims and reinforcing bands made of metal. The S-shaped, single handle observed here had also come to be traditional. Smaller cups of a similar shape, but lacking covers, are known as "mugs."

During the mid-Georgian period the taste for large-scale items made of silver waned somewhat, but concommittantly, there evolved an especial attraction to the use of rich, formally arranged ornamentation of the sort encouraged in France under Louis XIV. The designs of Juste-Aurèle Meissonier (ca. 1693–1750) were widely influential, as they were to be known both in France and abroad from his lavishly illustrated publication of his designs. (Unfortunately, few of the actual pieces made from those designs were destined to survive, being melted down for the raw value of their precious metal.) In England, Paul de Lamerie (1712–1751) became the leading exponent of the new, Rococo forms initiated in France. Their intricately compounded linear designs, replete with floral elaboration, were often graced with fanciful inventions inspired by current tastes for chinoiserie. At another level, the love of luxury and display sustained by the privileged classes in the age of the Rococo was accompanied by an equally demanding hunger for diversion. Such pastimes as games of chance, especially those involving playing cards, became

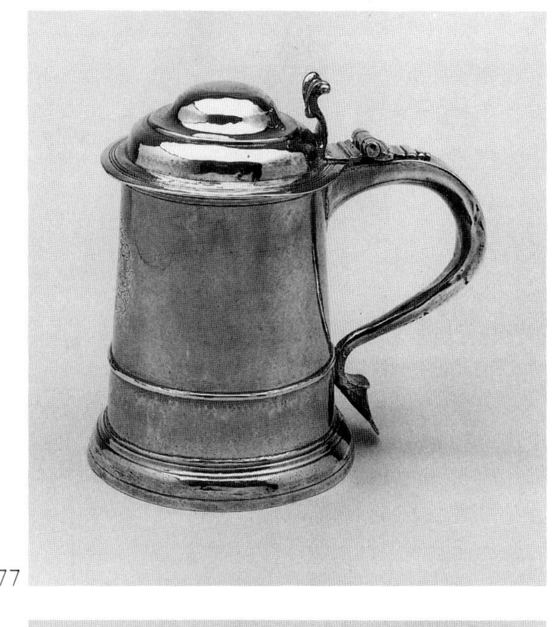

77

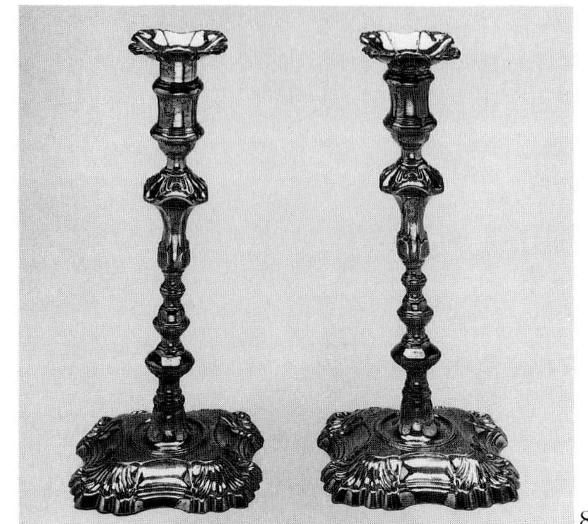

80

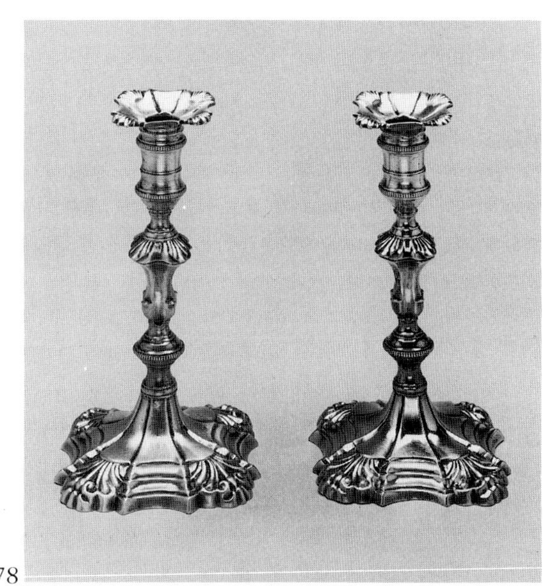

78

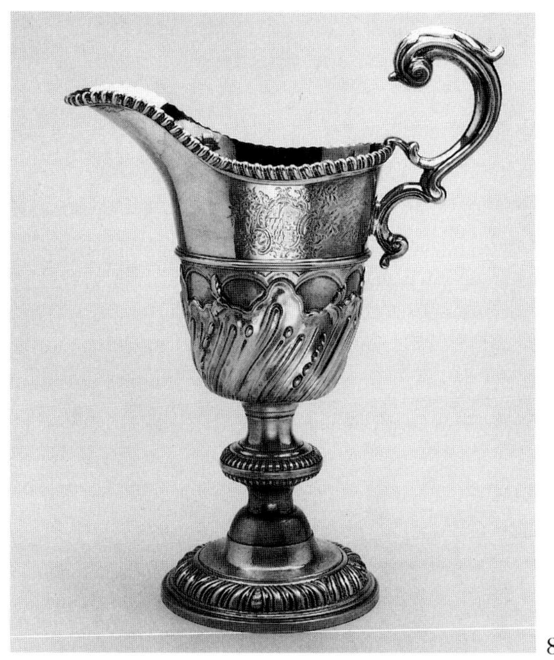

81

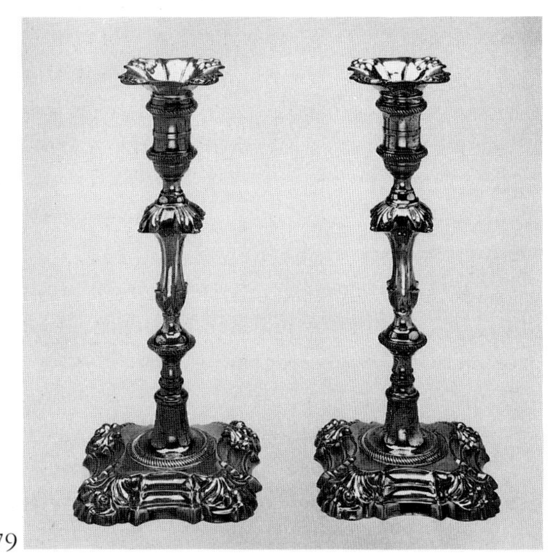

79

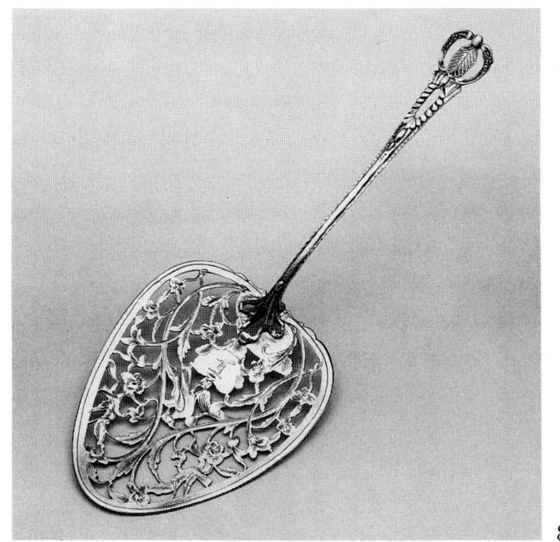

82

popular. Gaming tables with places to set candlesticks, usually four in number, or writing cabinets with slides to hold pairs of candlesticks were devised so that the enjoyable pursuits of gaming and writing could be more comfortably pursued into the evening hours. Enthusiasms of the kind provided a new luxury market for silversmiths in their provision of appropriate lighting fixtures.

Three pairs of Georgian candlesticks have been included, all of them solid cast pieces. The earliest and smallest pair (No. 78) shows the baluster stems then prevalent. Repoussé shell designs enliven the square bases, but typically, some expanses of silver are left fairly plain, to permit a reflection of light. (Mirrors were also used extensively to magnify light.) By this time, the candle was placed in a socket—in this case, in removable ones that facilitated cleaning. Socket candlestcks had first come into use during the sixteenth century. Much the same composition occurs in a slightly later and larger pair of candle holders (No. 79), in this case bearing the distinguishing designs of a winged horse on the squared base, along with an engraved inscription under the banner: LABOR OMNIA VINCIT. A third pair of candlesticks (No. 80), again with baluster stems and irregular square bases, are somewhat smaller but even more elaborate. The sockets of the upper balusters and the bases are decorated with a stylized leaf pattern, while crests on each base show a small bird with a branch in its beak.

One of a pair of ewers (No. 81), dating from the same years shows the taste for lavishness that prevailed. Typical of their class of table furnishing, this piece has an inverted helmet-shaped body, richly ornamented with a coat of arms on one side and a crest on the other, as well as gadrooning. An upward flaring lip and complexly devised scroll handle sustain a lively, curvilinear rhythm that is based upon the column support with its round, molded foot. By this time, the ewer (and the basin that was sometimes made to match) had become essentially decorative. Originally, they were used for washing at the table and were especially favored in Italy, in the years before the fork was invented. By the Georgian era that once useful form was anachronistic and is consequently rather rare.

Of more practical value were serving pieces made for the table. Although the usual forms of flatware have not been included in the present selection, two serving pieces of special interest do appear. One of them is a pastry server (No. 82), which has a pierced handle and a flat, pierced, triangular bowl with a crest. Knives and other cognate implements were not made with silver handles before 1700. Closely related is a fish slice (No. 83), with an open-shaped bowl or slicer pierced with a flower-and-branch design, terminating at the handle in a plain end that bears the monogram *RL* within a circle. The hollow handle is here ornamented with a bead motif. Satisfying other needs were condiment pieces, a form which is here represented by two of a set of six salts (No. 84). In this case, the basic shape is in accord with the classical dispositions that rapidly manifested themselves with the advent of the Adam period (1771–1800). Oval or boatlike in shape, they have gracefully curved handles. The interiors are fitted with removable partitions at the midpoint, while the outside of the bodies are fluted and further embellished with winged designs on the side.

The latest examples in the present selection date from the Regency period (1800–1830), when the rather eclectic personal preferences and enthusiastic patronage of George, Prince of Wales, the future King George IV, were widely manifested. Although the Regency lasted only from 1811–1820, that term applies to the longer span of years of the future king's influence on matters of taste, ending with his death in 1830. While the archeological flavor of much of the silverware of the time does not make itself felt in

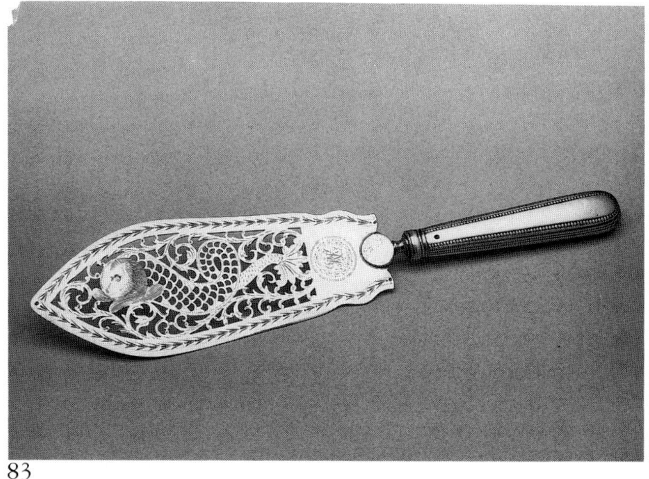

83

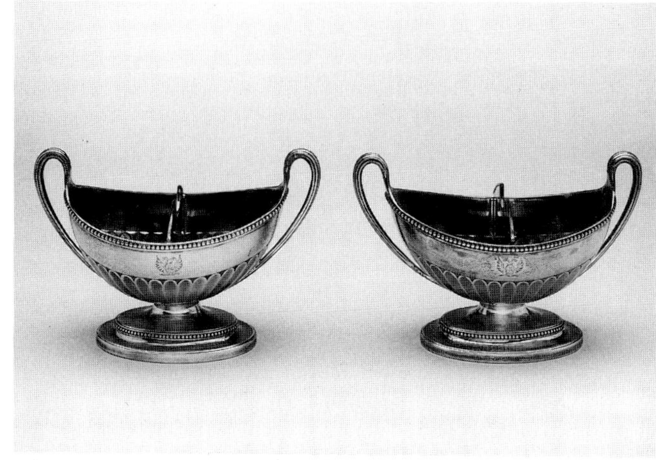

84

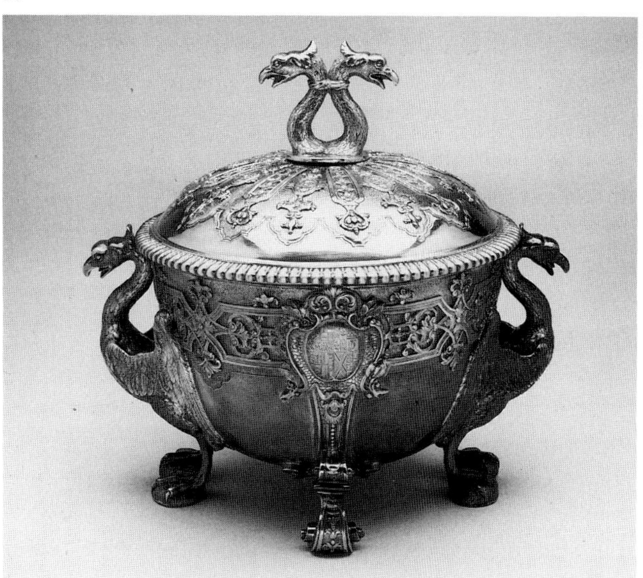

85

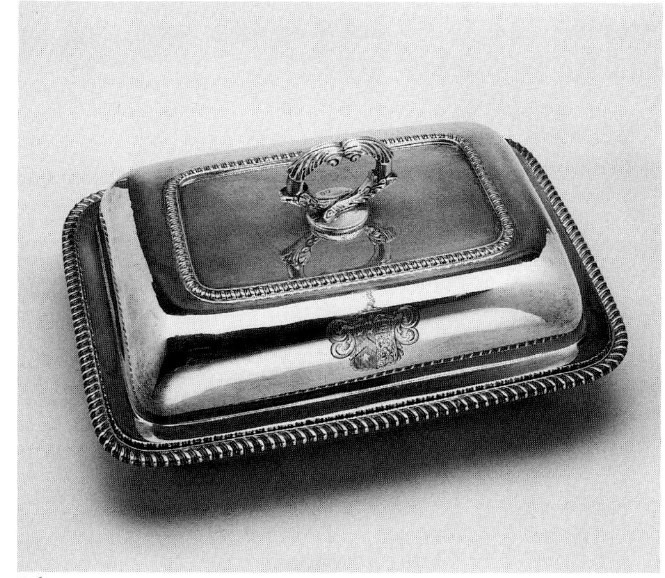

86

the Regency examples shown here, a recurrence of the Rococo which also occurred during that period does show itself in the bowl and cover (No. 85), one of a pair now in the Amherst College collection. Robustly ornamented with gadrooning and strap work contrasting with a mat ground, the body of the piece is supported on the major sides by two fantastic birds, each with outspread wings and scrolled feet. Nicely worked, but lesser supports mark the minor axis. The detachable cover is surmounted by a finial in which the bird motif recurs. Although somewhat awkward in overall proportion, the whole of this piece is so vigorously conceived and nicely treated in its detail that it possesses a special charm.

Much plainer, but satisfying in its own way is a covered dish (No. 86) dating from the same period. It is oblong in shape with a gadrooned edge on the dish and a molding on the cover. In addition, the cover boasts a removable ornamental handle. Since kitchens of the time were usually located far from the dining area, serving pieces of this kind were useful in keeping the food warm in the process of transporting it from kitchen to table. When necessary, the handle could be removed to convert the cover into an additional serving dish. In observing details such as this the viewer comes to appreciate yet again the ingenuity as well as the tastefulness of craftsmen who melded artistic invention with the service of utilitarian needs in the age of *The Grand Tradition*.

69. Charles II side chair, late 17th century. Walnut, 47¾ x 20 x 16 in. (121.3 x 50.8 x 40.6 cm). Bequest of Herbert L. Pratt, '95 (1945.363)

70. Queen Anne chair, 18th century. Carved walnut, 38½ x 22 x 17 in. (97.8 x 55.9 x 43.2 cm). From the Herbert L. Pratt, '95, Estate (1945.456b)

71. Queen Anne side table, 18th century. Inlaid walnut, 33 x 43¾ x 21½ in. (83.8 x 111.1 x 54.6 cm). From the Herbert L. Pratt, '95, Estate (1945.32a)

72. Pair of George I or II side chairs, 18th century (one shown). Walnut, 39 x 23 x 18½ in. (99 x 58.4 x 47 cm). Bequest of Herbert L. Pratt, '95 (1945.288a)

73. Needlepoint box. Textile, 12¼ x 19½ x 13¼ in. (31.1 x 49.5 x 33.7 cm). Gift of Mrs. Marjorie Merriweather Post (1959.57)

74. Queen Anne coffee pot. William Gamble, London, 1707–8. Silver, 8¾ x 4⅜ in. (22.2 x 11.1 cm). Bequest of Herbert L. Pratt, '95 (1945.171)

75. Queen Anne "lighthouse" coffee pot. Richard Green, London, 1712–13. Silver, 9½ x 4½ in. (24.1 x 11.4 cm). Bequest of Herbert L. Pratt, '95 (1945.193)

76. Queen Anne tea kettle and stand. John Fawdery, London, 1717–18. Silver, H. 15 in. (38.1 cm). Bequest of Herbert L. Pratt, '95 (1945.197)

77. George I tankard. Thomas Mason, London, 1719–20. Silver, 7 x 4¹¹⁄₁₆ in. (17.8 x 12.5 cm). Bequest of Herbert L. Pratt, '95 (1945.167)

78. George II candlesticks. John Cafe, London, 1755–56. Silver, H. 5½ in. (14 cm). Bequest of Herbert L. Pratt, '95 (1945.172a,b)

79. George III candlesticks. Ebenezer Coker, London, 1763. Silver, H. 10 in. (25.4 cm). Bequest of Herbert L. Pratt, '95 (1945.160a,b)

80. George III candlesticks. William Cripps, William Cafe, or William Caldecott, London, 1770–71. Silver, H. 9½ in. (24.1 cm). Bequest of Herbert L. Pratt, '95 (1945.153a,b)

81. Ewer. London, 1762. Silver, 13 x 10 in. (33 x 25.4 cm). Bequest of Miss Susan Dwight Bliss (1966.49b)

82. George III pastry server. Richard Mills, London, 1768–69. Silver, L. 11½ in. (29.2 cm). Bequest of Herbert L. Pratt, '95 (1945.203)

83. George III fish slice. T. Daniel?, London, 1781. Silver, L. 12 in. (8.9 cm). Gift of Mrs. Stanley King (1965.3)

84. George III salts. John Wakelin and William Taylor, 1782–83. Silver, 3½ x 5⅛ in. (8.9 x 13 cm). Bequest of Herbert L. Pratt, '95 (1945.183c,f)

85. Bowl and cover. J. W. Story and W. Elliot, London, 1810. Silver, 11 x 10 in. (27.9 x 25.4 cm). Bequest of Miss Susan Dwight Bliss (1966.50a)

86. George III covered dish. London 1814–15. Silver, 5¾ x 8½ x 11½ in. (13.3 x 21.6 x 29.2 cm). Bequest of Herbert L. Pratt, '95 (1945.156b)

BIBLIOGRAPHY

PAINTING

Boase, T. S. R. *English Art, 1800–1870*. Oxford: Clarendon, 1959.

Burke, Joseph. *English Art 1714–1800*. Oxford: Clarendon, 1976.

Cummings, Frederick, and Allen Staley. *Romantic Art in Britain: Paintings and Drawings, 1760–1860*. Philadelphia: Philadelphia Museum of Art, 1968.

Fry, Roger. *French, Flemish and British Art*. New York: Coward-McCann, 1951.

Hussey, Christopher. *The Picturesque: Studies in a Point of View*. London and New York: Putnam's, 1927.

Irwin, David and Francina. *Scottish Painter at Home and Abroad*. London: Faber and Faber, 1975.

Leslie, C. R. *Memoirs of the Life of John Constable*. London: Phaidon, 1951.

Maas, Jeremy. *Victorian Painters*. London: Barrie and Jenkins, 1969.

Pevsner, Nikolaus. *The Englishness of English Art*. London: The Architectural Press, 1956.

Redgrave, Richard and Samuel. *A Century of British Painters*. London: Phaidon, 1947.

Reynolds, Graham. *Victorian Painting*. New York: Macmillan, 1966.

Reynolds, Sir Joshua. *Discourses on Art*, various editions.

Taylor, Basil. *Painting in England, 1700–1850: Collection of Mr. and Mrs. Paul Mellon*. Richmond, VA: Virginia Museum of Fine Arts, 1963.

Waterhouse, Ellis. *Painting in Britain, 1530 to 1790*. Baltimore: Penguin, 1953.

Wood, Christopher. *Dictionary of Victorian Painters*. London: Antique Collectors' Club, 1971.

WATERCOLORS

Hardie, Martin. *Water-colour Painting in Britain*. Edited by Dudley Snelgrove, Jonathan Mayne, and Basil Taylor. 3 vols. New York: Barnes and Noble, 1966–68.

Mallalieu, H. L. *The Dictionary of British Watercolour Artists Up to 1920*. London: Antique Collectors' Club, 1976.

Williams, Iolo A. *Early English Watercolours and Some Cognate Drawings by Artists Born Not Later Than 1785*. London: The Connoisseur, 1952.

PRINTS

Guichard, Kenneth M. *British Etcher, 1850–1940*. London: Robin Garton, 1977.

Hind, Arthur M. *A History of Engraving and Etching*. London: Constable, 1923.

Ivins, William Mills. *How Prints Look*. Boston: Beacon, 1958.

Laver, James. *A History of British and American Etching*. New York: Dodd, 1929.

Pennell, Joseph. *Etchers and Etching*. New York: Macmillan, 1936.

Salaman, Malcolm Charles. *The Great Painter-Etchers: From Rembrandt to Whistler*. Edited by Charles Holme. London and New York: The Studio Ltd., 1914.

Sparrow, Walter Shaw. *A Book of British Etching*. London: John Lane, 1926.

Zigrosser, Carl. *Six Centuries of Fine Prints*. New York: Covici-Friede, 1937.

FURNITURE

Edwards, Ralph. *Georgian Furniture*. 2nd ed. London: Victoria and Albert Museum, 1958.

Gloag, John. *Georgian Grace: A Social History of Design from 1660–1830.* New York: Macmillan, 1956.

Harris, John. *Regency Furniture Designs from Contemporary Source Books, 1803–1826.* London: Alex Tiranti, 1961.

Hayward, Helena, ed. *World Furniture, an Illustrated History.* London: Hamlyn, 1965.

Heal, Sir Ambrose. *London Furniture Makers from the Restoration to the Victorian Era, 1660–1840.* London: Batsford, 1953.

Jourdain, Margaret and Rose Fred. *English Furniture: The Georgian Period, 1750–1830.* London: Batsford, 1953.

Macquoid, Percy, and Ralph Edwards. *The Dictionary of English Furniture,* 2nd ed., revised by Ralph Edwards, 3 vols. London, 1964.

Symonds, R. W. *Furniture Making in Seventeenth and Eighteenth Century England.* London: The Connoisseur, 1955.

Wintersgill, Donald. *English Antiques, 1700–1830.* New York: William Morrow, 1975.

Silver

Ensko, Stephen G. C., and Edward Wenham. *English Silver, 1675–1825.* New York: Robert Ensko, 1939.

Hayward, J. F. *Huguenot Silver in England, 1688–1727.* London: Faber and Faber, 1959.

Jackson, Charles James. *An Illustrated History of English Plate . . .* 2 vols. London: "Country Life" Ltd., 1911.

Jones, E. Alfred. *Old Silver of Europe and America: From Early Times to the Nineteenth Century.* Philadelphia: J. B. Lippincott, 1928.

Oman, Charles. *English Silversmiths' Work.* London: Her Majesty's Stationery Office, 1965.

Wenham, Edward. *Domestic Silver of Great Britain and Ireland.* New York and London: Oxford University Press, 1931.

Wyler, Seymour B. *The Book of Old Silver.* New York: Crown, 1937.

The Amherst College Collection

Mead Art Building, Amherst. *The Amherst Family Portraits.* Exhib. cat., 23 October–12 November 1967.

Morgan, Charles H. *The Development of the Art Collection of Amherst College, 1821–1971.* Amherst: Amherst College Press, 1972.

Trapp, Frank A., ed. *British Art.* Mead Museum Monographs, nos. 6, 7 (Winter, 1985/86).

————, et al. *Decorative Arts at Amherst College.* Mead Museum Monographs, no. 3 (Winter, 1981/82).

Authors's note: Monographs on individual artists have not been included.

The Henry Luce Foundation
Andrew W. Mellon Foundation
Mobil Foundation, Inc.
The Mabel Pew Myrin Trust
The New York Times Company
    Foundation, Inc.
PepsiCo Foundation Inc.
Pew Charitable Trust
Pfizer Foundation
Phillips Petroleum Foundation
Primerica Foundation
Samuel and May Rudin
    Foundation, Inc.
Security Pacific Foundation
Sherman Fairchild Foundation
L. J. Skaggs & Mary C. Skaggs
    Foundation
The Soros Foundation
Xerox Foundation

NATIONAL PATRONS

Mrs. Robert C. Warren
    Chairman
Mrs. Robert E. Linton
    Director of the National Patron Program
Mr. & Mrs. James W. Alsdorf
Mrs. Sharon Bender
Mr. & Mrs. Winslow W. Bennett
Mrs. Edwin A. Bergman
Mrs. George F. Berlinger
Mr. & Mrs. Charles M. Best
Mr. & Mrs. Van-Lear Black, III
Mrs. Brooke Blake
Mr. & Mrs. Leonard Block
Mrs. Robert H. Bloom
Mrs. Donald J. Blum
Mr. & Mrs. Duncan E. Boeckman
Edgar & Elizabeth Bottler
Mrs. Leo Brady
Mr. & Mrs. Eli Broad
Mr. & Mrs. R. E. Brooker
Mary Griggs Burke
Mr. & Mrs. Peter M. Butler
Mr. & Mrs. Vincent A. Carrozza
Mr. & Mrs. Carroll L. Cartwright
Mr. & Mrs. Norman U. Cohn
Mr. & Mrs. McCauley Conner
Elaine Terner Cooper
Mrs. Gardner Cowles
Mr. & Mrs. Donald M. Cox
Edwin L. Cox
Mr. & Mrs. Earle M. Craig, Jr.
Mr. & Mrs. James F. Crumpacker
Mrs. Catherine G. Curran
David L. Davies
Dr. & Mrs. David R. Davis
Mrs. Julius E. Davis
Mr. & Mrs. Walter Davis
Mr. & Mrs. Kenneth N. Dayton
Mr. & Mrs. Robert Henry Dedman
Mrs. John de Menil
Beth & James DeWoody
Mr. & Mrs. Charles M. Diker
Mr. & Mrs. C. Douglas Dillon
Mr. & Mrs. Herbert Doan

Mr. & Mrs. W. John Driscoll
Mr. & Mrs. Gilbert S. Edelson
Mr. & Mrs. Maurits E. Edersheim
William S. Ehrlich
Mrs. Lester Eisner
Mr. & Mrs. Edward E. Elson
Mr. & Mrs. Arthur D. Emil
Madeleine Feher
Mr. & Mrs. David Fogelson
Mr. Leo S. Guthman
Mr. & Mrs. John H. Hauberg
Mrs. Wellington S. Henderson
Mr. & Mrs. Henry L. Hillman, Jr.
Mr. & Mrs. A. Barry Hirschfeld
Mr. & Mrs. Theodore S. Hochstim
Ronna & Eric Hoffman
William J. Hokin
Jan & James L. Holland
Mrs. Eunice W. Johnson
Mrs. Samuel K. Ketcham
Mr. & Mrs. Peter Kimmelman
Mr. & Mrs. Gilbert H. Kinney
Mr. & Mrs. C. Calvert Knudsen
Mr. & Mrs. Robert P. Kogod
Mr. & Mrs. Oscar Kolin
Mr. & Mrs. Anthony M. Lamport
Mr. & Mrs. A. R. Landsman
Mr. & Mrs. Richard S. Lane
Natalie Ann Lansburgh
Mr. & Mrs. Leonard A. Lauder
Mr. & Mrs. Edward H. Leede
Mr. & Mrs. Albert Levinson
Mr. & Mrs. Irvin L. Levy
Ellen Liman
Mr. & Mrs. Joseph Linhart
Mr. & Mrs. Robert E. Linton
Mr. & Mrs. Lester B. Loo
Mr. & Mrs. David B. Magee
Mr. & Mrs. James H. Manges
Mr. & Mrs. Melvin Mark, Jr.
Mr. & Mrs. Irving Mathews
Mr. & Mrs. Alan M. May
Mr. & Mrs. Frederick R. Mayer
Mrs. Robert B. Mayer
Mrs. Walter Maynard, Jr.
Roderick A. McManigal
Mr. & Mrs. Paul Mellon
Robert & Meryl Meltzer
Mr. & Mrs. William D. Miller
Mr. & Mrs. Ellison C. Morgan
Mr. & Mrs. Roy R. Neuberger
Mrs. Peter Roussel Norman
Mrs. John W. O'Boyle
Mr. & Mrs. William B. O'Boyle
Mr. & Mrs. Peter O'Donnell, Jr.
Mr. & Mrs. George O'Leary
Mrs. & Mrs. Dean Pape
Mr. & Mrs. Robert L. Peterson
Mr. & Mrs. Donald A. Petrie
Mr. & Mrs. Nicholas R. Petry
Mr. & Mrs. Charles I. Petschek
Barbara J. Pfouts
Barbara & Max Pine
Mr. & Mrs. John W. Pitts
Mr. & Mrs. Lawrence S. Pollock Jr.
Mr. & Mrs. Peter O. Price
Mr. & Mrs. Jerome Pustilnik

Françoise & Harvey Rambach
Mr. & Mrs. Walter S. Rosenberry, III
Mr. & Mrs. Milton F. Rosenthal
Selma & Lawrence Ruben
Dr. & Mrs. Raymond R. Sackler
Mr. & Mrs. Douglas R. Scheumann
Mr. & Mrs. Mort Schrader
Mr. & Mrs. Rudolph B. Schulhof
Rev. & Mrs. Alfred R. Shands, III
Mr. & Mrs. George A. Shutt
Mr. & Mrs. Herbert M. Singer
Barbara Slifka
Mr. & Mrs. David M. Solinger
Ann C. Stephens
Mr. & Mrs. James G. Stevens
Mr. & Mrs. W. T. C. Stevens
Mr. & Mrs. John W. Straus
Mrs. Norman Tishman
Mrs. George W. Ullman
Mr. & Mrs. Michael J. Waldman
Mr. & Mrs. Robert C. Warren
Mr. & Mrs. John R. Watson
Mr. Paul L. Wattis
Nancy Brown Wellin
Dr. & Mrs. William T. Weyerhaeuser
Mr. & Mrs. Dave H. Williams
Enid Silver Winslow
Mr. & Mrs. Howard Wolf
Mrs. Bagley Wright
Mr. & Mrs. Howard S. Wright
Mr. & Mrs. T. Evans Wyckoff
Two anonymous